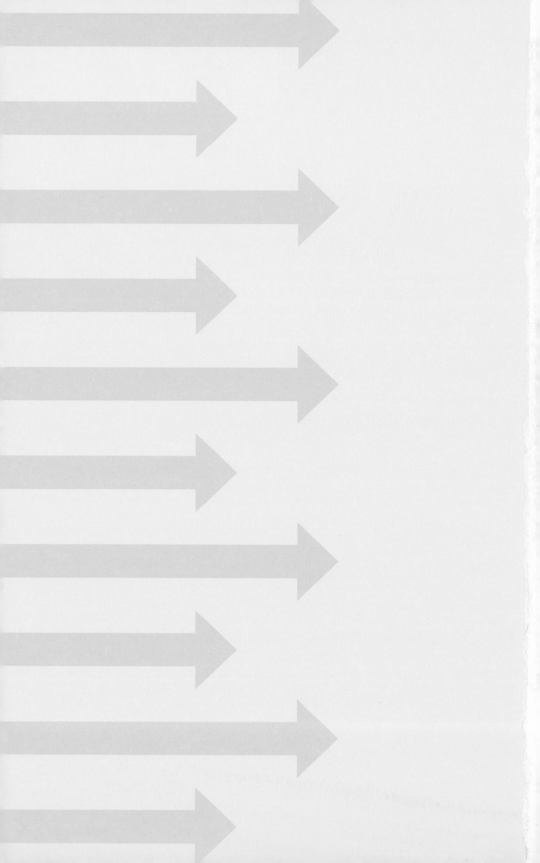

Praise for *Leading to Greatness*

"Jim Reid has dedicated his life's work to coaching and developing leaders, and to being a leader himself, at high levels of organizations. What most impresses me is his unquenchable drive to learn and to apply his accumulated wisdom to help leaders become both more humane and more effective. He is a true artist of the leadership development craft."

JIM COLLINS, AUTHOR OF *GOOD TO GREAT*

"Jim Reid is a master at supporting organization design and redesign, and in developing critical skills and competencies across an entire enterprise while helping gifted talent achieve their full potential. He is simply the best leader I have ever worked with."

GERARDO CHIAIA, CEO, LOGOPLASTE

"Jim Reid's great storytelling brings the leadership journey alive. His advice in *Leading to Greatness* is both practical and inspiring—a great reminder that leaders can learn to be great!"

MARY FEDERAU, EXECUTIVE VICE PRESIDENT, MATTAMY ASSET MANAGEMENT

"*Leading to Greatness* is masterfully done. Jim Reid is an exceptional leader and coach who generously shares his learnings and insights; his tips, tools and workbook will help those looking to build strong, cohesive teams, and immeasurably transform their leadership."

ANNA FILIPOPOULOS, EXECUTIVE VICE PRESIDENT AND CHIEF PEOPLE AND CULTURE OFFICER, FOUR SEASONS HOTELS AND RESORTS

"Jim Reid's passion for leadership is rooted in a genuine desire to help people grow, develop, connect to one another and live meaningfully. *Leading to Greatness* distills a lifetime of experience and knowledge into an accessible and transformational set of principles that will speak to every leader and aspiring leader looking to build and support a winning team."

DR. SONIA K. KANG, PROFESSOR OF MANAGEMENT,
UNIVERSITY OF TORONTO

"Jim Reid's years as a successful senior executive and coach have enabled him to develop a powerful +5 Leadership Development Model that enables executives to excel in the most difficult of circumstances."

DEEPAK KHANDELWAL, FORMER GOOGLE,
ROGERS AND CIBC SENIOR EXECUTIVE

"A work full of wisdom on what's at the heart of great leadership. Jim Reid is a caring coach and mentor with deep insight into human dynamics and how leaders can engage people and teams to achieve outstanding performance. *Leading to Greatness* is a must-read for anyone interested in being the best leader they can be."

JANET KO, CORPORATE AFFAIRS EXECUTIVE

"This book is a must-read for anyone interested in improving their leadership abilities and becoming the best they can be in their work and life. It comes at a time when the world is full of contradictory thinking and advice on great leadership and when the world has never needed this advice more. What makes this book great and special is its author, Jim Reid. He is probably the best Chief Human Resources Officer I know. Jim is an extraordinary leader, but more importantly, he is a lifelong student of leadership. *Leading to Greatness* is a product of his decades of studying and practicing what the very best leaders do differently, and it outlines a framework to enable us—mere leadership mortals—to become great."

CARL LOVAS, CHAIRMAN AND CEO,
ODGERS BERNDTSON CANADA

"Jim Reid is a person who has a passion for people, culture, values and organizational dynamics. *Leading to Greatness* lays out in clear, easily understandable steps how leaders can transform their organization through a deep understanding of themselves and others in order to build teams that drive results through values and purpose."

JOHN ROGERS, FORMER CEO, MDS INC.

"Creating a vibrant and innovative workplace demands that we harness skills that have previously been underweighted and address realities that have for a long time been ignored. These challenges require the kind of leadership that Jim Reid brings to the table, and that I have relied on to lead our teams to success. Jim not only understands the genesis of high performance but manages to share his skills in a way that has helped me both professionally and personally. *Leading to Greatness* is a must-read for any leader or aspiring leader looking to make lasting impact."

MELINDA ROGERS-HIXON, DEPUTY CHAIR,
ROGERS COMMUNICATIONS INC.

"*Leading to Greatness* is a straightforward and common-sense approach to business leadership. Jim Reid connects with his readers by demonstrating relevant examples that clearly describe the lessons learned throughout his very impressive career."

LOU SERAFINI JR., PRESIDENT AND CEO,
FENGATE ASSET MANAGEMENT

"*Leading to Greatness* is both insightful and practical in bringing to the reader a platform for personal leadership development that is rich with personal insight, backed by real-life storytelling and enveloped in practical guidance."

ALAN TORRIE, BOARD CHAIR AND FORMER CEO

"Jim Reid is the most outstanding HR leader I have ever worked with. He is empathetic yet always straight and to the point with a great set of values. He epitomizes what leading by example really means when it comes to shaping a values-driven culture."

DIRK WOESSNER, CEO,
COMPUGROUP MEDICAL

"In *Leading to Greatness*, Jim Reid captivates readers by bringing together the best research on what drives high performance and how those principles have impacted him on his incredible leadership journey. Through skillful storytelling and engaging case studies, Jim describes what talented leaders do differently to achieve exceptional results."

JOCELYN YACOUB, CEO AND FOUNDER,
YACOUB ELITE SEARCH

LEADIN
GREA

5 PRINCIPLES TO TRANSFORM YOUR LEADERSHIP & BUILD GREAT TEAMS

G TO

TNESS

JIM REID

Figure.1
Vancouver / Toronto / Berkeley

Cataloguing data is available from Library and Archives Canada
ISBN 978-1-77327-171-2 (hbk.)
ISBN 978-1-77327-172-9 (ebook)
ISBN 978-1-77327-173-6 (pdf)

Jacket design by Naomi MacDougall
Interior design by Ingrid Paulson
Author photograph by Emma Turner

Editing by Steve Cameron
Copy editing by Marnie Lamb
Proofreading by Alison Strobel
Indexing by Marnie Lamb
Permissions research by Mary Rose MacLachlan

Efforts have been made to determine copyright holders and to obtain permission for the use of copyrighted material. The publisher apologizes for any errors or omissions and would be grateful if notified for future printings.

Printed and bound in Canada by Friesens
Distributed internationally by Publishers Group West

Figure 1 Publishing Inc.
Vancouver BC Canada
www.figure1publishing.com

Contents

INTRODUCTION   How Small Steps Can Transform a Life · 1

PART 1   The +5 Leadership Development Model · 7

1   Self-Insight Drives Purpose · 11

2   Play to Your Strengths—Live with Passion · 23

3   Finding the Right People and Building a Strong Team · 39

4   Getting to Full Engagement · 53

5   Inner Discipline · 73

PART 2   The +5 Team Coaching Model · 101

6   Building a Winning Team · 105

7   Driving Successful Change · 129

8   Crisis Leadership · 147

9   The Leader as Coach · 161

10   Coaching Individual Transformation · 183

PART 3   Leadership Coaching Techniques · 203

Epilogue · 235

Acknowledgments · 240

Notes · 243

Credits and Permissions · 255

Index · 256

How Small Steps Can Transform a Life

> The most durable results happen as a series of good decisions that accumulate one upon another over a very long period of time. This creates a massive compounding effect.
>
> — JIM COLLINS

Most of us know a great leader when we are led by one. We intuitively sense something fundamental at work deep within that person that makes them a high-impact leader. But what is that fundamental something? And how do we harness it?

It is no secret that most leaders are looking for a leg up. They're searching for insight that can translate into practical action. Unfortunately, because theories on leadership abound, the popular thinking on what it takes to become a great leader is full of contradictory advice that can discourage even the most motivated of individuals. An additional frustration with leadership discourse is that it often has a failing grade in real-world application. It can be too academic, too narrow or too dismissive of the work needed to change culture and drive improved results.

That's why I've tried to keep my message to you as simple and straightforward as possible. What is that message? At the core, it is that the best leaders who drive real impact in their life follow a path to personal growth and success that is founded on five key principles:

1. Clarify and live your purpose and values in life every day.
2. Play to your strengths and passions—always.
3. Make the right people decisions.
4. Be fully engaged.
5. Be disciplined and relentless about driving extraordinary results.

In this book, I present two proven frameworks. The first is a model for high-performance leadership (Figure I.1; see page 9) that will enable you to build on success, use your potential and build a transformative life. The second framework (Figure II.1; see page 103) will enable you to apply a linked set of elements to develop your team. The concepts are derived from two significant sources.

First, the ideas are based on the best research that has been done on high performance, shaped by some of the current leading management thinkers, all of whom personally shared their ideas and advice with me. These thinkers include Harvard's John Kotter (*Leading Change*), Stanford's Jeffrey Pfeffer (*Power: Why Some People Have It—and Others Don't*), the University of Michigan's Ross School's Dave Ulrich (*Reinventing the Organization*), Jim Loehr (coauthor of *The Power of Full Engagement*) and Jim Collins (author of *Good to Great*, and coauthor of *Built to Last* and *Great by Choice*). Perhaps the deepest insight has come from the executives I have coached and worked with over many years of facing tough business turnarounds, challenges and crises.

Second, the framework is grounded in the real world, outlining what really works when leaders are tested by challenges that thwart ambition and strategy. I have spent over three decades observing what the very best leaders do differently from those who are less effective, so the frameworks I outline have been tested by the best of the best.

· · · · ·

This book is organized into three parts. In Part 1, I introduce you to the five principles that—if understood and lived—will significantly increase your effectiveness as a leader in the real world. In Part 2, I explore these principles in action, such as when we face a crisis, need to implement change, and work to strengthen our teams and culture. I also examine the leader's central role as coach and how coaching enriches a career. Part 3 is the leadership development workbook, which consists of activities and exercises related to the content in each chapter. My recommendation is that you complete the activities and exercises for each chapter as you read the chapter. The exercises are full of simple frameworks, practical tips and coaching questions that are designed to take your leadership to the next level.

From Getting My Wings to Earning Business Wisdom

Undoubtedly, the crucial experiences in our lives shape what we believe, who we are and how we live our lives. My first career was that of a military officer and pilot. Getting my wings was one of my most rewarding and challenging accomplishments. I had no experience as a pilot when I walked through the door to attend my primary flight-training program. I was not naïve, knowing that it had a failure rate of over 40 percent. But I listened, learned, threw myself at the challenge and graduated. I learned what discipline is by observing firsthand how some officers led by building followership, and others, even of the same rank, failed to do so, often by putting their own needs ahead of those they were leading. The difference in quality of leadership I witnessed was rooted in how certain officers deeply cared about the soldiers, sailors and members of the air force they led. Those officers served their country by honoring the people they commanded, developed and protected.

After my time in the military, I decided to further test myself not by flying with the airlines (as many of my fellow pilots did) but by moving into business. The second phase of my career began after I completed my MBA and took a role in operations at MDS Inc., a high-growth global life-sciences company. I was mentored by extremely talented executives such as CEO John Rogers and Alan Torrie, who would go on to become CEO of Morneau Sobeco. Together, they took a chance on me and promoted me to run one of the key business units in the company at the young age of thirty-three.

While at MDS, I completed the Advanced Management Program at Harvard University. John Rogers moved me on to the top executive team as the chief human resources officer (CHRO), with a mandate to expand the company's workforce and ensure that our culture could support our People Plan as the company's revenue grew from $500 million to over $2 billion. My work as CHRO at MDS was an exhilarating ride. I learned about the nature of teams and how business must change to adapt to evolving customer needs.

John saw potential in me, which I did not know how to realize, and I came to understand that seeing potential is a key role played by a good coach. By getting behind my development, he opened my eyes to how large-scale change can happen. It revolves around building the right culture and onboarding the right talent. While I was in this role as CHRO, I met Jim Collins, author of *Good to Great.* Jim continues to be one of the most influential people in my life, and his insight on what it takes to achieve great performance has indelibly influenced how I think about high performance. No question, while there are many great management thinkers today, Jim Collins has followed in the tradition of heavyweights like Peter Drucker to be in a class of his own as a courageous thinker, and a humble and inspiring leader.

· · · · ·

What does all this mean for you? I want to offer a fresh perspective on the legacy topic of leadership, give you the tools to create a framework to guide and measure your development, and provide you with a path to continuous learning. Specific to this framework is that it is applied to your whole life—work and personal—because behavior that is inconsistent at work and at home will frustrate the kind of authentic, consistent leadership needed to behave your way to a better place.

As the old adage goes, a journey of a thousand miles begins with a single step. I'm a firm believer that success is cumulative. It is about building momentum. The small steps we take—if taken in the right direction with purpose and passion—can take us places we could only previously imagine. Each step builds upon the other like a fifty-ton flywheel (to borrow Jim Collins's phrase). Initially, the effort to turn the flywheel is huge, but the longer we stick with it and the harder we push, the less effort it takes and the faster the flywheel spins. In many ways, self-development is like the power of compound interest—compounding can turn a modest sum into a small fortune over time—but only if you have the discipline to stay with it.

The steps outlined in this book will set you on the right path. They begin with the simplest of actions and end with the capacity to build something far greater than the sum of the parts of the individual frameworks. To stay on this path requires effort, however. Setting a new course and making a change in your personal trajectory requires courage, commitment and an openness to taking a new approach.

So join me on this journey, and make the choice to take your leadership to the next level. If you do, I promise you'll not only improve your impact at work and in life, but you'll also make the world a little better!

PART 1

THE +5 LEADERSHIP DEVELOPMENT MODEL

The +5 Leadership Development Model is the clearest and most grounded strategy for enriching your life and your leadership. It is deceptively simple yet incredibly challenging. However, there is no better toolkit than the five principles outlined in Figure 1.1. Throughout the book, I refer to the most talented leaders as +5 leaders. They are the leaders who live the five principles every day, and as a result, drive extraordinary results in their work and life. The +5 model requires discipline, dedication and self-examination. It is an all-encompassing framework you can use to navigate through good times and bad. I have witnessed the profound effect these principles have on 1) organizational culture, talent development, customer satisfaction and employee engagement; and 2) the critical elements any business requires to win in the complex, competitive marketplace we face today.

I have also witnessed the principles in the +5 Leadership Development Model in the actions and behaviors of the most talented leaders I have observed, coached and known personally. These actions and behaviors are simple and timeless, and can help you in transformative ways to live up to your full potential as a leader.

PRINCIPLE 1: **VALUES AND PURPOSE**	+5 leaders are crystal clear about their purpose and values, and they use this clarity to make effective decisions and show up as authentic, consistent leaders. Effective leaders understand how purpose and values are interrelated. These leaders are clear on what not to change in their life (values and purpose), while being open to changing everything else (strategy, priorities, culture, etc.), because they lead in a dynamic and fluid time.
PRINCIPLE 2: **STRENGTHS AND PASSIONS**	Each of us has a unique set of talents that differentiates us from everyone else. +5 leaders have a deep understanding of their DNA. They know their strengths, and leverage those strengths with persistence and passion to achieve extraordinary results. And they never, ever deviate.
PRINCIPLE 3: **THE RIGHT PEOPLE**	High-performing leaders look for passionate individuals to join their team. These individuals align with the team's values and purpose, and bring skills that augment the team's strengths. The signature action of these leaders is making the right people decisions—Right People. Right Seats. Strong Teams.
PRINCIPLE 4: **FULL ENGAGEMENT**	High performers tap into positive energy at every level—physical, emotional, intellectual and spiritual—so they are always fully engaged and inspire others to become engaged. They understand that life is not a marathon, where you must pace yourself, but rather a series of sprints followed by recovery. These are two aspects of culture I will discuss (among others) that inspire effective leadership.
PRINCIPLE 5: **DISCIPLINE**	High achievers engage in disciplined actions and behaviors. They create a disciplined culture that fosters engagement and constructive disagreement, to achieve exceptional results.

Self-Insight
Drives Purpose

1

To win over the most complementary talent requires [...] not just talking about *what* you do, but *why* you do it.

—PWC, *PUTTING PURPOSE TO WORK*

I clearly recall the day that a friend's nephew, a software engineer in his late twenties, called me for advice. He told me that his company, a legacy software firm, had lost its mojo, and he felt like he was drifting in his career. Despite being well paid, he was frustrated by the lack of challenge in his job and questioned why he should stay. We talked about the things he believed were most important: curiosity, tenacity, innovation and teamwork. He explained that his purpose in life was to do meaningful work that had the potential to make a difference. It was not my place to advise him to leave or stay at his company. What I could tell him was that if the values and purpose that guided his actions were absent in his workplace culture, he should reassess his future with that organization.

A few weeks later, he called to say that he had resigned from that company and moved to a much smaller software firm. The new firm's success depended on the hard work of a small and motivated team.

He was making less money, but the company's values were, as he said, "totally in sync" with his own, while the company's purpose—to create cutting-edge data science software designed to make work life easier and more productive—offered him truly meaningful work. Purpose and values. Values and purpose. They work in sync.

Jim Collins and Jerry Porras view values and purpose as the core ideology of companies that are "built to last." Values and purpose are foundational for these companies: "A set of basic precepts that plant a fixed stake in the ground: This is who we are; this is what we stand for; this is what we're all about."[1] Values are the *what*: they are what an organization believes. Purpose is the *why*: it is why an organization exists. Clarity on both is essential for success.

Walmart's core values were acknowledged by its founder, Sam Walton: "If you're not serving the customer, or supporting the folks who do, then we don't need you."[2] Those values still drive the company today, over seven decades later. That's who Walmart is. The company's purpose, however, is its why: to save people money on essential goods.

Disney's core values are imagination and wholesomeness. That's who Disney is. Disney's purpose, its why, is to entertain, inform and inspire people around the globe through the power of unparalleled storytelling. Walmart and Disney live and breathe these values. They come from within. They are not borrowed from a competitor. Collins is a firm believer that values aren't born from an intellectual exercise where executives figure out which values are most profitable or sound the best. Value creation is an inside-out exercise, one person at a time building up to a shared ideology that provides a framework for decisions and actions.

When done deliberately with careful attention to consistent execution and application, value creation can be the difference between a good company and a great company. According to a 2018 study by global leadership consulting firm DDI,[3] organizations without a clear purpose are rudderless and underperform their competitors financially by 42 percent. Let that sit in the back of your mind for a moment while I tell you about the time Jim Collins changed my life.

Meeting Jim Collins

For as long as I can remember, I've been interested in building people, teams, cultures and companies. But I've always wanted something more, to build something that not only lasts, but is also worthy of lasting. Something that's excellent, resilient and respected for its contribution to the world and society. This has always been my purpose, my North Star, and I thought I had the right focus and mindset to achieve my goals until I attended a leadership conference at Stanford in the 1990s. That's when I first met Jim Collins.

After Jim presented a class on leadership, in which he discussed his latest research that informed the concept of *Built to Last*, I approached him and asked what the data said about how best to approach organizational change that had the best chance of success. He looked puzzled by the question and said, "Jim, why are you here?" I said I was running a business, our business model was being turned on its side, and I needed to figure out what to change to ensure our continued success.

He stopped me right there. "That's the wrong question. The right question to ask when you're thinking about change is, first, what *not* to change." He went on to explain that the companies that stood the test of time and consistently outperformed the market had created an architecture for success. During their long years of research for their book, *Built to Last*, Collins; his coauthor, Jerry Porras; and their team had discovered that the companies that were built to last embraced something called *the paradox of change*.

The paradox of change is this: On one hand, you don't ever want to change your core—your foundational values and purpose. On the other hand, you need to be willing to change everything else—including your strategy, your culture, your practices. Why? Because the world is going to be a different place in five to ten years, and the companies that continue to outperform learn how to adapt better than most. They remain true to their core values, beliefs and purpose, and are open to changing everything else: priorities, processes, the makeup of teams, technology and so on.

Once I understood the paradox of change, and what it takes to build a company that endures and achieves exceptional results, I asked myself, "Could this apply on an individual level?" If you could have an architecture for building an enduring institution or company, if purpose and values are foundational to becoming a successful organization, why couldn't the same architecture apply at an individual leadership level?

The Relationship between Values, Purpose and Character

When I think back to my experience working on the leadership team at MDS, I recall examples of great leadership from the top down starting with John Rogers. MDS was a company with a higher-order purpose: making a distinctive contribution to people's health and well-being. As the former CHRO, I can tell you that the entire organization was inspired by that purpose. We all felt a deep sense of satisfaction and pride in being part of something larger than ourselves. It was important to everyone that we were making the world a better place.

+5 leaders not only have laser clarity on purpose; they are relentless in pursuing purpose no matter how difficult the obstacles. In his book *Leadership BS*, Jeffrey Pfeffer recounts the tale of Amir Dan Rubin. Rubin was appointed CEO of Stanford Hospital and Clinics, an underperforming healthcare facility noted for its high levels of hospital-acquired infections and chronic patient dissatisfaction.[4] Rubin's task was to transform one of America's worst quality-of-care institutions into one of the country's best.

To accomplish this massive task, Rubin focused on developing a core mission and vision that everyone could rally around. His mission statement became "to care, to educate, to discover." His vision statement became "healing humanity through science and compassion." What's the difference between mission and vision? Rubin's mission—caring, educating and discovering—clearly represents the organization's values: "What do we believe in?" The mission is about what's truly important, not just to the CEO but to the leadership team and ultimately to all the employees. Rubin's vision statement— healing humanity—is clearly the organization's purpose: "Why are we in business?" The vision pinpoints the organization's fundamental reason for existing.

Mission and vision = values and purpose. Pfeffer goes on to explain that Rubin adopted a performance management operating model (incorporating Toyota's lean production methods to execute its strategy and manage day-to-day operations) and hired a leadership team skilled at performance improvement to implement the model. Rubin made sure to bring on leaders that understood and accepted the company's values and purpose. Even more importantly, the values and purpose were translated into practical strategies and actions that the entire workforce of the hospital got behind. Rubin drove alignment from the top executives to the frontline healthcare workers and everyone in between. As a result, waiting times shrank while patient satisfaction soared from the 14th percentile to the 90th percentile. Best of all, Stanford Hospital and Clinics continues to be ranked as one of the best hospitals in the United States a decade later—even after Rubin moved on to become CEO of an exciting new start-up called One Medical.

Another example of a leader focused on a relentless sense of purpose is newspaper publisher Katharine Graham. She took over the reins of the *Washington Post* in 1963 after her husband—the paper's owner—died by suicide. In addition to dealing with this deeply traumatic event in her life, she faced three major hurdles: she had no hands-on experience in the newspaper industry, she had few allies in the business and she was a woman. In those days, that was a big negative in corporate America. Yet many believe she was one of the great leaders of the twentieth century, and I agree. In an interview with Farnam Street's Shane Parrish, Collins noted:

> While she was dealing with her own personal grief [...] there were people who were saying, "Well, Katharine, who are you going to bring in to run it?" Meaning, what man are you going to bring in to run it? And in a wonderful, almost Aretha Franklin–like way [she said], "Thanks, I think I'll do this myself." She grabbed onto it and grew into becoming a great chief executive. But what's interesting is that she felt that the *Post* had a noble role in the world. And she had to step up to guard and protect and lead around that. [*The Knowledge Project Podcast* Ep. 67]*

That singular purpose—journalistic excellence that would rival the standards of the *New York Times*—helped her overcome her grief and transform the paper from mediocrity into a much stronger institution.[5] But before she could become a great leader, she had to suffer through many trials and tribulations. Years later, in front of a Harvard Business School audience, Graham revealed: "I had participated, at least by osmosis, in the long struggle my father and my husband had waged to make the *Post* a success. But I was a long way from becoming an effective executive and leader. That was something I had to learn by doing."[6]

But "doing" is not easy, not when you are surrounded by a pack of hardnosed newspapermen and even tougher investors. Graham also had to deal with the political environments—at the paper itself and at the White House. Then–U.S. president Richard Nixon was an adversary. Graham relied on her deep convictions, along with a select group of mentors, to guide her through the legal turmoil and massive organiza-

---

* fs.blog/knowledge-project/jim-collins/

tional risk that erupted when she decided to publish the *Pentagon Papers*. Graham came out the other side an even stronger and more determined leader, taking a newspaper scraping along with $84 million in revenue and transforming it into a media titan generating $1.4 billion in sales twenty years later when she stepped down.[7] She would eventually be recognized as one of the great chief executives of the twentieth century, with another president, George W. Bush, noting that Graham "was a true leader and a true lady, steely yet shy, powerful yet humble, known for her integrity and always gracious and generous to others."[8]

Amir Dan Rubin. Katharine Graham. These are leaders with great clarity and insight into their personal values and purpose. They brought this clarity and conviction to their role as CEO in the organizations they led. Further, they deliberately ensured that their values and purpose informed every organizational decision. For instance, when the *Washington Post* built its first website, it didn't change its values and purpose; it simply changed the venue where its values and purpose could be found. The news landscape was shifting, and the *Washington Post*—values and purpose intact—was shifting with it.

However, when an organization's values and purpose are unclear or are dictated by a leader who is not living those values and purpose authentically—leading in a way that may, in the moment, be best for the bottom line while damaging the long-term health of the organization—performance will ultimately suffer.

Take the case of General Electric. For many years, people idolized Jack Welch and the Jack Welch School of Management. If a division at GE wasn't first or second in its industry, Welch sold or closed it. He believed that organizations had to cut the bottom 10 percent—the low performers—if they wanted to keep "winning." He was all about winning, and even his autobiography was called *Winning*. Employees referred to his approach as "rank and yank."[9] Welch believed that "failing to differentiate among employees—and holding on to bottom-tier performers—is actually the cruelest form of management there is."[10]

His leadership methods led to higher profits, but were the methods going to result in a sustainable company? Over the long term, what Welch was really doing was putting employees on alert, rather than affirming them, Dr. Tim Gilmor told me. Welch was essentially saying, "I'm watching you, and if you don't perform to my standards, you're fired." "Sadly, what that approach produces over time is an organization running on fear," said Gilmor, "and ultimately the followership fades because people know it's not safe to follow that kind of leader—unless you're that kind of person and you endorse those kinds of values yourself."[11]

Having a passion to fly is essential for great pilots. Having a passion to lead is essential for great leaders.

What Has Passion Got to Do with It?

When I was with the military, my fellow pilots and I debated whether great pilots were born with the necessary character, temperament and skills or nurtured them. I found my answer one gorgeous summer afternoon at our air base in Moose Jaw, Saskatchewan. We were in the officers' mess one Friday after a very challenging week when in walked one of the most respected pilots on the base. As aspiring jet pilots, we saw him as a living legend, a test pilot, and clearly someone we admired and looked up to. He just had the full package. He spoke to us for a few minutes, and then, the floor was opened to questions. One of the student pilots stepped up and said, "It's easy for you to talk about being a great pilot, but you were born a great pilot."

This admired pilot took his time to answer: "I've heard that before, and I'm going to give you the same response that Chuck Yeager gave in *The Right Stuff*. Colonel Yeager said: 'The best pilots I know are the ones who are most passionate about flying. They fly the most. They're the most committed to flying. And that is why they are the best! It's just that simple.'" His answer surprised me. "It cannot be that simple," I thought to myself. I was expecting something different, something more profound. Years later, however, I began to realize he was right. High performance is a choice. And I learned that perhaps the most important word he was using— though he seldom uttered it—was the need to have true *passion* for what you do!

The Balcony and the Dance Floor

I've coached hundreds of leaders, and in our discussions, we routinely recognize that leaders consistently face two types of change: daily change, adapting to the everyday events that require small changes and decisions; and lasting change, engaging in an ongoing process of self-awareness, adaptability and lifelong learning.

Most leaders are good at daily change. However, it is easy to get caught up in the churn of daily decisions and lose sight of the bigger picture, the lasting change. Unfortunately, many of us try to implement lasting change that will not prove effective, because we lack an objective perspective. The Balcony and Dance Floor is an excellent metaphor about how change happens in life at a personal level. My wonderful colleague Dr. Nancy Nazer and I stumbled across this metaphor in a blog written by Shayne Tilley[12] when we were designing a creative leadership development program at Rogers.

The Balcony and the Dance Floor goes like this. If you want to become a better dancer, it's difficult, if not impossible, to do it while you're wrapped up in your dance steps on the dance floor. To achieve sustainable change and become a better dancer, you need perspective. To get it, you need to go up to the balcony from time to time, look down at yourself and see how you are dancing. Take a moment or two to study and reflect on your moves without self-criticism or judgment. What kind of moves are working for you and what needs to change for you to become better?

This powerful metaphor offers a simple way to begin the process of gaining the laser-like clarity that +5 leaders have about their personal values and purpose in life. By taking the time to step back and view things from afar, leaders can see themselves and their organizations more clearly. The leader's ability to focus on their own purpose and values, as well as those inherent in their work culture, is paramount to strengthening the organization. A clearly defined purpose and set of values creates clarity for people in how they relate to one another. People working for a leader and an organization with well-articulated and enacted foundational beliefs feel safe and confident. They can just be themselves. That leads to better engagement, and better engagement leads to better results.

In Chapter 2: Play to Your Strengths—Live with Passion, we link core values and purpose to a leader's strengths and passions, or as the epigraph for Chapter 2 reads, courtesy of Katharine Graham, "Caring about and loving what you do for a living will make you feel like the luckiest person in the world." Please turn to Part 3 and complete the activities and exercises based on the topics covered in Chapter 1.

CHAPTER 1 TAKEAWAYS

> The paradox of change can provide an architecture for growth in sustainable high performance in any individual, team or organization. The best research completed on this topic is found in *Built to Last*, coauthored by Jim Collins and Jerry Porras.

> The paradox of change is framed in two key questions:
1. What should not be changed? The answer almost always relates to an individual's or company's core values and purpose.
2. What should be changed? People and companies need to adapt to the changing world around them. The world will be a different place in five to ten years, and those companies and individuals who adapt better than most will be the most successful. As a result, strategy, priorities and culture all must adapt to maintain performance.

> Clarity of values and purpose means that the team can expect the leader to be authentic, consistent and predictable.

> Clarity of values and purpose enables others in the organization to excel and function with confidence because the leader and team members' values and purpose are aligned and shared.

> The metaphor of The Balcony and the Dance Floor is a powerful reminder about how real change happens in life.

Play to Your Strengths—Live with Passion

2

Caring about and loving what you do for a living will make you feel like the luckiest person in the world.

—KATHARINE GRAHAM

The fox knows many things, but the hedgehog knows one big thing. So goes a two-thousand-year-old saying attributed to the Greek poet Archilochus and later repurposed by Isaiah Berlin in his essay "The Hedgehog & the Fox." Berlin argued that there are two kinds of people: hedgehogs and foxes. The fox's thinking "is scattered or diffused, moving on many levels." In contrast, hedgehogs "relate everything to a single central vision [and] a single, universal, organizing principle."[1]

Jim Collins famously adapted Berlin's thinking on human behavior as a framework for corporate success in his 2001 book *Good to Great*. After years of conducting well-documented research, Collins concluded that companies that made the leap from being good to being great had leaders that "used their hedgehog nature to drive toward what we came to call a Hedgehog Concept for their companies." Conversely, Collins and his research team found that the leaders of underperforming companies, or companies that would stagnate at the *good* phase of business, "tended to be foxes, never gaining the clarifying advantage of a hedgehog concept, being instead scattered, diffused, and inconsistent."[2]

Don't act like a fox, Collins warned. Don't be an organization that tries to be all things to all people. That's a recipe for mediocrity. Instead, act like a hedgehog—an organization that knows One Big Thing. Being a hedgehog should not be the goal of an organization, however. Rather, it is an understanding that begins with a deep insight into what an organization can be best at and what it cannot be best at. Understanding the distinction between what a company can and cannot be best at, Collins found, is a crucial aspect for companies looking to move from simply being good, to being great.

Collins and his fellow researchers decided that three elements create an organizational hedgehog concept:

1. What can the organization be best at?
2. What are people passionate about that becomes expressed through the organization?
3. How does the organization make money, and is it sustainable?[3]

The point at which the three elements overlap is the sweet spot for organizations—the point where leadership and organizational strengths, passions and profit come together to amplify each other. Figure 2.1 illustrates the hedgehog concept.

If you haven't read *Good to Great*, I highly recommend you do. It is full of amazing organizational insights, and Collins and his team prove over and over again the power of the hedgehog concept as a key defining difference in companies looking to leap from good to great.

FIGURE 2.1: THREE CIRCLES OF THE HEDGEHOG CONCEPT

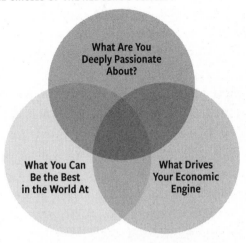

Source: Jim Collins, *Good to Great*, HarperCollins 2001, p. 96.

But what about the hedgehog concept can we apply specifically to leadership? Is there a similar process for consistently ensuring that you as a leader embrace your inner hedgehog, as opposed to fox, nature?

Define Your Personal Hedgehog

How does a personal hedgehog work? Let me give you a simple example involving my daughter Carolyn. Before she graduated from university, she asked me if I would help her get focused on her career. At the time, she was passionate about the theater. I drew the three intersecting circles on a piece of paper, and I asked her to fill them in. (To create your personal hedgehog, see Figure 2.2.) One circle was for what she thought her deep strengths are, the second for what her passions are, and the third for how she could marshal these to make a living. A couple of days later, she handed me the paper with the circles filled in. I could see that her strengths are creativity, empathy and relationship building, complemented with a strong drive, and she was passionate about being part of a theater company, and putting her love for acting and entertaining to work. She was also passionate about her family and friends, and she loved to read and learn.

I said: "I know you're passionate about acting and being part of a theater troupe, and I know you have talent. My question to you is this: 'Do you stand out as one of the *best* among your fellow actors?'" She admitted she didn't. To me, that was a red flag, because it meant she wasn't particularly differentiated, strengths-wise. I was concerned about this, but I kept my thoughts to myself and asked her about Karen, a fellow actress. Karen was someone Carolyn liked and admired. "What does Karen do?" I asked. "How does she make a living? How many weeks a year does she get to act?"

"Well, it's a really hard industry, Dad," Carolyn responded. "She gets a commercial or two, then a leading role in a production. And when she's not working as an actress? She does part-time jobs to get by." I paused for a moment and then asked her, "What do most actors do when they're not working?"

"They do what they can to get by, Dad! Some are bartenders; some work in restaurants," she replied glumly, knowing exactly where I was going with this line of questioning. "Do you see the problem?" I asked, as gently as I could. "You can't pick a set of strengths and a set of passions without circle three kicking in as well. You have to have all three. And you should consider a growing industry to work in because that is where the opportunity will be for you."

As an aside, many people ask me about getting into the television industry, because that's where my wife, Pattie, works. It's a glamorous field, for sure, but it's a tough business, and while someone may have all the poise, stamina, strengths and passion to be on television, to build your career in an industry that is under increasing pressure means you have to be one of the very best. It's not impossible to do—just harder. Further, everyone's economic needs for making a living

FIGURE 2.2: CREATE YOUR PERSONAL HEDGEHOG

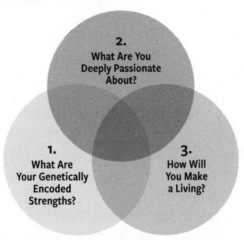

1.
What Are
Your Genetically
Encoded
Strengths?

2.
What Are You
Deeply Passionate
About?

3.
How Will
You Make
a Living?

Source: Adapted from Jim Collins, *Good to Great*, HarperCollins 2001, p. 96.

will be different. Waiting tables and acting is perfectly viable for some, especially if they are pursuing their passion.

Carolyn realized that her strategy of being a great actress and loving her job wasn't going to be enough for her. The "making a living" part wasn't where she wanted it to be. So instead of taking up an acting career, she completed a bachelor of commerce at one of Canada's top universities, went into financial services at TD Waterhouse and learned the business. A few years later, she shifted into human resources at TD Canada Trust, where she still works today, and she loves her work. She took her genetically encoded strengths (I'll cover what this means shortly), and her empathy for people and coaching, and built a great career at the bank. Her passion for seeing opportunity in change and innovation, coupled with her strength in helping people aspire to learn and develop, have enabled her to move into an exciting new area involving robotics and artificial intelligence, where she is doing a lot of value-added work helping organizations prepare for the digital transformation. And she says her job doesn't feel like a job! As her dad, I am so proud of the path she has created for herself.

The Hiring Questions I Ask

When I interview executives, I focus on a few questions to help me discover the information I am looking for. I set up the questions by saying: "Listen, you have a great background. I've read your résumé, so it is clear you've got some terrific and relevant experience. But here's my first question: 'What are the things in your life that have shaped you into who you are today?'"

My first question probes the candidate's values and purpose, because I'm looking for the right people for the team: those with the right values. As I mentioned in Chapter 1, values are critically important when it comes to fit, and +5 leaders—and potential +5 leaders—demonstrate a strong sense of who they are, what they believe in and why. These characteristics define *fit*.

To preface my next set of questions, I explain the hedgehog concept and the research in *Good to Great,* and explain that I was one of Collins's critical readers. I say, "I'm interested in knowing what your hedgehog is—your personal hedgehog." Then, I ask the first of the second set of questions: "How do you see yourself in terms of your deep strengths? Not what you're good at—I want to know the deep strengths that your DNA would define." My second question in the set probes passions: "I also want to know why you get up in the morning, what fuels you, what motivates you? In other

Carolyn's journey is an example of the personal hedgehog working at its best. But it didn't come overnight. Like many individuals I've coached in my thirty-year career, Carolyn at first struggled to get clarity. Often, people in this situation will tell me things like "I'm not enjoying my job," "My boss is not happy with my performance" or "I don't know where I'm going with my career." In many cases, when I sit down with these people and explain the three circles, they see how achieving clarity is empowering and can put them on a path to success. I encourage them to think about being the best they can be, and when they work on their hedgehog, get-words, what are you passionate about doing? What's your goal for that day? What will drive you to achieve that goal?"

With these questions, I'm probing for character, self-knowledge and self-awareness. I'm testing to see how clear the job candidates are about their strengths and passions. I have conducted thousands of executive interviews where some people respond in a bang-bang way: "This is me; this is who I am." They give it to me in ninety seconds, and then, we talk about it. Other people are all over the map, and I often have trouble following the bouncing ball as they fail to present who they are with any sense of clarity.

In my interviews, I mostly focus on circles one and two: genetically encoded strengths and passions. But if you're early in your career and deciding what industry to work in, or you're later along your career path and considering changing from one industry to another, circle three, making a living, becomes really important. Regardless of the person's situation, when we're hiring someone, we hire first on fit (values and purpose) and second on strengths and passions (what is needed for the role). It's a disciplined and focused process.

ting clarity on it often changes their life trajectory in a big way. Suddenly, they start looking for the kind of work and opportunities that are in their wheelhouse, and soon enough, they find those opportunities and discover they love what they do.

The Personal Hedgehog Process

In case you are wondering about my personal hedgehog, I have locked it down, although doing so took hard work and self-reflection—and some professional help. I've had the benefit of working with

FIGURE 2.3: JIM REID'S PERSONAL HEDGEHOG STATEMENT

To be the best in the world at helping people get on, and stay on, a high-performance trajectory in their life.

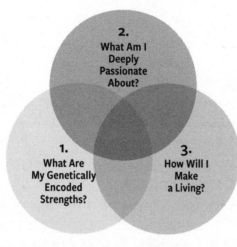

1. Deep Strengths (Differentiators)
   a) Driven to deliver
   b) Ability to build high-trust relationships
   c) Deep curiosity about people
   d) Very strong problem-solving skills

2. Passion (What fuels you?)
   a) Spending time with my family
   b) Making a difference in people's lives
   c) Building teams and culture
   d) Tackling complex change and challenge

3. Making a Living
   a) Work as CHRO of a large company
   b) Coach individuals and teams to outperform and drive impact

Source: Adapted from Jim Collins, *Good to Great*, HarperCollins 2001, p. 96.

several organizational psychologists over my career. If you haven't had the chance to work with an industrial psychologist or a skilled executive coach, I highly recommend it. If cost, timing or location is an issue, some helpful exercises are included in this book.

Figure 2.3 shows my personal hedgehog using the three circles of the hedgehog concept. Together, they address the goal that I always try to coach people to achieve: find a good job where work does not feel like work. For as a wise person once said, "When you love what you do, you will never have to work a day in your life."

I always encourage leaders to identify a primary performance strength as part of circle one. For me, that is "driven to deliver," which means if somebody asks me to do something and I say, "Okay, I'll do it," nothing will stop me from getting it done. I'll just do it. This performance strength is especially important for executives and includes, for example, having a strong results orientation or an ability to consistently deliver. It's not good enough for a leader to be great with people and a good team builder. You have to deliver. If you are a top-level executive and you want to be seen as a strong, high-performing leader, delivering has to be one of your differentiated strengths.

Circle 1: Identifying Our Genetically Encoded Strengths

What are genetically encoded strengths? How do you find them? Test them? Validate them and get clarity?

Without taking too deep a dive into genetics, I will note that our genetic makeup is based in four molecular subunits called *nucleotides*. They are chemically linked and form strands we know as deoxyribonucleic acid, or DNA. This basic structure of our chemistry means that from person to person, we are 99.9 percent alike. Yet we are readily able to know how we are different from family members, friends and coworkers. Research has proven that a mere 0.1 percent of our genome—a copy of which is present in every one of our nucleic cells—is unique to each of us.

While those differences may be accounted for in 0.1 percent of our genome, the human genome is made up of three billion base pairs, so that tiny 0.1 percent represents three million base pairs. It's those three million little differences, says Sharon Briggs, a senior scientist in the field of genomics, "that give you red hair instead of blonde, or green eyes instead of blue."[4] These three million base pairs also help explain why we have different strengths and capabilities. In business, strengths such as empathy, resilience, a strong drive, analytical skills and problem-solving abilities are valued.[5] So that is what is meant by genetically encoded strengths: they are the things you excel at, those which come to you naturally, without effort or thought. Where do you find them? These strengths are often things you've been aware of in some way since you were a child. They are as much you as your eyes or your smile.

FIGURE 2.4: DO YOU USE YOUR STRENGTHS EVERY DAY?

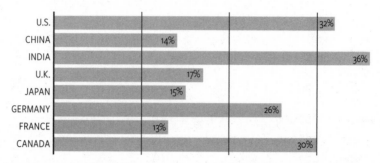

Percentage reporting they have "the opportunity to do what they do best every day" at work.
Based on Gallup's 2007 global client database.
Source: Gallup Organization, 2007.

The famous management consultant Peter Drucker liked to argue that if you focus on your strengths, you make your weaknesses irrelevant. I believe that because I see it every day. Sadly, working with strengths appears to be something few people get to do. *Strengths-Based Leadership*, published by Gallup, contains a revealing chart. It summarizes the responses of thousands of working people to one simple question: "Do you use your strengths every day?" You can see the results in Figure 2.4.

In Canada and the United States, only about a third of workers say they use their strengths every day. That means they're working with one arm tied behind their back, metaphorically. Even more interesting is what the chart is also telling us about that third who are playing to their strengths every day. They are almost certainly the high performers because they have something that the others don't—clarity. They have clarity about their strengths. I believe they arrived at that clarity through relentless self-examination and self-acceptance. Strengths and passions go together like purpose and values, but unlike strengths, passions are often more difficult for people to precisely define. So let's turn to an investigation of passions.

There's an old saying that every college student seems to have saved in their memory: "Find something you love to do, and you'll never have to work a day in your life."

Circle 2: Defining Our Passions

A few years ago, I had the opportunity to coach a high-performing leader named Steve who happened to be the head of strategy for a multibillion-dollar company, and I have chosen his experience to illustrate the idea of defining our passions.

CASE STUDY

Matching Role to Strengths and Passions

Steve was smart and strategic, outstanding at process and program management, and a great team builder. In fact, he was emerging as one of the best heads of strategy in North America. He was one of those executives whom people admired, and he was also on every executive search consultant's short list. But Steve wasn't happy: he aspired to be a CEO, not to head up a strategy team.

Over the course of several coaching sessions, Steve laid out his strengths and passions for me, and we talked about his career aspirations. Through our discussions, we focused on two possible outcomes. He could stay on the path he was on and be seen as one of the best strategy leaders in the industry. This path did not excite him. Alternatively, he could build off his strategy experience and pursue a CEO role at another company—a goal he was deeply committed to. In our discussions, I learned he was passionate about being a builder. He loved a challenge and was not afraid to step into messy situations. He recognized he might not have all the deep strengths a CEO needed, but he was convinced he could get there. So he resigned and went off to pursue his dreams, which meant leaving for another city.

Several years later, we bumped into each other, and he told me that despite his passion to lead an organization, he'd not succeeded as a CEO. He had come to realize that, at best, he was an average chief executive. He simply did not have the commercial strengths he needed to be successful, and he told me he was moving back into the strategy space. The good news is this: he had become more differentiated by having this CEO experience. He's still passionate about leading, but now, he is leading within an area of his greatest strength.

Steve realized that passions need to be supported by strengths. Clarity of passions comes from putting together a series of successes. The more you play to your strengths, the more success you have, the more you enjoy your work and the more informed you become about what you love to do. "It's like running every morning," Steve told me. "I've always been a good long-distance runner, but I never ran every morning, not like those dedicated guys you see. It was hit or miss. But I knew it was time for me to get fit again, so I decided to try and make running a regular part of my week. And you know what? The more I did it, the better I got, and the better I got, the better I felt ... before I knew it, I was running every morning."

Steve's passions for building and for taking on the role of a CEO had to be matched by the right set of strengths. He knew going into a CEO role that he had weaknesses, but he was not one to back down from a challenge.

Steve had hit on an important truth. There's an iterative relationship between what people like to do and their deep strengths. The better a person gets at something, the more they like something, and eventually, they discover they can drive impact; they can make a difference. Ultimately, they might realize that more than just really enjoying that something, they are really good at it, too. That trajectory builds confidence. I think one of the reasons the best leaders are so successful is that they're so clear about their passions and their strengths. And that gives them confidence. They just own it. But they didn't start there. They started on likes and dislikes while getting clarity on strengths. They iterated back and forth. They tightened the relationship between strengths and passions over time, and began to make more of a difference and achieve more of their goals. Then, they became more and more locked in and more confident as a leader. Later, when they built their teams, they didn't build them so that everybody mirrored the leader. Instead, these leaders built strength in areas where they weren't strong, because no one is strong in all areas. But many people can share the same passions, and that is key to a strong team.

Circle 3: How Will You Make a Living?

Before we go further, I want to provide some insight on the third circle of the personal hedgehog framework. Circle three is purely about leveraging your strengths and passions into a successful career and life. It addresses the decision you make about what industry you decide to work in. Is it a growing industry where opportunities for people like you not only exist, but expand over time?

When I am coaching individuals who are early in their career, we always begin by discussing the first element of circle three, industry. A growing industry is a springboard for career success. You do not have to pick a growing industry. But if you select an industry that is facing headwinds and shows negative growth year over year, you have to be even better in your role to grow your career simply because the number of opportunities will be fewer.

The second element of circle three addresses your career path. This brings all three circles together to define the kind of work you can do to earn a living and ideally, increase your earning potential over time. The goal is to play to your deep strengths, live your passions every day and select an industry where you can step into a role that gets you into your wheelhouse.

Putting It All Together

I began my career in the military. I had a passion for serving others and strength for leading people. During my time in the military, I deepened and gained insight on my passions and strengths. However, I chose to leave the military and move into business, where I began to discover my passion for operations. Then, I moved into general management and finally into human resources, reporting to the CEO. Along the way, I discovered that my true passions were building people and teams, and stepping into complex business challenges and turnarounds. My career decisions have allowed me to earn a great income, and create wealth for me and my family. But my journey started in the military with circles one and two, which is where your personal success comes to life every day.

One of the reasons people become great leaders is that they understand that clarity allows the leader to focus on what they need to know. I believe we absolutely need to know how our leadership behaviors affect other areas in our lives. So if you engage me as your coach, we will first discuss your values and purpose, and then, I will ask you to articulate your deep strengths and passions. If you can't clearly articulate your strengths and passions, I will say, "Fine, here's your homework assignment, which is to complete your personal hedgehog."

As you work on the assignment, you'll start to get a feeling of insight, change or renewal, a positive feeling like putting on a piece of clothing and finding that it fits perfectly. Because you need to get to the point where your hedgehog fits like a glove, I'll tell you to take a week or a few weeks to think deeply about your life and ask yourself fundamental questions like these: "When you're at your best, what strengths are you leveraging? What passions are you following?" When you've written down your reflections, I'll ask you to share them with your spouse, partner or someone you deeply trust—someone who's got your back and wants to celebrate your success. No half measures. It has to be all the way. You have to be willing to take a risk and be emotionally vulnerable for the process to work effectively.

That's the first part. Next, I'll ask you to express your personal hedgehog to colleagues or friends who you know will offer an honest assessment and to say to them: "I'm trying to get clarity on my genetically encoded strengths and my passions. Can I share this with you and speak to you about it, and can you give me some feedback on it? I need to know if this reflects who I am." You will ask them questions like, "When I'm at my best, do you see me playing to these strengths and following these passions?"

These are hard questions which will sometimes be answered with hard-to-hear truths. But that is why they are reserved for the people who know you best, whom you trust and whom you respect. Completing a personal hedgehog can be a difficult and sometimes emotional journey. But it is also liberating. However, to effect real change and gain true perspective, you must commit to the process. If you do, you'll be better for it. Trust me.

· · · · ·

In this chapter, you have been asked to continue a process of self-discovery which began in Chapter 1: knowing your values and purpose, strengths and passions. You take your authentic self to the team, and in turn, you will expect authenticity to guide team members' behaviors and actions. This sets up the discussion for Chapter 3: Finding the Right People and Building a Strong Team, and as you will discover, I believe without a doubt that the most important decisions we make in life relate to people. To make the right choices, we need to know who we are, what our passions are and how we can match role to strengths to earn money but also increase our earning potential.

Please turn to Part 3 and complete the activity and exercise based on the topics covered in Chapter 2.

CHAPTER 2 TAKEAWAYS

> One of the most powerful concepts that came out of Jim Collins's *Good to Great* research is the three circles of the hedgehog concept (see Figure 2.1). The personal hedgehog concept (Figure 2.2) is about clarity and focus. Research proves that the most significant impact comes from leaders and organizations which operate at the intersection of the three circles.

> A personal hedgehog concept is not a goal to be the best, a strategy to be the best, an intention to be the best or a plan to be the best. It is about developing a deep understanding of what you can be the best *at*. The top leaders operate this way every day.

> Playing to your strengths and passions is the path to your greatest success.

Finding the Right People and Building a Strong Team

I consider my most important job to be recruiting, because the greatest people are self-managing. —STEVE JOBS

The most important decisions we make in life relate to people. The choices we make about who will journey through life with us, who we will count on as friends and who will make our time at work that much more rewarding—these decisions have the power to be life altering.

To choose as best we can, we need to understand who we are. That is why it is necessary to discuss purpose and values, strengths and passions. Doing so openly and authentically will help you find clarity about who you are and what is important to you. Purpose directs our actions. Values reveal who we are and what we believe in as individuals. Strengths are those things we are genetically encoded to do, and passions are where all of the above coalesce to create an expression of how we can live our best life.

All of this is also true of organizations. Our collective actions are an expression of the organization's purpose. We work hard to ensure that the organization succeeds and thrives. Getting clarity on these foundational principles, personally and organizationally, is the first step on your journey to becoming a +5 leader. The next step is to translate this foundation into tangible results. In other words, the question now becomes, "How does the work get done and who's going to do it?" This leads us to the third principle of personal growth and organizational success, which is building a high-functioning team.

Up until Jim Collins's research was published, the prevailing wisdom on building a great company followed frameworks and models devised by many of the global consulting companies. For example, McKinsey devised the 7-S Framework, which started with the creation of a strategy that needed to align to structure, systems, style, staff and skills all wrapped around a shared set of values.[1] McKinsey essentially asked its clients, "Where are you today as a company, where do you want to get to, and how do you want to compete?" In other words, to borrow Collins's analogy from *Good to Great* of a business being like a bus, the underlying question in the model McKinsey devised was, "Where do you want the bus to go?" McKinsey's model focused on strategy first.

In contrast, Collins's research team discovered that the good-to-great companies began their transitions differently. They put people before strategy! This insight completely upended conventional thinking. Instead of asking, "Where do you want the bus to go?," Collins said organizations should ask, "Who do we want on the bus?" After years of research, Collins discovered that all the good-to-great companies focused on people first. They got the right leader in place, who in turn set about building the right executive team even before a vision was forged. Perhaps the classic example of this strategy is Hewlett-Packard, a company whose greatest idea wasn't even a product; instead, it was something called the HP Way. In his book of the same name, David Packard explained the HP Way: "The Hewlett-

Packard Company believes that the best results come when you get the right people, trust them, give them freedom to find the best path to achieve objectives, and let them share in the rewards their success makes possible."[2]

The HP Way describes Hewlett and Packard's unquenchable desire to get the right people on the bus before anything else could be accomplished. Only then did they try and figure out their strategy—what direction they should take the company in. History shows that HP outperformed the general market and one of its major competitors, Texas Instruments, by a significant margin from 1957 to 1990.[3]

The best leaders I've seen over three decades of working in the corporate world are the ones that consistently make the right people decisions. In fact, I believe that making the right people decisions is the signature quality of a +5 leader. So how do you get the right people on the bus and in the right seats? "It's about being rigorous without being ruthless," said Collins.[4] It's about being methodical and, above all, disciplined. In *Good to Great*, Collins laid out what the research said are the most critical people practices or disciplines for leaders to follow to drive consistent high performance. I've outlined Collins's findings below and provided some examples from my thirty-plus years in organizational management to back up Collins's claims.

It goes without saying that every leader wants to hire well, but surprisingly few know how to do it on a consistent basis.

The Three Disciplines[5]

1. If in Doubt, Do Not Hire

I contend that hiring right has little to do with a candidate's credentials, education or experience, but everything to do with the fabric of an individual. I am referring to what an individual is made of. Don't get me wrong—at the end of the day, the people you hire must be able to do the job and do it well. But a hiring practice that prioritizes knowledge and experience is going to hinder selecting the right people for your team.

The first thing the best leaders do is determine if a candidate is the right fit. What are some of the telltale signs that a candidate might not be the right fit? It could be a lack of enthusiasm for the organization's purpose. It could be a work ethic that while strong may not be sufficiently collaborative to align with the democratic way the team gets things done. It could be that academic achievement is off the charts, but people skills are wanting.

Whether a candidate is capable of doing the job is irrelevant if they are not aligned with the purpose and values of the team and organization. Fit flows from values and purpose, so the leaders who want the best for their team begin with an inside-out orientation of people. My top qualities are values, purpose, work ethic, character and intelligence. It's that simple. When I interview, I probe deeply to find out whether or not candidates humanize their world. Do they care about people? Are they coachable? Are they open to giving and receiving feedback? Do they have humility? Do they have a sense of humor? Is their outlook on life positive?

You might think, "That all sounds great, Jim, but human beings have biases and filters, and it is a known fact that leaders hire in their own image." The effects of biases can be diminished by always bearing in mind that the best hiring decisions—or said more strongly, the only hiring decisions—seek to identify people who believe in team and culture as long-term drivers of performance.

Once an individual passes the "right fit" goal post, the next questions are the following: "What seat should they be in? What skills and strengths are needed to complement a team that is already high functioning? What role is best for the candidate?"

That role may be defined by a candidate's strengths that moderate a leader's weaknesses. No leader is strong in all areas, not even a +5 leader. So the goal is to build a team that complements rather than replicates the leader's strengths. You're looking at trying to find the right combination of capability, skill, background and experience while never trading off between experience and fit. Because a +5 leader is a mentor and coach, and has attracted and retained talent by ensuring that the organization has a learning culture, I'd argue that experience is the least relevant metric when it comes to hiring. Hire the person who has the right fit with the team. Experience will come.

Leaders often ask me, "Is there ever a time where you might hire based on skill and experience, even if the fit is not ideal?" My answer is yes, but only in areas where the people management demands are not large and where the demand for deep, relevant experience is critical to getting the work done well—areas such as digital transformation, cybersecurity and software programming. Even if someone isn't a perfect fit in terms of being the right person, even if they don't pass all the criteria—assuming you've determined that their integrity is sound—I would still go forward with one proviso. I would make sure their influence on the team and the size of their team are manageable. If you do that, you minimize the risk while filling a critical hole.

We can look to Netflix as a prime example of hiring the right people based on fit. Patty McCord, the company's chief talent officer from 1998 to 2012, said hiring for fit helped transform Netflix into a juggernaut:

> If you're careful to hire people who will put the company's interests first, who understand and support the desire for a high-performance workplace, 97% of your employees will do the right thing. Most companies spend endless time and money writing and enforcing HR

policies to deal with problems the other 3% might cause. Instead, we tried really hard to not hire those people, and we let them go if it turned out we'd made a hiring mistake.[6]

2. Put Your Best People on Your Biggest Opportunities— Not Your Biggest Problem

This second discipline, a result of Collins's research, is classic. Assigning your most creative and innovative executives to solve the organization's most pressing problems can make your organization good, but asking your most creative and innovative executives to capitalize on the largest opportunities can make your company great. Collins illustrates this discipline with the case of Joe Cullman, CEO of Philip Morris during the 1960s. In the 1960s, the largest market for the tobacco company was domestic. To expand its market beyond North America, Cullman assigned his top executive, George Weissman, to get it done. At the time, Weissman was managing a thriving domestic market, and by comparison, international sales were paltry, at about 1 percent. For the number-two person in the company, this decision appeared to be a massive demotion. "I didn't know whether I was being thrown sideways, downstairs or out the window," Weissman said. "Here I was running 99 percent of the company and the next day I'd be running less than one percent."[7] However, Cullman's decision turned out to be a brilliant move because under Weissman's masterful direction, international became the largest and fastest-growing division in the company's history.

3. When You Know You Need to Make a People Change, Act!

For many leaders, having to move a member off the team or fire them is hard. But this was another dimension identified in Collins's research. When it comes to getting the wrong people off the bus, I always coach leaders in the following way: "Take your time, and take as long as you need to, because you're making a decision that's going to affect people's lives and going to affect the team. But once you've made your decision, act."

However, often leaders take longer than they need to make the call. Or they decide to make a change and then procrastinate. They typically think, "Well, it's better to stick with Julie or Jayman for the time being because I need somebody in that job." But the truth is most leaders should act quickly for their sake, the organization's sake and the employee's sake. The employee is under stress, aware that their level of performance is falling behind and that the team is being affected. Often, when you make the change in a respectful way, the employee is relieved. That feeling goes both ways, because when I talk to people about hiring and firing decisions, the thing I hear most often from a leader is, "I waited too long."

A leader who has the right people on the team need not worry about team morale when someone needs to be moved off the team. Let's say you have recently taken on a role with a new company and have seven managers reporting to you. The organization is undergoing a turnaround, and you are to contribute to the initiative. You assess all the managers based on fit and decide to let three go. The four remaining managers will see the value they have to the organization, and you will ensure that their value is acknowledged and rewarded.

That's the beauty about the "right people" approach. Getting the right people on the bus, the wrong people off the bus, and the right people in the right seats, and building a high-performance team works. Not only does it work, but it's also uplifting for people. It gets all the negative energy out, and it clears the way for progress. It liberates the team. It cuts out all the politics. People are now more committed to what you're trying to do, not less. They're less worried, not more. That's the beautiful thing about getting it right.

CASE STUDY

The Three Disciplines and Team Building

When I came into my current job as chief human resources officer at Rogers Communications, one of Canada's largest companies, I inherited a very hard-working HR team, but at the same time, the company was struggling to recover from some missteps after the passing of its celebrated founder, Ted Rogers. The business had lost momentum, and changes had to be made. Meanwhile, the organization looked at HR as a young, talented and dedicated team but one that did not bring a lot of value to the table. If we at Rogers wanted to get back to number one in our space, the executive team had to reinvent our whole approach to building leaders, teams and culture. As a result, I completely rebuilt my top team in HR. Only one of the seven people who reported to me survived the change. These were tough decisions, but I had to get the right people on the bus. That was phase one. Only then did we as a team start to figure out, from a people and culture perspective, exactly where we were going to drive the bus.

We needed to answer the challenge: "How were we going to help the company outperform the competition?" To make that happen, we established a fresh set of people practices, and we began the process by engaging our three thousand people leaders in the challenge. Then, through communication and a commitment to building the coaching skills of our people leaders, we drove the process deep into the heart of the company. By this, I mean we followed the three disciplines. We hired for the right fit, put our best people on our biggest opportunities, and acted quickly once we had made those difficult decisions on where we needed to upgrade talent.

Our efforts paid off. Performance radically improved. We drove engagement from a percentage in the high 60s (which is below the median in North America) to 87 (which is in the top quartile). The HR team didn't do that on its own, but the company couldn't have done it without the right team in HR. A lot of people counted the company out after our founder died. We were told we couldn't win without his vision and leadership. Well, we proved them wrong, and we did it by making the company one of the best places to work in the country eight years in a row. We were recognized with a Most Admired Corporate Cultures award. I think Ted Rogers would have been proud.

The "Right People" Principle and Our Personal Life

If the "right people" principle is key to building high-performance teams and companies, it is even more critical in your life. Some of my most insightful coaching discussions with leaders arise when I ask if they are surrounded by the right people in their work and life, and if not, how to deal with it and set things on a better path. Just think for a moment: perhaps the most important decision any of us makes in our lives is who we want to spend it with. Why? Because our partners and closest friends are important enablers of our success. The most important people in our lives are the people who have our backs, who celebrate our successes even more than we do, and who are there for us in the good times and especially in the tough times. This cannot happen if values are not shared, if our purpose in life is not respected and believed in, or if our strengths and passions are not celebrated throughout our lives.

These principles came home to Pattie and me when our daughter Jane came over one Friday night to have a "fireside chat" with us—a ritual we enjoy with all our children. Jane is a remarkable young woman. She is confident, poised and a gifted athlete, and she lights up the room when she walks in. She always applies herself to the best of her ability. After graduating with her master's degree and subsequently being hired, she appeared to be on a roll career wise. But she had a big problem she needed to solve. Jane was in love with a terrific young man and outstanding teacher who lived ninety miles away. She wanted to be with Nick, and we could see from the look on her face that she needed to talk things through. We talked about her decision and shared our own story with her. For Pattie and me, our decision to build a life together was based on our love and our knowledge that we shared common values and life goals, and we could not imagine a life without each other. Once we had told our story, silence fell in the room. Then, Jane looked at us, smiled and told us that she was moving on to build her life with Nick. She quickly landed a new job, and is weaving the same magic she always has and excelling at what she does. We are so proud of her and the amazing person she has become.

I'm a big believer in keeping things simple, and the right people principle is as simple as it gets. If you're wondering how to make the right people decisions, you can't go too far wrong with the following section of my personal playbook. It's an important part of my coaching guide for leaders, it has worked for me for years, and it will keep on working for years to come. The formula for the Right People Playbook is this:

1. Get the right people on the bus.
2. Get the wrong people off the bus.
3. Put the right people in the right seats.
4. Build a high-performance team.

Shared Values + Unique Strengths = The Building Blocks for High-Performance Teams

Today's teams need to think about how they work, which means responding and adapting to change that is constantly accelerating. Artificial intelligence and data analytics are upending the way we work and think, customer demands are intensifying (response time is often expected in minutes instead of hours or days), and a new generation of employees is searching for a different kind of purpose and engagement. Successfully managing this kind of tumultuous change takes great leadership within the team.

No one realized this more clearly than Abraham Lincoln. When Lincoln became president in 1861, the United States was tearing itself apart at the seams. The dispute between the pro-slave and anti-slave forces as well as the growing division over economy and trade was so intense that several southern states had already seceded from the union, more were threatening to leave, and civil war would break out just weeks later. The president desperately needed strong leadership to get through what he already knew would be an unprecedented period in American history. Fortunately, Lincoln possessed the self-awareness and self-confidence to realize that he needed the best people by his side. These were "people who were leaders in their own right and who were very aware of their own strengths," said Lincoln biographer Doris Kearns Goodwin in an interview with the *Harvard Business Review*.[8] Lincoln astounded his political foes by including in his cabinet three of the most powerful men in America—William H. Seward, Edward Bates and Salmon P. Chase—each of whom had bitterly lost the Republican nomination against the relatively unknown Lincoln. For good measure, Lincoln brought in three members of the opposition party as well.

A huge part of Lincoln's leadership strength was his ability to surround himself with people who could debate with him and question his assumptions, said Goodwin. "It particularly helps if you can bring in people whose temperaments differ from your own," she noted, adding that CEOs, not just political leaders, can learn from this. But Goodwin was quick to point out that keeping your friends close and your enemies closer is not entirely accurate. "The idea is not just to put your rivals in power—the point is that you must choose the best and most able people."[9] Although the top executive is critically important to building a great executive team, the reality is that great teams drive great companies. No CEO can drive a company on their own.

Phil Knight, for instance, built Nike into one of the world's most iconic companies, but he relied on a superb team of passionate people every step of the way. His team was sometimes described as a bunch of misfits, something Knight readily admitted. "Johnson couldn't cope in the so-called normal world of nine-to-five," he wrote. "Strasser was an insurance lawyer who hated insurance—and lawyers. Woodell lost all his youthful dreams in one fluke accident. I got cut from the baseball team. And I got my heart broken."[10]

But Knight's team had a complementary set of unique strengths and an abiding passion for their purpose. Jeff Johnson was a relentless salesman, Rob Strasser turned out to be an incredible negotiator and Bob Woodell was a supply-chain guru. They may have been misfits, but they were brilliant, each in their own way. And each carried a chip on their shoulder, so they fit together like fingers in a glove. As the company grew, its rate of growth accelerated so fast that Knight often had to reorganize the roles of his top executives twice a year. But they seldom complained. No matter how chaotic it got, the team never stopped believing in the vision or its CEO. And Knight never stopped believing in his team: "I trusted them wholly," he recalled in his memoir, *Shoe Dog.* "I didn't look over their shoulders, and that bred a powerful two-way loyalty."[11]

· · · · ·

Organizations have no trouble presenting a public face about who they are. Enron famously carved its values (Respect, Integrity, Communication, Excellence) into its lobby wall. Words to live by. The trouble was that top leadership didn't live them. The culture of Enron was poisonous. People lied and went to jail for their mendacity.

What is a leader to do when an organizational culture is slipping away from the values and ethics that are its stabilizer? First, the leader must know and understand their own values, purpose, strengths and passions. Next, they must get the right people on the bus—people with shared values and complementary strengths. Then, they need to build a high-performing team by getting the right people in the right seats. The result is a workplace that is safe, welcoming and

Leaders help shape and build the culture within their teams, and culture is changed one leader at a time, one team at a time. You behave your way to restoring a culture to its center or starting a new culture. That's what getting the right people on the bus is all about.

engaged to its full potential. Only then does the leader decide where to drive the bus.

But what if the workplace is not engaged to its full potential? What happens to the organization? Is the lack of engagement the fault of the leaders? The employees? Or both? What, if anything, can be done to raise the level of engagement, and how is it done? The answers to these questions lead us to the main topic for Chapter 4: Getting to Full Engagement. But first, please turn to Part 3 and complete the activities and exercise for this chapter.

CHAPTER 3 TAKEAWAYS

> Instead of asking, "Where do you want the bus to go?," Collins said organizations should ask, "Who do we want on the bus?" His research challenged the assumptions in many organizational design models, including the 7-S Framework by McKinsey.

> The three disciplines are
> 1. If in doubt, do not hire. (And when you do hire, hire for the right fit.)
> 2. Put your best people on your biggest opportunities—not your biggest problem.
> 3. When you know you need to make a people change, act!

> Our partners and closest friends are important enablers of our success.

> Although the top executive is critically important to building a great executive team, the reality is that great teams drive great companies. No CEO can drive a company on their own.

> Leaders help shape and build the culture within their teams, and culture is changed one leader at a time, one team at a time. You behave your way to restoring a culture to its center or starting a new culture.

Getting to Full Engagement

4

Energy and persistence conquer all things.

—BENJAMIN FRANKLIN

My thinking about high performance changed materially when I met Dr. Jim Loehr at a two-day conference about engagement. Loehr and his colleague Tony Schwartz had penned a best-selling book, *The Power of Full Engagement,* which sought to educate executives about managing energy, not time. I found the book profoundly useful in life and in the workplace. I learned from Loehr and Schwartz that life is not a marathon but a series of sprints, that there is a delicate balance between two forces (stress and recovery) and that achieving balance between the two is critical in managing our lives.

Before Dr. Loehr turned his research to what he calls "corporate athletes," he spent thirty years working with world-class sports stars as he searched for the secret to consistent high-level performance under immense pressure. What did he find when he measured the likes of Pete Sampras, Monica Seles, Mark O'Meara, Eric Lindros and Grant Hill? Elite-level champions—the titleholders, the best of the best in every sport—managed their energy differently than their fellow competitors did. They went through a process of energy expenditure and renewal which not only enabled them to perform at the highest level, but also allowed them to perform at that level on demand.

After spending those two days with Loehr, I walked away with a deeper insight into what drives extraordinary performance. This insight wasn't only about the sports field or the workplace. In fact, I began to understand that engagement is really the core of what a life well lived is all about. So how do we stay engaged? How do we tap into our purpose, values, strengths and passions to grow as individuals and as leaders? How do we take this personal growth and transfer it to building great teams? We do it through the power of full engagement.

The Power of Full Engagement and the High-Performance Pyramid

Loehr and Schwartz defined The Power of Full Engagement as "the skillful management of energy, individually and organizationally."[1] To illustrate this point, Loehr quoted Jack Nicklaus, a renowned golfer whose focus and will to win enabled him to win a record eighteen majors:

> I can't concentrate on nothing but golf shots for the time it takes to play 18 holes. Even if I could, I suspect the drain of mental energy would make me fuzzy-headed long before the last putt went down. In consequence, I've developed a regimen that allows me to move from peaks of concentration into valleys of relaxation and back again as necessary [...] My focus begins to sharpen as I walk onto the tee, then steadily intensifies as I complete the process of analysis and evaluation that produces a clear-cut strategy for every shot I play. It then peaks as I set up to the ball and execute the swing [...] I descend into a valley

as I leave the tee, either through casual conversation with a fellow competitor or by letting my mind dwell on whatever happens into it. I try to adhere to this pattern whether I'm playing my best or worst.[2]

In his own way, Nicklaus spelled out Loehr and Schwartz's paradigm. Despite Nicklaus's legendary powers of concentration, even he admits that he couldn't concentrate on the game for an entire round of eighteen holes. Instead, he managed his energy, sought stress and used his downtime as productive time systematically, at multiple levels—physically, mentally and emotionally. This enabled him to maintain a supercharged focus for those critical moments when he was sizing up a shot and swinging the club. During the four hours it takes to complete a competitive round, losing concentration at key moments is easy. Nicklaus avoided this by developing a set of rituals which enabled him "to move from peaks of concentration into valleys of relaxation and back again." See Table 4.1 for a summary of the new paradigm of engagement, as demonstrated by Nicklaus.

It is this carefully calibrated movement back and forth between stress and recovery (peaks and valleys) that gives high achievers the remarkable ability to reach what Loehr called our "Ideal Performance State." This state enables us to be at our peak when we need it

TABLE 4.1: THE POWER OF FULL ENGAGEMENT

Old Paradigm	New Paradigm
Manage time	Manage energy
Avoid stress	Seek stress
Life is a marathon	Life is a series of sprints
Downtime is wasted time	Downtime is productive time
Rewards fuel performance	Purpose fuels performance
Self-discipline rules	Rituals rule
The power of positive thinking	The power of full engagement

Source: Jim Loehr and Tony Schwartz, *The Power of Full Engagement*, Free Press 2003, p. 6.

most. No one can be at their best 24/7: "When we expend energy, we draw down our reservoir. When we recover energy, we fill it back up. Too much energy expenditure without sufficient recovery eventually leads to burnout and breakdown."[3] When Loehr and Schwartz began testing and measuring the effects of their model on thousands of corporate executives, they found that performance increased dramatically when their model was employed, and that those who used the model had improvements in their health and well-being.

In my experience, most executives are super athletes. However, unlike athletes, who spend most of their time in practice, the typical executive may work as long as ten to twelve hours a day with no practice time but big consequences for failure. Their career may span thirty to forty years. That's a long haul. And that is why the best leaders have a deep understanding of energy management and its link to high performance.

As shown in Figure 4.1, Loehr and Schwartz's High-Performance Pyramid is a bottom-up approach to building and maintaining four separate but highly related human capacities. Each is important in and of itself. However, when combined through the use of ritual—an action that is beneficial to recovery but also done almost without thinking—Loehr and Schwartz argue that we will not only improve our performance but also lead longer and happier lives.[4]

Physical Capacity

Physical capacity, the first building block of the High-Performance Pyramid, is essentially being ready to play. An elite-level athlete would never stand a chance if they didn't have a healthy diet, get adequate sleep and employ an appropriate exercise routine. Corporate athletes are no different. Without these basics, it becomes incredibly hard to perform to the best of your abilities.

Sports science research conducted over the past decades has proven that the key to building strength and stamina is finding a way to strike a

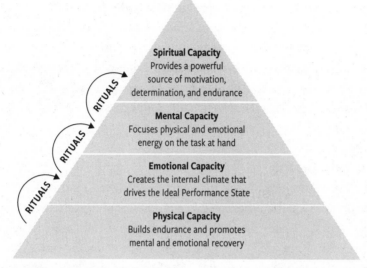

Source: Jim Loehr and Tony Schwartz, *The Power of Full Engagement*, Free Press 2003, p. 12.

balance between work (i.e., stress) and recovery (i.e., rest). For physical fitness, if we give our bodies an adequate recovery period from times of stress—usually two days—our muscles not only heal but grow stronger. Conversely, if we don't work our muscles, they grow weak and atrophy.

On a micro-level, Loehr and Schwartz observed this stress/recovery relationship with elite athletes in moments as small as the fifteen to twenty seconds between points of a tennis match. They reported that the athletes who consistently engaged in routines or rituals that promoted an alternating rhythm between stress and recovery—something as simple as visualizing the next point while adjusting their strings— were able to lower their heart rates "as much as 15 percent to 20 percent between points."[5]

Conversely, players who lacked these rituals failed to perform at an optimum level. Why? Because their bodies and minds weren't allowed to de-stress. As a result, the energy they expended was not allowed to rebuild, so the athletes became vulnerable to frustration, anxiety and loss of concentration. They became, as Loehr and Schwartz not-so-delicately put it, "far more likely to choke under pressure."[6]

For +5 leaders, similar routines and rituals might include breathing exercises, a quiet moment to reflect, a water break or a short walk. Marathon meetings are commonplace among top-tier executives, and finding subtle and unique ways to engage in recovery tactics during such sessions is key to keeping fully engaged.

Emotional Capacity

The second building block in Loehr and Schwartz's framework is emotional capacity. When we use our emotional capacity, we create the internal climate that helps strive for the ideal state of engagement: a super-focused calm and an optimism about the task at hand. I remember watching Canada's Mike Weir win golf's Masters Tournament in 2003, and in post-match interviews, he emphasized how calm he was throughout the round despite the enormous pressure he faced trying to win his first major. Weir had clearly entered an Ideal Performance State, what many of today's athletes call "the zone."

Managing our emotions is essential to sustaining peak performance, but managing emotions is not always easy. At the conference I attended, Loehr told the story of a corporate client whose colleagues found him difficult to deal with. This individual had an anger management issue, and eventually, it began to affect his team's performance. With Loehr's support, the client agreed to undertake a series of rituals designed to help him take control of his negative emotions. He began the process by learning to become more aware of his body's signals—telltale indicators like a racing heart and chest tightness that told him he was on edge. He engaged in breathing exercises to calm down and made an effort to soften the tone of his voice. He worked on putting himself in the other person's shoes. The final step was to focus on framing his response to people in a different and more positive way. Learning to be more emotionally flexible allowed this individual to experience a broad range of emotions and deal with them effectively, even if the emotions were negative.

Mental Capacity

The third building block of the High-Performance Pyramid is mental capacity: the ability to sustain high-level focus and to shift seamlessly across different trains of thought and points of view. Performance management coaches are increasingly turning to cognitive therapy to enhance their clients' performance. But for Loehr, cognitive performance therapy includes more than just positive self-talk and effective time management. It includes such rituals as meditation along with other recovery activities. For corporate athletes, these can include deep breathing and visualization exercises. Visualization helped golfer Tiger Woods excel like few others in any sport. Earl Woods taught his son from an early age to create a mental image of the ball going into the hole before every shot. Corporate athletes prepare for meetings by finding quiet places where they can visualize the outcome of their meetings before they take place. The mental capacity building block of the pyramid becomes increasingly important as we grow older, because we must systematically stretch ourselves cognitively to protect against age-related mental decline.

Spiritual Capacity

The building block at the top of the pyramid is our spiritual capacity. The word *spiritual* may seem a little out of place in a business setting, especially when we are focusing on high performance, but what Loehr is referring to is the energy we derive from a strong sense of purpose and values. I think of this as the purposeful level, which provides us with the drive and motivation to accomplish more than we believed we were capable of. Every great leader in history—from Winston Churchill to Abraham Lincoln to Josephine Baker to Nelson Mandela—has been driven by a larger sense of purpose. Churchill's higher purpose was to secure victory against fascism, Lincoln's was to abolish slavery, Baker's was to fight racism, and Mandela's was to end decades of injustice and oppression.

As Loehr and Schwartz state, "Spiritual strength is reflected in the commitment to one's deepest values, regardless of circumstance, and even when adhering to them involves personal sacrifice."[7]

CASE STUDY

The High-Performance Pyramid in Action

Let me give you an example of how the pyramid can work in everyday life. David was a second-year business commerce student at one of Canada's premier universities. Prior to heading off to university, he worked with an organizational psychologist to help him figure out the career path that was most likely to be fulfilling for him. The assessment results showed that David was intelligent, personable and quick witted, and that he had a zest for life. But the psychologist flagged one caveat. It seemed that while David had all these qualities that aligned with career success, he was not ready or able to fully engage in his studies. At Christmas break in his second year, David called me in a panic. He had failed three of his five courses and had to meet with the dean of the business school to make a case for continuing his studies.

In our coaching session together, we focused on three key questions: "What's going wrong? What does success look like for you? What are you going to say to the dean of the business school in your meeting tomorrow to remain in the program?" We also discussed the High-Performance Pyramid (Figure 4.1) and what he was experiencing that was getting in the way of his engaging in his studies. He agreed that his biggest deficit was the need to commit to some simple rituals that reinforced both his emotional calm and optimism as well as the need for more focus to tap into his mental capacity to succeed.

After we finished our coaching session, David dusted himself off, looked in the mirror, pulled himself together from a physical, mental and emotional point of view, and most importantly, set some near-term goals, established rituals and committed to living according to a set of personal values. He turned his academic situation around in a very big way. Today, he is distinguishing himself in sales at one of Canada's top financial institutions. I have coached David for years, and I am especially proud of him because he happens to be my son!

The Importance of Rituals

The High-Performance Pyramid works equally well for both elite athletes and high-achieving executives because it embraces the broad concept of stress and recovery through rituals on all four levels. Why are rituals important? Loehr explained it to me with a question: "If you can't perform a particular task effectively when you're feeling relaxed and unpressured, how likely will you be able to do so when the pressure is high, or you are in the midst of a crisis?" Building precise rituals makes it possible to push away the distractions and fears that arise in high-stress situations. High performers stay fully engaged on a personal level by managing their energy on multiple levels: physical, emotional, mental and spiritual/purposeful.

You might find that your recovery rituals for each level are similar. If you develop a meditation ritual as part of your mental recovery, you'll likely find that the physical sensations and calm you develop via meditation are akin to the benefits from the deep breathing exercises you use as an emotional ritual. The pyramid works because it is intuitive, interconnected, simple and effective. Achieving a personal state of ideal performance requires making choices that will advance and not derail your progress in each of the four high-performance levels. And because you are a leader, your progress will have beneficial effects on the physical, mental, emotional and spiritual/purposeful energy of your colleagues generally and your team specifically.

Given that high achievers learn how to manage their energy and reach their Ideal Performance State on demand, can organizations reach a collective high-performance state? Is it wishful thinking to consider that committed and energetic leaders can influence an organization's culture to the extent that employees will somehow be energized as well and turn around engagement numbers?

Getting to Higher Engagement Means Taking Stock

When it comes to engagement, most leaders are winging it. After all, improving team and individual engagement is clearly in every leader's best interest, yet the numbers continue to show that most leaders could do a better job.[8] With all the time, effort and money being spent driving employee engagement, why are so few people inspired by their jobs? What can leaders do to transform disengaged employees into team members that are inspired by their work, play to their strengths and learn and grow every day?

It is unprincipled and unfair for a leader to expect and demand full engagement if the leader is not demonstrating total engagement. We often think that the least engaged are the rank-and-file employees, but that simply isn't true. In fact, a staggering two-thirds of managers are unengaged. And the primary reason? They are not given enough support from their own managers. "Shifting how your company trains and supports managers, and repositioning them as coaches," said James Harter, Gallup's chief scientist, "is essential for helping managers to change culture."[9]

But again, what about those team leaders? How many of them have checked out, why, and what is the impact on the employees who report directly to these leaders? Good leaders don't begin the process of engagement building by presenting a model or process and asking that it be followed. Rather, they start with results. They analyze the behaviors of high-performing teams within the organization. They look outside the organization at the competition, to find out why they are not beating the competition. Then, these leaders do something more—they take stock of themselves and their leadership team.

+5 leaders make sure they are fully engaged by managing their energy along every layer of the High-Performance Pyramid. They ask themselves the following:

> Am I, and is my leadership team, laser focused on where we are going as an organization and why we are going there? If not, why not?
> Has a crisis or a variety of external demands made me lose sight of my purpose or affected my passions?
> Have I got the right people on the bus?
> Am I managing my energy well? According to Patrick Bliley of executive search firm Spencer Stuart, leaders "must never lose sight of the outsized impact their energy and their behavior can have on others who are working for them."[10]

Only after these fundamental questions are addressed is it time to ask best practices questions:

> What are the best-performing leaders doing to engage their teams?
> What are the best-performing companies doing to engage their employees?
> How might some of their practices work for my teams and organization?

I have some examples to give you of two companies in very different businesses that have taken employee engagement to a higher level.[11]

CASE STUDY

Employees Are Given Opportunity and a Clear Growth Path

What's not to love about Costco—especially for its employees, who consistently rank it as one of the best places in the world to work. Jim Sinegal, Costco's founding CEO, established a people-first culture that offers learning, training, opportunity to grow and good compensation. In return, however, the company expects its employees to take full ownership of their work. If you've been to a Costco lately, you've experienced that expectation in person. Every employee seems to know where everything is and is happy to help you find it, and they work calmly under pressure, no matter how busy the store gets. (And it's always busy!)

There's a good reason employees take ownership, according to HR consultant Josh Bersin. Costco empowers its employees by cross-training them to handle many positions. "They manage cash registers, stock shelves, rearrange the store, develop promotions, and manage others. The result is both a set of highly empowered teams that have the training and freedom to be both autonomous and productive as well as above-average retention and engagement rates."[12]

There's more to it than that, of course. Current CEO Craig Jelinek also makes sure the right people are on the bus and that a clear path to advancement within the company exists. Over 70 percent of employees are hired internally:

> Our view is we want to have a company for the long haul and continue to grow the sales and grow the profits fairly and make sure

there's always opportunity for our employees to grow. If you look at the last 30 years, our stock has grown about 15%–16% a year in value, and we think we've got a pretty fair return for our shareholders.[13]

Costco has given a pretty fair return to its employees as well, as the data on employee engagement show. Turnover is a remarkable 1 percent at the management level and less than 5 percent at the hourly level.[14]

CASE STUDY

Employees Are Given Excellent Benefits

Fast-rising software company Salesforce ranks near the top of *Fortune*'s list of 100 Best Companies to Work For because CEO Marc Benioff makes sure employees are fully engaged in life outside their work, not just in it. In an interview he gave to the *New York Times*, Benioff said that he made a pledge to himself when he was a young man: "When I start a company, I will integrate culture with service." Today, Salesforce is a $100 billion company, and Benioff has made good on that promise. Every employee understands what service means, because it starts on their very first day of work. Benioff described what happens after new employees are shown around the offices: "We take them out and they do service in the afternoon. They'll go to a homeless shelter or they'll go to the hospital or go to a public school. This is a very core part of our culture." Salesforce lives and breathes engagement at every level because Benioff and his leadership team want a company where employees "are excited to come to work every day, where they feel good when they get here."[15]

To that end, the company offers employees seven full days of paid time to volunteer in their local communities and up to $5,000 every year to spend on any causes they like. At the same time, the company's Wellness Reimbursement Program offers employees $100 each month to use any way they want, whether toward physical fitness, therapy, nutrition or something else. Meditation rooms have been installed throughout the offices so employees can rest and recover, and if they need tips and tools to help them eat right, sleep well or practice mindfulness, employees can visit Camp Pono—Salesforce's virtual wellness site—any time they wish.[16] It's all part of Salesforce's employee-centric culture.

Getting to Higher Engagement, One Person at a Time

Besides an exceptionally high level of employee engagement, Costco and Salesforce have something else in common: a clear sense of purpose, along with leadership that is itself engaged on multiple levels. Employee engagement filters down and up the organization, but it always starts at the top. Leadership must walk the walk if employees are to get fully engaged. That said, leaders can only do so much.

TABLE 4.2: EMPLOYEE ENGAGEMENT PLAYBOOK

1.	Alignment: With purpose, values, strategy and priorities (at organizational and team level)
2.	Expectations: By leadership and employees
3.	Feedback: As timely and constructive, with praise for good work
4.	Opportunities: For personal and career growth
5.	Psychological Safety and Trust: In that employees' voices are valued and encouraged, and they have high trust in managers and executives
6.	Training: In the skills and tools people need to succeed

Source: Created by Jim Reid.

Ultimately, engagement must emerge, develop and grow organically. It can't be manufactured. The employees' collective desires and energies have to be in sync with a higher purpose in order for the employee experience to be people focused and fulfilling.

A rich employee experience begins when employees awaken to the possibilities of what they can achieve as a true partner in the organization they work for. For this to happen, a number of positive factors must be in place. Based on decades of research by Gallup and others, and in combination with my own experience and research, I created a playbook that helps guide me and my team.[17] To keep it as simple as possible, I distilled the process of achieving engagement into six qualities that must be present in an organization's culture. Table 4.2 lists these qualities.

These six drivers—alignment, expectations, feedback, opportunities, safety and training—collectively create an exceptional employee experience. This in turn creates high levels of employee engagement, which leads to a willingness to take ownership of one's work, which creates a natural desire to go the extra mile with customers. The happier the customer experience, the stronger the financial results. Together, these drivers represent a simple but powerful value chain, illustrated in the graphic below, that leads to extremely high levels of performance.

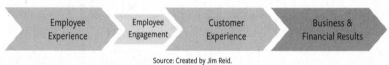

Source: Created by Jim Reid.

If you build an exceptional employee experience, you create a more inspired employee. Inspired employees produce stronger customer experiences, which drive superior business results. A study by Jeff Cava, CHRO for Starwood Hotels and Resorts Worldwide, showed how direct the link can be between employee engagement and customer experience. "Increased collaboration between departments in the hotel, self-reported by employees, was very predictive of reduction of customer complaints," said Cava in a recent interview with McKinsey. "We intuitively knew that employees' attitudes had a massive impact on client satisfaction, but this time it was real data!"[18] It's no accident that Starwood employees are engaged because they fully understand Starwood's purpose, which is to consistently exceed their guests' expectations of Starwood's products and services.

The Path to Top Quartile Engagement

Without a doubt, engagement should be the core people metric that every organization needs to measure. No matter what your starting point is, these six simple steps will improve your engagement baseline score over time:

1. It's important to adopt a consistent set of questions to measure engagement. I have always based engagement at the individual, team and company level on four dimensions. The questions below are drawn from a company called Kenexa and have been widely recognized as a global standard:

   > *Pride*: I am proud to say I work for company X.
   > *Advocacy*: I would recommend company X as a great place to work.
   > *Loyalty*: If I were offered a comparable job with similar pay and benefits at another company, I would stay at company X.
   > *Satisfaction*: Overall, I am satisfied with company X as a place to work.

2. Wrap the four engagement questions around a set of additional questions that address all six elements in the Employee Engagement Playbook. Try to keep the total number of questions to a maximum of between thirty and thirty-five, if possible. Having more than one question per element is often a good idea to give you better feedback from your teams.

3. Annually, conduct an employee survey to get feedback from your teams on what is working and what needs to improve. Ensure that you emphasize that the survey is about making the company stronger, so their employee experience will improve over time. Participation rates above 75 percent are needed to gather the best insight and data from your teams.

4. Once the survey is complete, analyze the data, and perform basic analytics to determine what the key drivers are for each team, each division or function, and the company. Almost always, the drivers of engagement will be drawn from the six elements of the playbook, but the analysis needs to be done at all three levels (team, division and company). Not every team is the same, so to improve team engagement, you need to focus on the strongest drivers of engagement for that team specifically.

5. Communicate the results openly and transparently to everyone. Best-practice companies often communicate results at the team, division or function, and company level. But the key is to hold each leader accountable for improving their team's score year over year. In my experience, it is not the absolute score a team gets that determines success; it is the degree of improvement in the score over time that matters.

6. Hold your leaders accountable for strongly communicating survey results, and building and implementing an action plan to improve year over year. This accountability is critical, but note that an engaged leader understands this and will need little reminding. This is another reason to have the right people on the bus.

Following these six steps can set you on the journey to build high-performance teams across your company. The cumulative impact of having high-performance teams builds a fully engaged culture, and a fully engaged culture wins in the toughest times as well as the good times.

. . . . .

Engagement is the core people metric behind sustainable high performance, and this is just as true of teams as it is of people. When they need to be at their peak level of performance, high performers consistently rise to the challenge and deliver. Also, because high performers are fully engaged at multiple levels—physical, emotional, mental and spiritual/purposeful—they are healthier and less stressed than their peers, and thus able to sustain their performance over the long haul.[19] Research and simple logic tell us that fully engaged employees are measurably more productive and happier than disengaged employees are, and likely healthier too. Organizations with high engagement levels measurably outperform their peers. So you might ask, "What qualities does an organization possess that enable it to sustain a high level of engagement and performance?" I believe that one quality in particular is the foundation to such a culture, and this quality is revealed in the title of the next chapter: Inner Discipline. Before reading that chapter, proceed to Part 3 and complete the activities and exercise for this chapter.

CHAPTER 4 TAKEAWAYS

> Life is not a marathon but a series of sprints; a delicate balance exists between two forces (stress and recovery), and achieving balance between the two is critical in managing our lives.

> When it comes to driving full engagement, leaders must not only lead the way; they must also set a good example.

> Our Ideal Performance State enables us to be at our peak when we need it most. No one can be at their best 24/7: "When we expend energy, we draw down our reservoir. When we recover energy, we fill it back up. Too much energy expenditure without sufficient recovery eventually leads to burnout and breakdown."[20]

> To achieve full engagement, we must be physically energized, emotionally connected, mentally focused and passionately aligned with a higher purpose.

> Good leaders don't begin the process of engagement building by presenting a model or process and asking that it be followed. Rather, they start with results and ask themselves, "What team practices will deliver these results?"

Inner Discipline

> An organization can only carry out its mandate if there is discipline, and where there is no discipline there can be no real progress.
> —NELSON MANDELA

chose to open this book with a spotlight on values and purpose because having clarity about these critical elements of leadership influences all the other competencies and skills of a +5 leader and how that leader gets things done. If you look back at Dr. Jim Loehr and Tony Schwartz's new paradigm in *The Power of Full Engagement*, the idea that purpose fuels performance speaks clearly to the power that values and purpose have: they are the essential foundation for excelling as a leader.

Two of the best leaders I have worked with in my career are Gerardo Chiaia and Dirk Woessner, and they are great examples of leaders who use values and purpose as the foundation for themselves and their companies.

I first met Gerardo Chiaia after joining Husky Injection Molding in 2008. I soon realized he is a gifted people leader—compassionate but tough, driven to win, authentic and inspiring. He lived his values and played to his strengths every day while building a stellar sales team across multiple countries and cultures. Not surprisingly, he was recruited to be CEO of multinational plastics company Logoplaste at a critical time in its growth history.

Dirk Woessner and I met in Toronto after Rogers launched a global search for a president to lead our $7 billion consumer wireless business. Like Gerardo, Dirk is a values-focused leader, relentless in his drive to win, and with tremendous energy and natural leadership skills. He understands that talent wins, so he quickly assembled a terrific team that took Rogers back to number one in telecom in three short years. In early 2021, this gifted leader was appointed CEO of CompuGroup Medical in Germany.

While both of these leaders have values and purpose as their foundation, they also share one more commonality: indefatigable discipline. This discipline gives them access to an even higher gear they can engage to excel.

Gerardo and Dirk embody the principles laid out in the first four chapters. They represent the +5 leaders who work at every level of the organization. I've seen them in action, in good times and bad, and they have figured out how to consistently perform at a high level. They can do it because they check the four boxes discussed so far:

1. They're crystal clear about their purpose and values.

2. They play to their strengths and do it with passion.

3. They know how to get the right people in the right seats.

4. They're fully engaged and create an environment in which their teams can be engaged and at their best.

But they also check a fifth box: inner discipline. They understand that a disciplined culture begins with self-discipline that is inculcated in the teams and organization. +5 leaders understand that self- and team discipline is the key to unlocking performance and delivering outstanding results. They put a laser focus on how people work together because they know that an agile, responsive and innovative team is the building block of an organization. The energy and enthusiasm of each single performance unit can infect an entire organization. How do you build a high-performance culture that provides people and the teams they contribute to with the support they need to work at an exceptional level? We will shortly arrive at the secret sauce, but let's first examine the relationship between culture and performance.

The Interplay of Culture and Performance

Peter Drucker famously said that culture eats strategy for breakfast. Every leader needs to cultivate a deep understanding of culture if they want to drive sustainable performance. The proof can be found in a multi-year study by John Kotter and James Heskett, published in their seminal book *Corporate Culture and Performance*. The study results showed that strong cultures (defined as those that "highly value employees, customers, and owners, and encourage leadership from everyone in the firm") outperformed other comparable companies by four times in terms of revenues and a whopping seven times in terms of profits.[1] Kotter and Heskett examined the cultures of two hundred companies and found incontrovertible evidence that a strong corporate culture produces strong financial results.[2]

As you can see from Table 5.1, the twelve companies described as having a "performance-enhancing culture" substantially outperformed companies that had a weak culture and did so in every major category.[3]

TABLE 5.1: CORPORATE CULTURE AND PERFORMANCE

	Average Growth for Firms with Performance-Enhancing Cultural Traits	Average Growth for Firms without Performance-Enhancing Cultural Traits
Increase of revenue	682%	166%
Expansion of workforce	282%	36%
Increase of stock price	901%	74%
Increase of net income	756%	1%

Source: Adapted from John P. Kotter and James L. Heskett, *Corporate Culture and Performance*, Free Press 2011.

Jim Collins and Jerry Porras, in their landmark study *Built to Last*, concluded that culture was a critical driver of performance. In his book *Good to Great*, Collins argued that a culture of discipline separates the great companies from their lesser-performing peers.[4] He defined the culture of a great company as one composed of disciplined people, engaged in disciplined thought, taking disciplined action. The kind of discipline he was referring to created freedom for people to act in the right way. Far from a straitjacket, it was a launching pad for greatness, because discipline provides people with the confidence to confront the brutal facts and adjust course when necessary. Discipline rooted in purpose enables people to rely on their purpose to guide the toughest of decisions.

Nevertheless, Collins pointed out that discipline in and of itself will not produce great results. He and his research team found "plenty of organizations in history that had tremendous discipline and that marched right into disaster, with precision and in nicely formed lines."[5] Collins illustrated this point by profiling two companies, Burroughs and Chrysler, both of which were led by powerful, highly disciplined leaders—Ray MacDonald at Burroughs and Lee Iacocca at Chrysler. Neither developed a culture of inner discipline, however. Instead, discipline was imposed. MacDonald and Iacocca personally disciplined their organizations through force. But there is a big difference between an organization that imposes discipline and one that lives discipline every day through its collective values, purpose, strengths, passions and engagement.

Without discipline, values can get washed out over time, purpose can become fuzzy, strengths can atrophy, passions can die out and many of the right people may leave. Without discipline, the four other principles lose their effect. Starved of motive force, the organization's flywheel begins to slow. A culture of inner discipline not only prevents this from happening, but it also keeps the flywheel moving at optimum speed.

Inner discipline creates resilience to maintain its direction and not get thrown off course by outside forces and internal adjustments.

Inner Discipline: The Secret Sauce of Performance

I have come to believe that great companies thrive because they possess an inner discipline at every organizational level. Inner discipline develops when organizations have the right leaders—those who are clear about their purpose, understand their deep strengths, take full responsibility for their actions, and do so with passion and skill. They

FIGURE 5.1: THE THREE CIRCLES

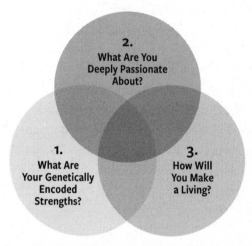

Source: Adapted from Jim Collins, *Good to Great*, HarperCollins 2001, p. 96.

operate within the three circles introduced in Chapter 2 and shown again in Figure 5.1.

The most talented leaders I've met, coached and observed view shaping a culture of accountability and progressiveness as an unswerving commitment. I've observed the teams these leaders build and coach, and how the teams play to the leaders' strengths, make decisions based on clear and consistent values, and are fully engaged in their work. People receive encouragement and support in a culture of psychological safety, where trust in each other is paramount. When leaders say, "We're all in this together, so let's move in the same direction," they demonstrate a team-first attitude. If they consistently act that way, their culture grows stronger because culture is behavior driven.

Conversely, if leaders show or tolerate unprofessional behavior (for example, if leaders bully people or if teammates use bullying tactics), the companies get the culture they deserve. If leaders fail to intervene to stop dishonesty, backstabbing or recriminations, a lack of accountability will poison the culture. The organization develops a me-first culture when leaders say: "If you're on my team, you're a friend, you're one of us; and if you're not on my team, you're the enemy." A me-first culture is a toxic culture, toxicity breeds poor performance, and poor performance worsens over time as the right people leave and those who remain become increasingly disengaged.

The Five Hallmark Behaviors of Great Leaders

To this point, I have focused on the principles that define a +5 leader. I am now going to turn the discussion to five behaviors that define the work of great leaders (that there are five is coincidental). Great leaders may each have a unique outlook on life, but they are consistent in their outlook and deliver results on a sustainable basis. The hallmark behaviors are

> practicing humility
> having a builder's mindset
> having clarity of mission
> displaying grit
> telling stories that make connections

This inside-out discipline of consistent behavior sets expectations for and within the leaders' teams and ultimately shapes the high-performance culture that all leaders strive to achieve.

Practicing Humility—Laying the Groundwork for Action

Humility is that wonderful leadership behavior that says *we* is bigger than *I*. Such leaders give others credit for their achievements, while shouldering the blame when things go sideways. These leaders are often naturally modest people who dislike the spotlight, and are frequently loath to pat themselves on the back no matter how much they accomplish or how hard they work. Practicing humility means listening well to and having empathy for others. It means genuinely caring about people and in return having people do their best work, because they feel respected and perhaps even honored.

Collins's research proved that humble leaders drive better results. While they may often be "self-effacing, quiet, reserved, and even shy,"[6] they are fiercely driven by a cause that is bigger than themselves, and people are drawn to leaders with this kind of selfless ambition. Another way of looking at Collins's findings is to see a connection between being humble and empowering others. A *Journal of Management* study by Professors Amy Ou of the National University of Singapore, and David Waldman and Suzanne Peterson of Arizona State University, reinforced the importance of humility. After studying over one hundred small-to-medium firms in the U.S. technology sector, the authors reported that "humble CEOs may be more likely to take a long-term perspective and, thus, may have stronger effects on long-term firm outcomes."[7]

Leaders who care deeply about people have a greater appreciation of their team members' strengths and contributions, said the study's authors. Humble leaders "actively gather information from various angles" and avoid rejecting information that contradicts their thoughts. As a result, they empower those around them. In contrast, ego-driven leaders tend to centralize power, which weakens their teams by rendering "others powerless and passive, thus eliminating the motivation for lateral collaboration."[8]

In *Good to Great*, Collins neatly summarized the concept of the humble leader with an analogy he called "The Window and the Mirror."[9] When things go well, what do humble leaders do? They thank the team. They look out the window and give credit to others: "Look at what we accomplished together," they might say. When results fall short, they look in the mirror and take responsibility. The buck stops here: "What we tried to do didn't work," they may tell their team, "and at the end of the day, I'm accountable for that outcome."

Team members will take on more responsibility under a humble leader, and decisions will be made collaboratively to achieve the goals the company has set. The strong followership produced by a leader's humility cannot be understated for the extraordinary outcomes that result.

Having a Builder's Mindset—Where Bold Vision Is Born

The second hallmark behavior of the most talented leaders, and the reason they are so likely to create sustainable success, is that they possess a builder's mindset. They not only love to build businesses; they also love to build and grow people, teams and cultures. Some gifted leaders build communities and even nations. Builders also love to learn, fueled by their curiosity to constantly build better teams and team members, which creates organizations where learning and development are open to all.

In *Built to Last*, Collins and Porras referred to these kinds of leaders as "Clock Builders, Not Time Tellers."[10] Clock Builders build something that tells the time forever, long after they are gone. They operate like architects and engineers because they build organizations and high-performing cultures that last. In contrast, Time Tellers have a special ability to tell people the time anywhere. They are able to time the market with a great idea, vision or product. While it is true that great visions and great ideas can propel a company forward, over time the world changes and a once-great idea begins to lose its appeal and relevance. It takes artistry and skill to be a Time Teller, but this skill often dies with the artist.

Clock Builders, however, do not rely on a single idea or vision like the Time Tellers do. Instead, the organization itself is the creation. Clock building is a great metaphor for how the best leaders think and operate. They think organization, not idea. They think people and culture, beyond profit and loss. They take the long view. If you were to talk to a Clock Builder, they would probably agree with this proverb: "Give a man a fish, and you feed him for a day; teach him how to fish, and you feed him for a lifetime." This is exactly what the best leaders do!

There's a poem that perfectly captures how the most talented leaders think about building things that matter and making a difference in the world. The poem was sent to me by one of the executives in my learning group when I attended the Stanford Executive Program on organizational change run by Jim Collins and Jerry Porras. My colleague told me that the poem, originally written by American poet Charles Benvegar, was quoted in a speech given by Lou Holtz, one of the most successful college football coaches at Notre Dame:

> I watched them tearing a building down,
> A gang of men in a busy town.
> With a ho-heave-ho and a lusty yell,
> They swung a beam, and the side wall fell.
> I asked the foreman: "Are these skilled—
> And the men you'd hire if you had to build?"
> He gave me a laugh and said: "No, indeed!
> Just common labor is all I need.
> I can wreck in a day or two
> What builders have taken a year to do."
> And I thought to myself as I went my way,
> Which of these roles have I tried to play?
> Am I a builder who works with care
> Measuring life by a rule and square?
> Am I shaping my deeds to a well made Plan,
> Patiently doing the best I can?
> Or am I a wrecker, who walks the town
> Content with the labor of tearing down?"

Beautiful and simple. Building—not tearing down or dividing—is what the best leaders do.

Having Clarity of Mission—Where Purpose Is Acted On

When I was a young military officer, I learned a great deal about mission. When I signed up, I agreed to serve my country even if that meant putting myself in harm's way. When I was given instructions, the priorities were clear. Follow-through was everything. The military has a relentless focus on results. The stakes are too high not to achieve the purpose of a mission. When leaders pursue a mission, everyone totally commits to support the goal. I saw it all the time. Whatever it took, all our energy, focus and effort was on delivering success. This commitment was a universal trait. When I trained with the U.S. and German militaries and other NATO forces while serving in Europe, that same level of commitment among my fellow soldiers was present.

Not surprisingly, a mission mindset exists in top-performing leaders and organizations. When Professors Thomas W. Malnight, Ivy Buche and Charles Dhanaraj launched a global study of the key drivers of high-growth businesses in 2011, they were surprised to discover a driver they hadn't considered at all: purpose. Although purpose had long been considered an add-on for companies wishing to improve employee morale and give back to the community, it was seldom seen as a core part of executing an effective strategy, wrote the study's authors:

> But as we worked with the high-growth companies in our study and beyond, we began to recognize that many of them had moved purpose from the periphery of their strategy to its core—where, with committed leadership and financial investment, they had used it to generate sustained profitable growth, stay relevant in a rapidly changing world, and deepen ties with their stakeholders.[12]

This is not a coincidence.

CASE STUDY

"A Family of Individuals United by a Single, Shared Mission"

Microsoft's Satya Nadella offers us a shining example of how an outstanding executive linking purpose, mission and results can restore a once-great company to its former heights. Under Bill Gates's leadership, Microsoft grew into one of the largest and fastest-growing companies in the world. Then came the dot-com crash of 2000, and Gates handed the reins to a new CEO, Steve Ballmer. The company began employing a ranking system of management similar to Jack Welch's at General Electric. People were graded on a curve, and one out of ten members of a team had to receive a "poor" rating, even if everyone in the group was an A player, wrote Kurt Eichenwald in *Vanity Fair.* "Every current and former Microsoft employee I interviewed—*every one*—cited stack ranking as the most destructive process inside of Microsoft, something that drove out untold numbers of employees."[13] The result: Instead of competing with other tech firms, Microsoft employees ended up competing with each other to keep their job, and teamwork was crippled. Twelve years of underperformance later, criticism built to the point that anonymous employees swarmed social media complaining that Ballmer was a tone-deaf manager.

Enter Satya Nadella. When he took over as CEO, he transformed the company from an old-world, inward-looking software firm into a cloud-driven powerhouse. Thanks to Nadella, everyone became absolutely clear about their mission, and the company became what he referred to as "a family of individuals united by a single, shared mission"[14] centered on "empowering every person and every organization on the planet to achieve more."[15] Nadella backed up his relentless focus on mission with a strong sense of empathy for others, especially customers. "I don't think [empathy] is simply a 'nice to have' but I believe it is at the center of the agenda for innovation here at Microsoft," he said. "Our core business is connected with the customers' needs and we will not be able to satisfy them if we don't have a deep sense of empathy."[16] The mission was to get employees to walk in the customers' shoes so they could deliver exactly what their customers needed.

Leading through empathy and other soft skills (that were once derided by corporate experts) gets results because the workforce is getting younger and the old ways of managing are disappearing fast. For Nadella, mission clarity trumps everything. "The only thing that I value and look for in other leaders," said Nadella, "really circles around the notion of: are they creating clarity and energy?"[17] The result: Microsoft's market value has quadrupled from the time that Nadella, a lifelong employee of the company, was named CEO in 2014. By 2020, Microsoft was vying to be the most valuable company in the Western world.

In his book *Start with Why*, Simon Sinek wrote that leaders can't lead until they know why they are leading. "It all starts with clarity," he said. "If you don't know *why* you do what you do, how will anyone else? If the leader of the organization can't clearly articulate *why* the organization exists in terms beyond its products and services, then how does that leader expect the employees to know *why* to come to work?"[18]

When Nadella was asked what he considered the hallmark behavior of the best leaders, his answer was simple: "The most important attribute that any leader needs to have—and it is often underestimated—is the need to create clarity when none exists."[19] He was talking about clarity of mission. Nadella provided that clarity when Microsoft needed it most, and he continues to provide it today.

Displaying Grit—Never Letting Go of Purpose

Think of a time when you hit a massive setback in your life, when you were knocked off your feet and you had to dig deep to recover, not just for a day or two, but for a prolonged period when you had to reach inside to find an inner strength you never thought you had. It is exactly this kind of hallmark behavior—I call it *grit*—that I see the best leaders display time and time again. It is a characteristic I look for when I coach and interview executives. What experiences shaped them in their life? What are they made of? What kind of adversity have they faced? How do they deal with failure? This inner grit is a discipline that almost always serves leaders well in work and life.

One of my favorite expressions is "steel gets hardened in a furnace." People get tested in the toughest of times, and how they navigate through this test shapes their character for years to come. In 2014, I was looking to hire an accomplished organizational development leader to help Rogers Communications make some transitions that included workplace culture. When I interviewed Nancy Nazer, who has a PhD in organizational behavior, she told me her story, and what a story it was.

She was born in Iran during a time when the political climate was very unstable. Nancy told me that her early childhood memories were peppered by bombings, shooting in the streets and sudden blackouts that left families feeling fearful and uncertain. Almost overnight, people lost their freedom. Her father, who held a very senior government position, decided to flee Iran just before the revolution led to further violence and privation. Nancy lived on three different continents before she was ten, and as the eldest child, she had no choice but to develop the kind of grit and inner toughness that only this kind of experience can bring about.

With only a suitcase full of belongings, Nancy and her family moved to England, where they had to learn a new language, figure out how to fit into a new culture and make new friends. During this time, she told me her parents remained optimistic, never wavering from the belief that they would put down roots in a country that would welcome them. Their next stop was Canada, where they began the process of rebuilding and connecting to a new community and way of life.

These early hardships shaped Nancy's way of looking at opportunities, challenges and the world, and propelled her to complete her PhD in her twenties and go on to become one of the most talented organizational development experts in North America. Her passions for people, belonging and culture helped her land her current role as CHRO at one of Canada's most successful global pension-fund companies with over $100 billion in assets under management.

Angela Duckworth wrote a seminal and highly recommended book called *Grit: The Power of Passion and Perseverance*. She defines grit as a combination of "passion and sustained persistence applied toward long-term achievement, with no particular concern for rewards or recognition along the way."[20] I think that's an excellent way to define this hallmark behavior of a +5 leader.

One of Duckworth's interviewees for the book was JPMorgan Chase's CEO, Jamie Dimon. Although at the top of his game and leading Citigroup to new heights as its president, he was fired by the bank's chairman (and his mentor), Sandy Weill. Dimon didn't fade away and fall off the business map like most leaders fired in such a public manner. Instead, Dimon dusted himself off, regrouped and became the CEO of one of the biggest and most successful banks in the world. He battled throat cancer and bounced back after a heart attack that required emergency surgery. Some doubted if he would return as CEO. They were wrong. After a few weeks of recovery, Dimon returned to work in fighting form: "Entering into a crisis is not the time to figure out what you want to be," he noted in his annual shareholder letter. "You must already be a well-functioning organization prepared to rapidly mobilize your resources, take your losses and survive another day for the good of all your stakeholders."[21] To this day, he believes his firing, and the year he took off to reflect and regroup, made him a better leader. In his words, actions, beliefs and sheer determination, Dimon epitomizes the word *grit*.

Telling Stories That Make Connections

The final hallmark behavior of +5 leaders is the ability to connect with others through the spoken and written word. Those leaders who seem to connect effortlessly and effectively have an ability to make the complex simple and connect mission to engagement through storytelling. They understand that context gives color to story, and a simple message is the best way to drive home the basis for change. Context and a simple story bring clarity, simplicity and relatability to these leaders' messages, which enables them to connect with large numbers of people. Leaders as storytellers connect to heart and mind, empowering people and fostering a high level of commitment to get the work done.

Consciously or not, +5 leaders seem to intuitively understand the basic principles of good storytelling. In his book *The Power of Story*, Jim Loehr suggested that storytelling has three rules: 1) purpose; 2) truth; and 3) action. "All good storytelling converges around these three ideas," he said.[22]

To illustrate how a great communicator employs these rules, consider Nadella's famous 3,187-word email to the workforce when he became Microsoft's CEO in 2014. He asked employees to help him transition the company away from its focus on "devices" and toward the cloud. He galvanized employees by communicating a message of purpose, truth and action. Here are key excerpts from Nadella's July 10, 2014, email:

> [Purpose:] We will reinvent productivity for people who are swimming in a growing sea of devices, apps, data and social networks [...]
> [Truth:] [In the past] we have described ourselves as a "devices and services" company. While the devices and services description was helpful in starting our transformation, we now need to hone in on our unique strategy [...]
> [Action:] We will obsess over our customers [...] You will see new investments in our workforce, such as enhanced training and development

and more opportunities to test new ideas and incubate new projects [...]
Finally, every team across Microsoft must find ways to simplify and
move faster, more efficiently.[23]

Look at the clarity of Nadella's mission statement and how bold it
was. He acknowledged the obsolescence of past strategy yet honored
how far it had taken Microsoft. He was clear on how Microsoft would
transform through customer focus, people development and innovation. Like any great story, Nadella's had a beginning, middle and end.

Disciplined, purposeful communication is an essential behavior of the most talented leaders because the world is flooded with
messaging, ideas and conflicting concepts. In order to mobilize a
workforce, you have to cut through the noise and create a narrative
for people, one which paints a picture of a better future—a future that
people believe will take them, their team and their company to a better place. Storytelling inspires people to go on the journey, to focus
their skill, engagement and energy on the actions needed to effectively change for the better. Stories humanize the work world, a
world where data and business jargon obscure the efforts of people
to produce results.

The Five Behaviors in Action

So how does this kind of discipline play out in the real world? Each
year, the *Harvard Business Review* lists the world's best-performing
CEOs, and the 2019 edition tells us something interesting. While the
average tenure of a CEO is about seven years, the average tenure of
the best-performing CEOs is fifteen years.[24] To see why, let's examine
some of these hallmark behaviors in action. I chose the following five
leaders because while they are completely different personalities,
they all personify what it means to be a humble, tenacious and
mission-driven leader.

Kevin Lobo, CEO, Stryker Corporation: Listen, Learn and Engage

When Kevin Lobo assumed the top job at Stryker—a Fortune 500 medical devices firm and one of *Fortune*'s 100 Best Companies to Work For—he enhanced an already strong culture by putting a laser focus on the company's eighty-year-old mission: "Together with our customers, we are driven to make healthcare better."[25] To update the mission, he established four new subthemes: globalization, innovation, collaboration and cost optimization. Under Lobo's tenure as CEO, Stryker's revenues have nearly doubled, from $8 billion to over $15 billion. Much of the company's recent growth has come from acquisitions. But each one was made with what Lobo called "an intense focus on customers," and each originated from one of Stryker's divisions, not from head office. This decentralized strategy is intentional because Stryker's goal is to keep the company close to its customers. "We spend 6.5 percent of our revenue on R&D but don't have any central R&D at all," Lobo said. "And even though we do a lot of deals, we only have two people in corporate business development. All the other business development people—28 people—sit in each of our divisions."[26] Lobo proudly noted that each business unit has full autonomy over its research and development, sales and marketing, and business development.

Lobo's low-key style is not only purposeful but also highly authentic. In an interview with the Rotman School of Management in Toronto, he recalled watching—and recoiling from—a video presentation he had made when he was a student at Rotman. "I was disgusted with what I saw—I didn't look like me. I came off very aggressive and too forward. It didn't fit with who I was. I realized that I had been changing to fit the culture of the companies that I had worked for, and it wasn't right."[27]

Lobo is a constant learner, so it's not surprising that his number one priority is listening. "You listen, learn, engage the teams, be transparent and open, identify areas of opportunity, align the team and focus on winning."[28] Today, a winning culture means a diverse culture, and diversity has become an important goal at Stryker. But diversity is not always easy to achieve; it requires a fierce commitment. To make sure the organization is diverse, Lobo insists that recruiters present him with a wide range of candidates when he is hiring new talent. "Leaders need to set the tone for the organization," he said. "Start by talking publicly about making diversity a priority and keep repeating that message. Then, you need to follow it up with action."[29]

Lobo's actions speak even louder than his words, and reflect a deep humility borne out of a constant desire to learn, grow and become a better leader.

Rob Bernshteyn, CEO, Coupa Software: Fiercely Determined to Build Trust

Rob Bernshteyn is the CEO of a fast-rising software firm called Coupa. The company helps organizations optimize and control their spending through a new cloud-based system of business spend management. Coupa has tapped into a huge and fast-growing market, but to achieve Bernshteyn's goal of building a future Fortune 500 company, he and his leadership team are relentlessly focused on three core strategies: making the customer successful, delivering results and creating a culture of excellence through collaboration. These strategies are inscribed on a wall at Coupa's head office and detailed in Bernshteyn's book *Value as a Service*.

According to the company's website, "the core values that we had when we were only 25 people are still the same core values we have today, and we plan to keep it that way." This statement ties into the company's clarity of mission and purpose. Bernshteyn noted that most Millennials want to build something that has meaning and be involved with something that has some sort of purpose, because they "want their lives to be related to something that has real meaning." That's why the company's culture is so focused on its mission and growing the company the right way. According to Bernshteyn, the company's values "create a commonality that helps form a strong bond between everyone in the organization, which gets all of us driving in the same direction."[30]

Bernshteyn has been a builder-entrepreneur since the age of eleven, when he began building a Major League Baseball trading card business that would ultimately fund his college tuition. But Bernshteyn doesn't just want to build a business; he wants to build trust and transparency with all his stakeholders—his employees, customers and suppliers:

> At the company level, we are open in spirit. As a public company, we show our financials openly. We share our strategy openly. We engage with customers openly. We share ideas and learn from each other, from our customers, and from our partners openly [...] These concepts are not abstractions for me. I came to this country from a place that was about as closed as can be: the former Soviet Union.[31]

Why is openness so important in business? Openness reduces friction, encourages collaboration and creates trust. For example, whenever Coupa demonstrates its software products to customers, it is very careful to present specifically what the products are and what they are capable of doing. This is less common than you might think in the software sector, said Bernshteyn. When a request for proposal comes in, "too many companies in the software industry say yes to everything, and then try to figure it out later." Bernshteyn and his team have embedded their core values so deeply into the company's DNA that they couldn't change them, even if they wanted to. "It's a binding force at our company. It is part of who we are."[32]

Alex Gorsky, CEO, Johnson & Johnson: The Mission Is Everything

When Alex Gorsky took over as CEO of Johnson & Johnson (J&J) in 2012, it was a tumultuous time in the company's long and storied history. Trusted brand names like Benadryl, Motrin and Tylenol were under attack from healthcare critics who were beginning to call into question J&J's grip on quality control. The critics were quickly silenced by Gorsky, who righted the ship in short order. Leaning on the leadership lessons he picked up at West Point and later as a captain in the elite U.S. Army Rangers, Gorsky understood the critical importance of mission. "There's a general attitude in the military of trying to do everything possible to accomplish the mission. We [at J&J] have the same kind of commitment to improving patients' lives. We face daunting challenges every day, and it's important to do our best to come up with solutions."[33]

I know from personal experience how he feels. When I was in the military, we all felt we were part of a mission that was greater than ourselves. We were like a band of brothers joined in a worthy cause, and those bonds run deep. (To this day, I stay in contact with many of the friends I made there decades ago.) "The cause really motivated people far beyond the day-to-day tasks that they do on their jobs," Gorsky noted.[34] I suspect he speaks from the heart when he says that joining "a company like J&J [that was] founded on values and a credo was just a great fit for me."[35]

Written nearly eighty years ago by Robert Johnson Jr., the son of one of the founders, J&J's credo begins with people: "We believe our first responsibility is to the patients, doctors and nurses, to mothers and fathers and all others who use our products and services. In meeting their needs everything we do must be of high quality."[36] Johnson made it clear that patients always came first, ahead of profits. Gorsky is no less clear about his company's mission and his role as its chief guardian. In an interview with Michael Useem and Adam Grant, Gorsky noted that no leader can be perfect, which is why they must work closely with their teams to get as close to perfect as possible. And that's where mission becomes so important. "How do you make sure every day—when decisions are made in many different areas around the world and in different business organizations—that the credo remains our moral compass, the glue that holds us together?" Gorsky asked. It's by "keeping this alive in the organization [...] that we make sure we do the right thing."[37] At a speech he gave in front of an audience of college students, Gorsky said he always tries to do the right thing, but it's a lot easier to do if you love what you do and do it well.[38] He clearly embodies both those ideals.

Colin Powell, Former Secretary of State: Never Give Up

As the son of Jamaican immigrants, Colin Powell, a four-star general and former secretary of state, learned to deal with adversity from an early age. Those lessons clearly paid off. Even as a young military officer, Powell was described by his superiors as "tenacious, yet polished, and able to deal with individuals of any rank," and "whose potential for a career in the military [was] unlimited."[39]

Through a combination of hard work and dogged determination, Powell rose through the ranks to eventually become chairman of the Joint Chiefs of Staff, along the way receiving multiple military decorations including the Purple Heart, the Bronze Star and the Legion of Merit.[40] Throughout his life, Powell overcame numerous hardships, including being injured in a helicopter crash. "Nothing will be handed to you," he told Howard University graduates in a commencement address. "You are entering a life of continuous study and struggle to achieve your goals; a life of searching to find that which you do well and which you love doing. Never stop seeking."[41]

When he became secretary of state, Powell was asked about the secret to his success. He always had the same answer. There's no secret, he would say. Success is "the result of preparation, hard work and learning from failure."[42] Powell never forgot who he was or why he became a leader. He recognized this at a very early stage in his military career. "I came to understand [soldiers] during my tour at Gelnhausen. I learned what made them tick, lessons that stuck for thirty-five years [...] They want to be part of a successful team. They respect a leader who holds them to a high standard and pushes them to the limit, as long as they see a worthwhile objective."[43] They also respect a leader who is willing to dig deep and climb any wall to make sure his troops succeed. That was Colin Powell. And that is true grit.

Susan Wojcicki, CEO, YouTube: Everyone Has a Story

More than two decades ago, Harvard-educated Susan Wojcicki, the daughter of a physics professor and a high school teacher, became the sixteenth employee of a fledgling search engine company called Google. She was hired as Google's first marketing manager, and with only a shoestring budget, she helped turn the company into an advertising giant. Wojcicki was a key player in the development of Google Ads, Google AdSense and Google Analytics—services that now contribute the lion's share of the company's bottom line. In 2006, Wojcicki persuaded Google's cofounders, Sergey Brin and Larry Page, to acquire video-sharing company YouTube for $1.6 billion. Eight years later, she became its CEO.

When she was asked why Google spent over a billion dollars to buy a company with no profits, she responded:

> We realized that people all over the world could upload something and that other people wanted to watch it [...] that anyone could be a creator, anyone could be a producer, that anyone would have a story or something they wanted to share, and that other people actually wanted to see that and enjoy that experience [...] People want to engage with other people. The stories that have come out of [YouTube], and the ways people communicate with a global audience is so powerful.[44]

From an early age, Wojcicki understood the power of storytelling. Her mother, Esther, taught journalism at Palo Alto High School. (She also published a book called *How to Raise Successful People: Simple*

Lessons for Radical Results. All three of her children are living proof: Susan Wojcicki's sister Anne is CEO of 23andMe, while Janet is a professor of medical anthropology.) Wojcicki likes to tell audiences the story of how Sergey Brin and Larry Page ended up living in her garage. At the time, she and her husband had just bought their first house:

> We didn't know if we could afford the mortgage, so we decided we were going to rent part of our house. Then it turned out that Sergey and Larry were starting their company and they needed office space [...] It was actually really hard to find office space. Our joint friend suggested, "Why don't you rent Susan's and Dennis's house?" So they showed up and they said, "Oh, this looks great."[45]

Later, she started using Google's search engine in her work, and when the service went down for a day, she suddenly realized how essential it had become to her research. So when Sergey and Larry approached her about becoming their marketing person, she didn't take long to say yes, even though, as she admitted to Reed Hoffman in a recent interview, she really didn't know what she was doing. In fact, she was a little scared because she had "never really been a marketer. And if I really had been a marketer, everything they would've said to me would've scared me away."[46]

Her story is inspiring because it illustrates the power of belief and purpose, and because it is a reminder that big things often emerge from modest beginnings. "We spent a long time building out our ad products" and monetizing the business, she said, referring to Google's multi-year evolution into a tech powerhouse.[47] Wojcicki noted that over fifty million creators contribute to YouTube today, and over two billion people watch YouTube videos globally every month. She is especially proud that many of the people who create YouTube content have become storytellers and media companies in their own right.

With global influence comes global accountability, however. Wojcicki took decisive action when she realized that YouTube had evolved from a video-sharing service to a (mostly unmonitored) information platform that was equally capable of delivering misinformation and depicting gruesome acts of violence. The turning point happened after the 2019 London Bridge terror attack. "[That's] when we started to get a lot of the questions of scrutiny," she said. A video on YouTube showed the attack as it unfolded, and the company was mentioned in countless news reports that followed. "As we got bigger," she noted, "we also attracted more bad actors who started to want to think about how to use YouTube for their own benefit [...] I read all the stories [...] of who these different actors were." After that, she "realized that we needed a completely different operating model."[48]

In response, she called an off-site meeting for 8:00 AM the next day. She flagged her notice with a Code Yellow, which is Google's sign that something is wrong. "I didn't really know what was wrong, but I knew [...] we needed to change how we operated."[49] Since then, YouTube has hired over ten thousand new employees in an effort to curb the surge in questionable videos and block the bad actors who were exploiting the service to "mislead, manipulate, harass or even harm."[50] The company's efforts have been largely successful, if not perfect. "But I also think that we have made tremendous changes, and we have tried to be responsive. And we have more work to do, I don't deny that."[51]

Wojcicki has built trust inside her organization and out, by being honest, straightforward and approachable. She has worked hard to create an environment where not only YouTube employees can feel safe—but so too can the global brands that advertise on the site. She and her team are continuously updating their algorithms and closely monitoring the service hour by hour to keep bad actors out and good actors happy. She also wants YouTube to be a premier source of skill building and online education, which is why so-called *EduTubers* (those who are able to build an audience of ten thousand or more) scoop up significant rewards. Wojcicki's goal is to enable hundreds of millions of creators to express themselves in unique ways, while making sure Google is "living up to our responsibilities [...and] working with governments around the world as we face increasingly complicated regulatory issues."[52] If she can pull off this feat, YouTube will remain atop the video storytelling universe for decades to come.

· · · · ·

Leaders like Lobo, Bernshteyn, Gorsky, Powell, and Wojcicki help instill a strong culture in their organizations through their behavior, passions and guiding purpose. Culture drives results, and the stronger the culture, the stronger the results. An organization with a disciplined culture consistently gets the right things done the right way because it is moving forward, as one, toward a common purpose. Culture always lives at the team level because, as the saying goes: "If you want to go fast, go alone. If you want to go far, go together." But again, the team must be powered by the right people in the right seats, people who are working with passion and strength, and who are engaged by purpose and inner discipline.

Organizations that outperform are filled with these kinds of leaders. They create and become part of a culture that is constantly growing, evolving and engaging. What separates +5 leaders from the rest are the five behavioral traits: humility, builder's mindset, clarity of mission, grit and storytelling. What separates great organizations from their peers are the five principles: values and purpose, strengths and passions, the right people, engagement and discipline.

How do the +5 leaders working within these organizations demonstrate these traits? How do they apply these principles in the real world? In Part 2, we turn to five common scenarios all leaders face, and to how the +5 principles guide leaders to make better decisions and take the best course of action. Our first consideration is building a winning team. Make sure you complete the activity and exercises in Part 3 for this chapter before moving on to the next section of the book.

CHAPTER 5 TAKEAWAYS

> The team is the building block of an organization. It is the performance unit. Its energy and enthusiasm can infect an entire organization, tweaking the culture while remaining true to the values and ethics that are the organization's permanent and foundational principles.

> A culture of discipline separates the great companies from their lesser-performing peers.

> Great leaders possess a disciplined drive for results. Inner discipline enables leaders to outperform on a sustainable basis, while a disciplined culture becomes the execution engine of any successful team or company. The best leaders create immense followership by setting a tone within their team, a tone that comes to life through five hallmark behaviors.

> Culture is the company's execution engine. A disciplined culture not only drives high performance, but it also helps sustain performance over the long term.

> The stronger the culture, the stronger the results. Culture is the only real source of sustainable competitive advantage we have.

THE +5

TEAM COACHING

MODEL

Theory is nice, but practice makes perfect. I'm a business practitioner and constant learner. As such, I invest my energy and time in learning that can have a powerful influence on my business career and personal life, and I pass on that learning to my teams. I look for pragmatic solutions that take us to a better place.

The second part of this book is about practice and applying the five principles presented in Part 1 (values and purpose, strengths and passions, the right people, full engagement and discipline) to real-world situations. In my practice, I've found that those real-world events can be broken down into what I call *the five situations*—the pressure cooker moments of truth which test a leader's mettle and test it often.

The Five Situations

> when the right environment needs to be created to nurture winning teams
> when the culture needs to have the capacity and capability to allow the team (and organization) to adapt and innovate
> when the leader needs to step up to deal with a crisis
> when the leader becomes a skilled coach capable of transforming a team
> when the leader becomes a skilled coach capable of transforming individuals

To help leaders and teams address these situations, I developed a team coaching model that I use in my own practice. Five building blocks, or elements, of team coaching apply to creating a high-performing team. The +5 leader can depend on the framework shown in Figure 11.1.

ELEMENT 1: THE RIGHT PEOPLE	The critical building block of any high-performance team is the right people. They share the core values of other team members, and are inspired by the purpose of the organization and the mission of the team. They are committed to delivering results.
ELEMENT 2: CLARITY OF MISSION AND PRIORITIES	All +5 teams share a common element: they are relentless about achieving their mission, and bring a consistent focus and tight alignment to the critical priorities that drive team success.
ELEMENT 3: TRUST AND PSYCHOLOGICAL SAFETY	All high-performing teams strive to create a work environment that has a high degree of trust and safety. Team members feel safe to debate, disagree and be who they are.
ELEMENT 4: ADAPTABILITY	These teams can pivot as needed to deliver on their mission. They continuously assess their capabilities and add new ones to adapt while remaining true to their core strengths, purpose and values.
ELEMENT 5: RESULTS	+5 teams are laser-like on pushing their objective across the finish line. They bring rigor to track progress, focus to avoid distraction and discipline to deliver.

Building a Winning Team

6

> Good leaders have the humility to know that they don't know everything. They foster an environment of openness and sharing. They earn trust and respect. —JAMIE DIMON

If I were to ask you, "So how are you getting along with your team these days?," how would the question land for you? You might think this: "Jim, it sounds like you're asking me about how I'm getting along with my spouse or my kids. Fine, thanks. But I'm not supposed to 'get along' with my team; my job is to get stuff done." Or you might reply: "Funny you should ask. There's some unhealthy friction going on. I welcome opposing points of view and energetic debate, because we end up with new ideas. But this is different, and I feel like I'm being tested." You might also say: "The truth is that we are not as good as we could be. The buck stops with me, and I have to figure this out."

There are myriad replies to my question. What might yours be? I ask because we are exploring a topic that I believe is at the heart of a successful organization: building a winning team.

As leaders, we get tested. Our teams get tested. We are all looking for ways to do things better than another leader, another team or a competitor. So much has been written on competitive advantage, but the hard truth is that long-term, sustainable high performance for teams that outperform has two components: 1) having the right people on the bus and in the right seats; and 2) coaching the team to a high level of collaboration and innovation.

Why is having the right team so important? The team is the ultimate performance unit of any organization, and the magic of getting any organization, department or group of people to outperform is rooted in teamwork. As changes in technology, competition and demographics continue to force companies to innovate and adapt, and the need for expertise continues to deepen, the reality is that we can accomplish very little without the outstanding contribution of a team.

A high-performance team is characterized by the deep level of commitment team members have to one another. This level of commitment may rival the commitment they experience in their strongest relationships in life: with their partners, best friends and families. It's not a coincidence that the most successful business and sports teams often refer to their teammates as "family." Recall what Phil Knight said about his team at Nike: "I trusted them wholly," he wrote. "I didn't look over their shoulders, and that bred a powerful two-way loyalty. I let them be, let them do, let them make their own mistakes, because that's how I'd always liked people to treat me."[1]

Knight's comment points to two keys to building great teams. Knight was brilliant at getting the right people on the bus—people who shared the same passion, brought similar and complementary strengths and had a laser focus on results—and Knight inspired them to an even higher purpose. Once they were on the bus, he trusted them with his business life. They appreciated his trust and repaid him in kind. He said his team was "more alike than different, and that gave a coherence to our goals and our efforts." They were also an exceptionally humble and unpretentious group. "There was none of that smartest-guy-in-the-room foolishness," Knight wrote. "Each would have been the smartest guy in any room, but none believed it of himself, or the next guy."[2]

To sum up, sustainable high performance depends on finding the right people and creating the right environment for the team to flourish (or in other words, innovate). Let's explore more fully these two key insights.

Building Great Teams

Key Insight Number One: Find the Right People

Onboarding the right people is a product of alignment with purpose, values and ethics. Think of this in terms of mission clarity; the right people will share the leader's values and believe in the organization's purpose. Nevertheless, getting the right people in the right seats is a rigorous, highly disciplined process requiring Jim Collins's three-pronged approach: 1) If in doubt, don't hire; 2) put your best people on your biggest opportunities, not your biggest problems; and 3) when you need to get certain people off the bus, act! I explored this key insight at length in Chapter 3. This chapter's focus is on the next key insight.

Key Insight Number Two: Create the Right Environment

People perform at their highest level when they possess a clear sense of purpose, and are led by an engaged, trustworthy and inspiring leader. The leader must unequivocally provide the team with the environment to create and innovate—a space to freely offer constructive ideas and opinions without fear of recrimination or ridicule. Team members need to feel psychologically safe. This is more than just feeling safe from harassment or ridicule. They need to feel that their ideas and concerns merit the attention of the leader and fellow team members. They need to believe that they can open up, share their emotions and occasionally make mistakes without being penalized or losing their job. According to psychologist and Stanford University professor Dr. Laura Delizonna, psychological safety results from the following beliefs:

> If I make a mistake, it will not be held against me.
> Members of this team are able to bring up problems and touchy issues.
> My unique skills and talents are valued and utilized.[3]

Let's assume you've done the work of getting the right people on the bus and the wrong people off it. In other words, you've assembled a team with a shared purpose, values and complementary strengths. The challenge now becomes the following: "How can you, as a leader, shape and build your team into a tight unit that has each other's back and is relentless about achieving the team's mission?" I would argue that the essential ingredients are trust and safety. As the leader, you must understand that your word is your bond. For your team members, safety is about being able to be authentic and listened to.

Let's look at an interesting example. In 2012, Google embarked on a mission to find out why some teams are effective while others are not. As part of what came to be called Project Aristotle, Google conducted hundreds of interviews with its employees over a two-year span while analyzing the key attributes of over 180 active Google teams. The results were surprising and full of insight. Julia Rozovsky noted on Google's *re:Work* blog:

> We were pretty confident that we'd find the perfect mix of individual traits and skills necessary for a stellar team. Take one Rhodes Scholar, two extroverts, one engineer who rocks at AngularJS, and a PhD.

FIGURE 6.1: GOOGLE'S FIVE DYNAMICS OF A TEAM

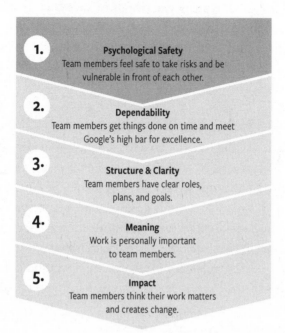

1. **Psychological Safety**
Team members feel safe to take risks and be vulnerable in front of each other.

2. **Dependability**
Team members get things done on time and meet Google's high bar for excellence.

3. **Structure & Clarity**
Team members have clear roles, plans, and goals.

4. **Meaning**
Work is personally important to team members.

5. **Impact**
Team members think their work matters and creates change.

Source: Julia Rozovsky, "The Five Keys to a Successful Google Team," *re:Work* (November 17, 2015), rework.withgoogle.com.

Voila. Dream team assembled, right? We were dead wrong. **Who is on a team matters less than how the team members interact, structure their work, and view their contributions.**[4]

Google discovered five dynamics, shown in Figure 6.1, that set the effective teams apart from their peers at Google. The top one? Psychological safety, which was defined in Google's study as "Can we take risks on this team without feeling insecure or embarrassed?"[5]

Psychological safety cascades into the other dynamics. Dependability: team members are comfortable keeping one another accountable. Structure and clarity: team members need not ever feel embarrassed about asking for clarification. They need to understand what they are being asked to do. Meaning: the purpose team members feel in their work can be both a shared and an individual experience but is always respected. Impact: constructive and continuous sharing of feedback is a hallmark of psychological safety, and it leads to the delivery of strong results.

A High-Performance Team Model

As a practitioner and coach, I look for timeless principles and frameworks that when applied will get you to a better place. I am a fan of a model Patrick Lencioni introduced in his book *The Five Dysfunctions of a Team*. This model provides a simple and actionable framework for developing a productive team and cultivating a teamwork culture by addressing the dysfunctions Lencioni identifies.

The five dysfunctions are presented in a pyramid composed of five upward-cascading layers (see Figure 6.2). In other words, each

FIGURE 6.2: THE FIVE DYSFUNCTIONS OF A TEAM

Inattention
to Results

Avoidance of Accountability

Lack of Commitment

Fear of Conflict

Absence of Trust

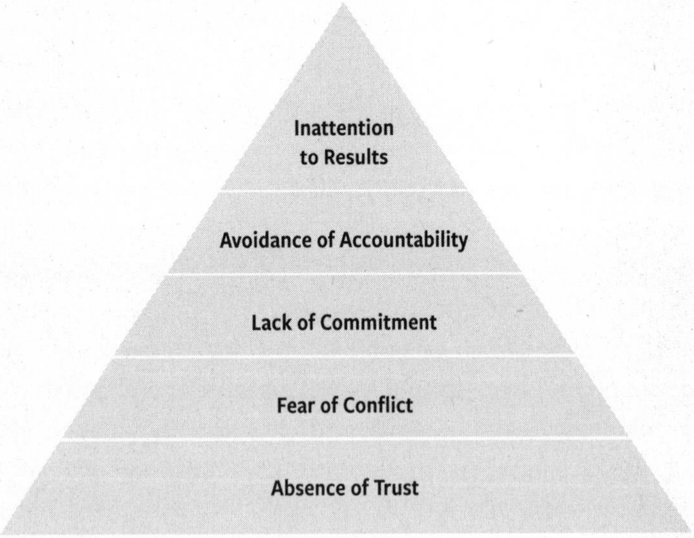

Source: Patrick Lencioni, *The 5 Dysfunctions of a Team*, Jossey-Bass 2002, p. 195.
Developed by Patrick Lencioni and The Table Group. Reproduced with permission of The Table Group.

layer or dysfunction influences the next level of the pyramid. Lencioni posits that *absence of trust* is the first dysfunction of a team. If trust is missing, people are afraid to be vulnerable or share their feelings and opinions, because they risk being exposed to reproach and recrimination. People who are defensive and insecure will have a *fear of conflict*. People avoid conflict out of a need to preserve what Lencioni calls an "artificial harmony."[6] But all this does is stifle productive debate and the expression of new ideas within the team. Without collaboration, without engaging in debate and blue-skying ideas, team members are ambivalent about committing wholeheartedly to the team's decisions. The resulting *lack of commitment* creates ambiguity and uncertainty, which prevents team members from sticking with the decisions they've made. Because team members don't hold each other accountable for their behavior, *avoidance of accountability* occurs, which undercuts team performance. In an environment where no one is held accountable, team members begin to pursue individual goals instead of focusing on collective success, and the final dysfunction, *inattention to results*, occurs.

Over the last decade, I've seen leaders address concerns with their teams by working through the Five Dysfunctions Pyramid to identify systemic problems and clean them up. To further simplify the model, Figure 6.3 shows what really works for leaders who aspire to build great teams.

Layer 1: Trust and Psychological Safety

Effective teams have a high level of trust, which Lencioni defined as "the confidence among team members that their peers' intentions are good, and that there is no reason to be protective or careful around the group."[7] Trust is incubated in an environment of psychological safety where people are "comfortable being vulnerable with one another."[8] Your role as a leader is to create this state and encourage the team to be vulnerable and open with each other about their mistakes

Source: Created by Jim Reid.

and weaknesses. This goes far beyond a state of tolerance because when people feel safe, they become willing to engage in constructive debate, or what I like to call *productive conflict*.

Layer 2: Productive Conflict

Productive conflict is the second layer of the performance playbook. When people trust each other and feel safe, they are encouraged to speak their minds, and engage in open and constructive debate. Teams come together because the conversations have a frankness and positivity that produce ideas and advance the mission. In contrast, members of teams that lack trust tend to avoid and even fear conflict, and productivity suffers.

Layer 3: Commitment

When people can debate without fear of recrimination, they are free to commit to action. As Lencioni wrote, "Great teams also pride themselves on being able to unite behind decisions and commit to clear courses of action even when there is little assurance about whether the decision is correct."[9] As the saying goes, analysis can lead to paralysis, and high-performing teams avoid paralysis at all costs because no decision can be made with absolute certainty. Teams will never have all the data they need to make a foolproof decision, but they can get the information they need to make a good decision. If that decision turns out to be a mistake, they'll learn from it.

Layer 4: Accountability

When teammates commit to a decision, even if some of them don't agree with it, they're able to hold each other accountable for delivering on that decision—provided they feel they were part of the decision-making process. If every team member's voice is heard, every member becomes accountable once the decision is made. As Lencioni noted, ambiguity is the enemy of accountability. Decisions that are hidden from view frustrate accountability. When a team collectively and publicly buys into a decision, that is powerful, because it motivates people to perform at a higher level and it makes accountability a shared responsibility among every team member.

Layer 5: Results

Results are the fifth, and final, layer of the performance pyramid. High-performing teams always put team results ahead of individual needs. You might be asking, "What other needs could there be?" Let's not forget that many team members also happen to lead their own teams. In a dysfunctional team, members might be worried about the impact of team decisions on their own budgets or resources, or the roles their subordinates are going to play to execute the decisions that have been made. Not so with great teams. They keep their focus on Team One—the larger team they are part of—not Team Two, the team they lead.

· · · · ·

The five layers of the performance pyramid can be summarized this way: The only way of ensuring a relentless focus on team results is to hold people accountable for those results, and this is achieved through a high level of commitment. Consensus is reached through debate, and a free exchange of ideas requires trust, which in turn requires that team members are vulnerable but also secure in the knowledge they will not be exposed to criticism, ridicule or lack of respect.[10]

CASE STUDY

Culture Change at Rogers

Now that we have our framework for building high-performance teams, how does this all come together to build a high-performing company? Dave Ulrich is one of the most prolific educators on leadership and culture whom I have met and worked with. He was ranked the number one management guru by *Businessweek*, profiled by *Fast Company* as one of the world's top ten creative people in business and was a top five coach in *Forbes*.

In 2018, we invited Dave to speak at a leadership conference for 150 of our senior executives at Rogers. He passionately made the case that the role of leaders is to drive customer value and create culture. Dave drove a big stake in the ground when he stated unequivocally that the biggest challenge leaders face is getting culture right. Why? Companies have to adapt to changing competition, changing

Leadership is not only about the leader but also about the value created by the team. Leadership isn't about telling others what to do; it's about inspiring others to do the right thing for the customer. By empowering others, leaders build winning teams and cultures.

customer expectations and rapidly changing market forces, and adaptation is about getting the culture right to deliver results.

I've said this before, but it's worth repeating: culture is the performance engine of the company. More than ever, I believe that culture is best changed one team at a time. To achieve culture change at scale, you need to do two things:

1. Hold leaders accountable to drive customer value and shape a winning culture. To achieve this, each leader should apply a proven framework for building high-performance teams (for example, The +5 Team Coaching Model, Figure 11.1, on page 103).

2. Scale the building of culture by driving a top-down change effort led by the CEO.

CASE STUDY

Top-Down Culture Change at Rogers

When the current CEO of Rogers, Joe Natale, joined the company in April 2017, he came with a clear game plan, and he passionately communicated his plan to all twenty-six thousand employees in his first sixty days during a series of town hall meetings. "Our goal is to be number one," he told us. "To be the best place to work, to deliver the best customer experience and to be seen by our shareholders as providing the best long-term return." He also told us that our journey to number one would take multiple years, but he showed us how coming along on the journey with him would create opportunities for personal growth and a rewarding career as part of a winning team. Joe made it safe for everyone to sign up because he really understood that one of the keys to driving this change was to engage our three thousand people leaders in a very real and meaningful way. To make this happen, he charged my team (HR) with building a People Plan that would capture the essence of how Dave Ulrich described the leaders' role—in other words, to drive value and shape culture.

Source: Created by Jim Reid.

Of course, this People Plan was built with the input of our executive team, but three individuals on my team played a crucial role: Dr. Nancy Nazer, our SVP of Organization Development, and two key members of her team, Kyle Novak, our senior director of Team Effectiveness, and Dr. Geoff Ho, our director of Research and Analytics. Here is their story.

Dr. Nancy Nazer: Accountability Instead of Finger-Pointing

"We put together a multi-year People Plan that aligned with our overall organizational strategy. And then, we worked backwards and asked ourselves these questions:

> What are our key markers in the sand, in terms of priority, that we know are going to be the most important drivers?
> What are the initiatives that are going to support the strategy?
> How do these various priorities build on one another, so that they continue to drive this cycle organically and the flywheel gathers momentum?

4 Point People Plan

1. Make Rogers a destination for top talent.

2. Accelerate re-skilling of our workforce to build key strengths for the future.

3. Evolve our people practices to meet the needs of a changing workforce.

4. Continue to drive best-in-class engagement.

Source: Created by Jim Reid.

"Our CEO, Joe Natale, has a great saying: 'Culture is what people do when no one is watching.' There's so much truth to that because culture resides in all of us, and we own the culture we create. Nobody else can change it but us. Early on in my career, I met a lot of people who would come into our HR programs and tell us that they had these seven steps to transform culture and so on, and if you followed them, you were going to be better and more collaborative, and have this winning culture. But I've come to recognize that culture change takes a whole bunch of little steps that people have to make together. And it requires all of us to make that possible.

"What I've experienced over the years is that we have to be accountable and aware of the culture that we create. When I first joined Rogers, before the transformation I sensed a lot of negativity among the senior leaders about the culture in the company. It wasn't surprising, because there had been a lot of change over the years, with three CEOs in the space of five years. So there was a great deal of uncertainty. People were pointing the finger at 'them,' and saying things like 'they are not collaborative,' and 'they are not holding up their end of the bargain,' and so on. So the most important shift that had to happen early was to get everyone to acknowledge that 'we' are the 'they.'

"Then, we went out and asked our employees to help us fix the problem. Once we started to understand what truly mattered to our people (growth and development being a top priority), not only did we measure it, as Geoff will explain, but we made sure there was accountability from the top, from our CEO on down. We were very transparent in terms of saying, 'We're doing well on this, but we're not doing well on other things.' When we surveyed our people, we asked them, 'What aspects of our culture are you most proud of?' and 'What is holding us back?' We created a video with their responses, both positive and negative. We wanted people to experience in their own words how they were describing our culture.

"We had a leadership program called The House, which helped our leaders focus on the culture changes they needed to create to drive greater performance. It wasn't about pointing fingers at people; it was about taking accountability and asking yourself, 'Why should I be a leader? Why should people be led by me?' It was a very experiential program, but it gave us great clarity about which aspects of our culture we wanted to preserve, and which parts would be irresponsible to tolerate, and which would hold us back. And we communicated the type of culture we wanted to build and shared this communication broadly, and then offered this program deeper in the organization to our director-level leaders, and then to some of our high-potential or top-talent managers. And then, we did exercises for them to think about: 'Okay, if this is where we're going, what do we need to preserve?' 'What do we need to change?' It was very real."[11]

· · · · ·

Having overseen that process with Nancy, I can say it still is very real, because our cultural change as a company is ongoing. Part of that transformation is changing the behavior of our leaders and their teams. That's not always an easy process, but as Kyle Novak points out, when people are willing to challenge each other on the things that they've agreed to do, commitment levels go way up.

Kyle Novak: What Kind of Environment Do You Want to Create?

"To encourage the behaviors we need to win, one of the things we do as a coaching team, even in the course of a single meeting, is run through an exercise where we will ask, 'What's the environment and culture that you want to create for the discussion today?' We'll explicitly get people to call that out. And so they'll typically say things like, 'We want it to be open, we want it to be honest, we want to be authentic, and we want to be able to challenge each other.' And what calling that out does is create a bit of a contract for the team for that meeting. It's a way to get their collective commitment up front, so that later on in the meeting, if the team doesn't feel they're doing those things, people will say, 'I thought we said that we were going to be X.' Without that kind of commitment and agreement up front, that would likely never happen.

"One of the concepts that we love is the idea of a Team One. When you're on a leadership team, who is Team One? Is it the team that you lead, or is it the team of your peers? Lencioni says that your first responsibility is to Team One, the team that you share with your colleagues, not Team Two, the team that you lead. I agree with that. The team that we actually lead is sometimes a more comfortable place to be. But when we prioritize the team we lead, we tend to focus on what that team needs to accomplish instead of on the collective goal. It's only natural. So to counter that tendency, we identify collective goals for each leadership team, the big things that they want to accomplish. Then, we help them figure out how their individual teams (Team Two) can work to support the Team One goals.

"Culture is changed through a combination of top-down and bottom-up approaches. In most large-scale organizations, the top-down approach is critical, because there is an existing power structure that has tremendous influence. You can't get away from the influence top executives have on people's feelings of safety and security. Simply put, if I think that a certain action is going to keep me gainfully employed with an opportunity to grow, then I'm likely to take that action. So I think the tone set by the top-down approach is incredibly important. But at the same time, bottom-up change is equally important. However, it requires leaders that are really willing to listen and learn, and not just ask questions but dive into what people say in response. And leaders must be willing to look beyond just getting confirmation of their own views, but to ask their people, 'What am I missing here?' and 'What do I have wrong?' If they're willing to bring this kind of leadership to the team, then culture can be heavily influenced from the bottom up."[12]

· · · · ·

The change process intensified when we began from the bottom up by acting on the simple suggestion made in our annual employee survey: we started to measure what our workforce believed was working well so we could understand what really mattered. Our research director, Dr. Geoff Ho, was an advisor on Google's Project Aristotle. He advised us that Google tested as many as forty different factors influencing team effectiveness, and that the researchers discovered that psychological safety was at the top of the list of drivers of the most effective teams. But Geoff was very clear that the results didn't mean that most teams didn't feel safe at Google. "The results just meant that psychological safety was foundational for team effectiveness," he told me. "That was the goal of the Google study, and since that study was published, Google has built entire coaching and training systems around safety and creating teams, and continues to measure team effectiveness through the five factors they identified." (See Figure 6.1 on page 109.) Instinctively, we understood this, and we brought this same disciplined, analytical approach to Rogers. "Show me the data" soon became one of our favorite expressions!

Dr. Geoff Ho: We Had the Data to Measure Team Performance

"One of the things I did when I first joined Rogers was look at our programs. One of them was called High Trust Teams, and Kyle and his team were leading that effort. We wanted to see if Lencioni's model applied to Rogers's best teams, because every company has its own context, and different teams have different contexts. So we took a look at the data that Kyle's team was compiling to help build trust and drive results. For example, we measured the extent to which every team felt effective or felt like they were hitting their performance objectives as a team, so we had a really solid data source across all the teams and for how effective they felt they were. We also ran the annual employee survey, so we knew how teams felt about everything under the sun, including whether they felt like they had the right goals and objectives, whether they had trust, whether they had the right technologies and tools, whether they felt included, whether they had the processes and procedures to help them do things well, and whether they had diverse teams. We had all that data.

"We tested about fifteen things, and what we learned was that the top three items that drove team effectiveness nicely converged with Google's study. And the most important one was having a foundation of trust and psychological safety. The next-most-important item was having clear goals that linked to the company's objectives, which ties into the accountability layer of Lencioni's pyramid. A third was about having the opportunity to innovate and bring up new ideas. This notion ties into the second layer of the Playbook for High-Performing Teams [see Figure 6.3 on page 112], which is productive conflict. And we found that organizational support was another important driver. We also learned early on that many of our teams felt they didn't have all the processes and technology needed to really be effective. Based on this insight, we worked hard to make sure the most critical aspects of every role of every employee at Rogers were captured in the engagement survey. After all, if the point of the survey is to increase engagement, we have to figure out what drives engagement.

"So we worked with many of our key stakeholders, both within the call center area as well as other areas of the company. And we worked with not just the big business units, but also the people who run the offices and the physical workspaces, and the people who run our compensation programs, and the people who run our training programs. We structured the annual engagement survey to capture those elements, so when we actually surveyed groups like the call centers, we were capturing the right elements of their experience. I think the results of our efforts to change the culture speak for themselves, because from 2014 to 2020, employee engagement went from 72 percent to 87 percent—a fifteen-point increase in just six years. That's quite a dramatic improvement. [See Figure 6.4.]

"One of the key things that we've been building in terms of culture is the collective mindset that it's all about the customer. I think Joe Natale really helped rally everyone around putting the customer first in everything that we're doing and thinking and feeling. When I ran the employee survey, we made sure to do the customer side of the analysis first, but now, the idea that the customer is first has become so ingrained in us that it's just taken for granted. I think that is an incredible example of how culture change has taken root at the company.

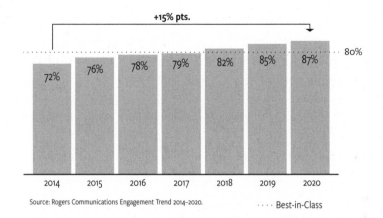

FIGURE 6.4: EMPLOYEE ENGAGEMENT

+15% pts.

80%

72% 76% 78% 79% 82% 85% 87%

2014 2015 2016 2017 2018 2019 2020

Source: Rogers Communications Engagement Trend 2014-2020.   ···· Best-in-Class

"I firmly believe that culture is changed one behavior at a time, and the right behaviors are part of how things work, and drive the decisions we make. I see an invisible set of assumptions guiding our behaviors, and behaviors are an outcome guided by the values of the organization. I've seen enough companies where they have a vision and a mission that sound good, but when you look more closely at the company, you realize there's a different set of assumptions; people don't actually believe in the vision, and maybe they're not actually trying to achieve it. Why haven't people bought in? Is the leader acting in ways that are in line with what they're saying is the vision? Is the company doing what it says it's doing? Vision can truly affect whether the culture is healthy or not.

"One of the key insights we got from the data was the discovery that growth and development is the top driver of engagement, and it's been that way for as long as we've been doing the analysis. And so every year after we validate the data, we take steps to continue building on this key area to make sure people are growing and developing, and that our leaders are fully behind the development of their people and teams. We're now at a point where a majority of the company, including our front line, has development plans and regular development conversations with their managers. We have a manager program that every manager goes through. We have an executive program that every executive goes through. So every year, we use that data and continue to look for opportunities to build on people's desire for growth and development."[13]

The Empathy Quotient

That's a window into Geoff's, Kyle's and Nancy's efforts and perspectives on our journey to change the culture. The responses we received from our teams confirmed a critical new insight: psychological safety was foundational to high-performing teams at Rogers. To create a feeling of psychological safety with a team, leaders need to model vulnerability. They do this in two ways, according to Dr. Laura Delizonna, who specializes in optimum performance and organizational culture change: they are honest about the uncertainties and risks the team may be facing, and they admit and reframe mistakes.[14] Their language might look like this: "Where I went wrong was...," "I don't have all the answers..." and "Thank you for telling me that I was wrong."

Psychological safety involves going beyond interpersonal trust to create a sense of belonging based on mutual reliance and respect where people can feel comfortable being themselves. This sense of belonging can become a team-wide trait only when team members are consistently willing to ask for help, ask other team members for input and express their own honest thoughts, and by so doing, expose their weaknesses. In other words, each team member must be willing to be vulnerable. Being vulnerable isn't about being weak or nice, however. Instead, it's about communicating openly and with empathy but also about sharing one's ideas with conviction.

You may recall from the previous chapter how Microsoft CEO Satya Nadella's empathic and collaborative approach helped propel

Microsoft to new heights. But empathy wasn't always natural for Nadella. In fact, he learned it the hard way after his son, Zain, was diagnosed with cerebral palsy and quadriplegia. "I struggled with it at first," he said, "partly because I had all these plans for what life would be. Then I realized I had to step up and do my duty as a father. I began to see the world through my son's eyes. That's what empathy is all about."[15]

The modern leader is quite different from the leaders of the past. In many ways, they must be, because the workplace and the workforce have changed. The people I work with tell me the same thing. Leadership isn't what it used to be. To which I say, "Thank goodness for that!" Leaders can no longer be dictatorial if they want buy-in from their teams. They need to care about their people and understand how their choices impact not just the company's bottom line, but the people who are the engine of that company.

High-empathy communication is just one element in building a high-performance team. Creating an environment for high-empathy communications begins with the right people who share similar values and a common purpose. This is not only how culture is forged at the team level; it applies to the organization as well. We as leaders shape culture every day, but given the myriad perspectives on culture, let's explore what culture really is.

Culture Is How Work Gets Done

Culture is the company's execution engine. It's how problems get solved and decisions get made. Cultures go wrong when behavior doesn't flow from shared values. In other words, you don't have the right people on the bus. You might have some of the right people and some of the wrong people, and that's enough to inhibit sustained high performance. Every organization's culture is different because its people are uniquely different and so are its purpose and values, and while most teams in successful organizations share similar values, each team has its own culture. For example, the culture in the marketing department is different from the culture in the accounting department. Structure and order might prevail in accounting, while innovation and creativity might dominate in marketing.

"Culture is really set by how you act," Okta CEO Todd McKinnon, one of the new breed of cloud-based technology leaders, said in a recent interview. "They don't care what you say, it's about what you do." He communicates openly with his team when times are good and equally as often when times are tough. "It really had a solidifying effect on the team," McKinnon said, referring to the early days of the company when investors were pushing for better results. "It made people rally together. It made people in the company feel like it was their company."[16]

Leaders Eat Last

I first began to understand what true teamwork is all about during my time in the military. As officers, we were taught that nothing is more important than achieving the mission, and the key to mission success is developing the soldiers or members of the unit you lead into a top-performing unit. In his best seller *Leaders Eat Last*, Simon Sinek laid out the case for the reasons "some teams pull together and others don't," the book's subtitle. Not only did the title of his book fully capture what I believe to be the essence of leadership, but Sinek's poetic introduction to the book put forth a statement on leadership and building teams that I carry around with me because it is so powerful, motivating and accurate, especially for ex-military officers like me:

> Leaders are the ones who run headfirst into the unknown.
> They rush toward the danger.
> They put their own interests aside to protect us or to pull us into the future.

Leaders would sooner sacrifice what is theirs to save what is ours. And they would never sacrifice what is ours to save what is theirs. This is what it means to be a leader.

It means they choose to go first into danger, headfirst toward the unknown.

And when we feel sure they will keep us safe, we will march behind them and work tirelessly to see their visions come to life and proudly call ourselves their followers.[17]

While the stakes are not as high for most civilian leaders, the same principles ring true. Most leaders are focused on delivering great results to help move their organization forward, to compete and win in an increasingly competitive world where underperformance is just not tolerated. But as Sinek pointed out, great leaders go one step further. Ample evidence of this is provided in Chapter 7, where I will show how change initiatives inspired teams and led to a turnaround in a challenging situation. While the topics from Chapter 6 are still fresh in your mind, please go to Part 3 and complete the activity and exercises.

CHAPTER 6 TAKEAWAYS

> Building high-performance teams requires people to develop a level of commitment to their fellow team members that rivals the level of commitment they have in their strongest relationships in life—with their partners, best friends and families.

> Putting together a high-performing team depends on two factors: finding the right people and creating the right environment, where people feel valued and respected. When leaders are clear about what they believe, where they are going and why, finding the right people is much easier.

> To build a high-trust, high-performing team, the best leaders use a framework. One of the simplest and most actionable frameworks is Figure 6.3: A Playbook for High-Performing Teams, inspired by Patrick Lencioni.

> Dave Ulrich's research suggests that the two primary roles of the leader are to create customer value and shape a winning culture.

> At the organizational level, strong cultures are built one team at a time.

> The value chain for building a high-performance organization begins with culture.

Driving
Successful
Change

The number one force shaping the world right now is the increasing rate of change [...] What differentiates the failures from the winners [...] is their ability to react effectively.

—JOHN KOTTER

I t's really hard to dislike Eric Agius. He is as positive, as smart and as strategic a leader as you're ever likely to meet. He is also a great people person, with a well-earned reputation for getting things done. So when Eric was summoned to meet with his boss at Rogers, Dirk Woessner, early one summer morning in 2017, he had every reason to believe he would have a collegial and productive meeting. However, he did not feel that way when Dirk gave him some unexpected news.

Dirk leaned forward and looked Eric squarely in the eye. "We have an idea," he said. Then, he paused.

"What idea?" Eric asked, puzzled.

"We want you to lead the transformation of Customer Care."

The more Eric listened, the more his heart sank. Eric was about to be tasked with the most difficult assignment of his business life. It was a lateral move into a notoriously challenging job: fixing the situation at the company's call centers. In addition, he'd been in his current role—heading up the transformation across the company's sales channels—for only a little over fourteen months, and it looked like things were starting to turn around. "I appreciate the offer, Dirk," Eric replied quietly. "But you hired me to transform the sales channels, and we're well down that journey. Things are working. I can see the light. I'd really like to finish that job."

But Dirk wasn't about to take "no" for an answer. "Until we find a way to fix our call centers, it's going to be difficult to complete the overall transformation of the company. Why don't you mull it over?"

Eric knew it was an important job—some would say important but impossible. Seven thousand people worked at the Rogers Communications call centers, and more than thirty million customer calls a year were handled across eight offices spanning the country from Vancouver to Moncton. Everyone knew there were problems. Customer complaints were rising, Net Promoter Scores were falling and morale was low. So when Eric went home that night and talked it over with Marcia, his wife, he worked on a strategy to convince Dirk to let him finish his work with sales and respectfully extricate himself from Dirk's "ask."

Eric reached out to me for advice too. "There are some things you just can't say no to," I told him. "This is one of them. We all want you to do this. We think you'd be great at it." Eric thanked me and hung up. A few days later, after much deliberation, he agreed to take on the challenge. Here, in his words, is the story of a turnaround.

CASE STUDY: PART 1

Transforming Customer Care: "Things Just Happen to Us and We Have No Control"

"I accepted the role with a lot of trepidation—and my qualms turned out to be justified. When I started looking under the hood to see what things were really like within the call center and the care organizations, what I found was alarming. I learned that the team—the entire care organization—felt alone and isolated, like they were an island. I heard the words 'us' and 'them' a lot in the focus groups and listening sessions. It was shocking to hear our call center employees talking about Rogers like it was a completely different company. 'Rogers does this to us and to our customers, and then, we have to explain it and fix it,' they would tell me. 'It's just us who are helping our customers,' they said. 'Nobody really cares about the customer.'

"I knew that wasn't true, but it was how they felt, and I had to respect it. I got a strong sense that our call center people felt abandoned. 'Things just happen to us and we have no control,' they would say. 'We're not part of the process; we don't have a vote, and we don't have a forum where we can help educate head office about what the customer wants and what the customer needs.' And this feeling wasn't coming from just the specialists who were managing the phones; it went right up to the leadership. They all felt this way, and these feelings manifested themselves in different—and costly—ways.

"We suffered chronic absenteeism, for example. Over 20 percent of employees were absent on any given day, which was the equivalent of an entire call center not being available to serve our customers at any given time. People who we expected to come in to work and serve our customers simply weren't showing up. We also had ultra-high attrition, so our turnover was stunningly high. What had we done as an organization to send things off the rails like this? After some digging, I learned why the situation had become so dire:

Why Do Change Initiatives Fail?

We'll find out how Eric turned things around in a moment, but let's step back for a second and get some context. To truly understand how change succeeds, we first need to understand why change fails. The leading expert on why change fails is a professor at Harvard Business School named John Kotter. In 1995, Kotter laid out one of the best and most useful frameworks for driving successful transformation when his journal article "Leading Change: Why Transformation Efforts Fail" was published in *Harvard Business Review*. John would shortly follow up with his groundbreaking book *Leading Change*.

Professor Kotter has had a profound influence on my own thinking about the change process ever since I became his student in the 1990s at the Advanced Management Program at Harvard Business School. When I met him, he had spent the past decade researching and analyzing change initiatives in over a hundred different organizations, spanning every kind of transformation from restructuring, reengineering and restrategizing to

> We'd made very little investment in our operations. The digital tools that our call specialists used were so convoluted it was difficult to serve the customer and solve customer problems.
> Our compensation levels were well below market—and had been for a number of years.
> High attrition rates made it difficult to attract top talent.
> The physical environment was dated and uninspiring.
> Our training was inadequate and out of date.
> Our first-level leaders—the most important level of leadership in any call center operations—didn't have a clear purpose. We were forcing them to behave like administrators, following checklists instead of spending time empowering their people.

acquisitions, downsizing and cultural renewal. His conclusion? "A few of these corporate change efforts have been very successful. A few have been utter failures. Most fall somewhere in between, with a distinct tilt toward the lower end of the scale."[2] In other words, the vast majority of change initiatives failed.

Why? Kotter discovered that most leaders failed to consider the psychological impact of change on the employees themselves, especially in large organizations where the behavior of thousands of people must be shifted en masse. "The change process goes through a series of phases that, in total, usually require a considerable length of time," Kotter wrote. "Skipping steps creates only the illusion of speed and never produces a satisfying result."[3]

Because people are creatures of habit, change is not easy. Change can produce a loss of control, which breeds uncertainty and anxiety among staff. To combat anxiety, leaders need to communicate often and well, as we'll see with Eric Agius's story.

"These missteps were reflected in our numbers. Our First Time Resolution was low, and so were our customer experience metrics. Our leaders were fixated on costs. For example, if we needed to hit a number by the end of a quarter, we opted to do it by reducing expenses with little regard to the impact on customer service or employee engagement. In short, things were a mess. But as gloomy as it all sounds, having lived through it every day, it was actually worse. In fact, it was a little frightening. Fortunately, there were glimmers, bright spots that gave me hope. There were people at the call centers who still believed, who felt that serving the customer the best way possible was the right thing to do. And not just the right thing—the only thing. They were the green shoots, and I began to realize they held the key to a solution. That was the light at the end of the tunnel, and it was the beginning of the turnaround."[1]

Change is less about strategy and structure, and more about attitudes and mindset. Great leaders accept the fact that many people instinctively resist change—even when morale is low and frustration is high.

CASE STUDY: PART 2

Transforming Customer Care: "The Plan Is a Living Thing, and It Was Going to Continue to Grow and Change"

"I knew right away that I was going to need a lot of support and resources. The job was just too big. One big bright spot for me was our new CEO, Joe Natale. Joe was completely driven and passionate to turn things around, as was our CHRO, Jim Reid. With their impetus, the entire executive team got behind me, and that gave me hope and courage. When I went out and started talking to the frontline teams across the country, they encouraged me and sometimes pleaded with me to do something different. And that gave me even more hope, because should your team not believe in a way forward—if they don't want to be part of something bigger—it's very difficult to build any kind of momentum.

"I was inspired by how committed and how passionate many of them were about the customer despite the problems we were having. Throughout my career, I've had a simple philosophy which proved especially important here, and it is this: If we can make our frontline teams feel like the most important people in the company, they'll make our customers feel like the most important people in the world. I truly believe that because it's the way I'm wired as a leader. I think you have to believe, and so I tried to find reasons to believe, and luckily, I found them. Of course, there were obstacles. Budget was one. I had a very big ask, and I got put through the wringer explaining the return on investment. But I've never in my whole career received approval to move forward as quickly as I did on this.

"Then, it was time to come up with a plan. I remember going into Joe's office, and as we sat beside each other, I made notes on a blank sheet of paper and walked him through all my observations. We started mapping out a game plan and a path to turn things around. It was an amazing experience. Before this, I'd never sat side by side with the CEO and created a plan together, but that's the kind of CEO Joe is. And the plan we created that day became our North Star, and it has guided us since. We deliberately kept it as simple as possible, so people could easily absorb it and apply it. We settled on four key goals that drove every action we took:

1. Change the culture within the call centers by getting our employees fully engaged.
2. Create customer and frontline experiences that are as frictionless as possible.
3. Make the call center operations more efficient through better investment, training and tools.
4. Change the way we talk to our customers about value.

"One of the most important things we did to change the culture was create a brand. I felt that if we could create a brand for the process, we could create an identity that our frontline people could connect with. I learned from my Nike days how powerful a brand can be because a brand is a promise—and a promise must be kept. So all the call center teams and the call center operations were branded as Care Nation. Corny as it may sound, Care Nation was a way to counteract some of the feelings of being alone, of being an island, of being victims, of not having a voice. I wanted people to feel supported and believe that they mattered. I wanted to spread this feeling out to as many people as possible as quickly as possible, so we began communicating it across the company, and it became the heart of our storytelling.

"Our story now had a character, and this character—Care Nation—was unbeatable and strong. Then, Joe started using the term *Care Nation*, and Jim started using it, and the executive team started using it, and everyone at the call centers started calling themselves Care Nation. And it became a really powerful vehicle for people to feel strong. Heather Arthur, one of the VPs that ran Rogers Care for me at the time, told me that the frontline teams wore Care Nation like a Superman cape 'because it makes them feel bigger, better and stronger.' I loved her analogy because it showed exactly what we were trying to do.

"Then, we started telling individual Care Nation stories, and we made sure they accomplished three things. First, they had to be believable. When our teams heard the details of our path forward, they had to believe it was real and executable and doable, and not just words on a page or a laundry list of bullets in a PowerPoint deck. Second, our stories had to be relevant. Our teams had to look at the plan and say to themselves: 'Yes, this is solving today's problems. This is real. They've heard me. This is what I have to deal with every day, and this plan is going to help solve our problems, not someone else's problems.' Third, the customer had to be at the core of all our stories. During our road shows, we told the frontline teams that if they weren't hearing our most important message—that the customer was at the center of everything we're trying to do—to call us out because something's wrong.

"Perhaps most important, we wanted to make Care Nation their story, not ours. When we talked about it, we never said: 'This plan is done. I am communicating the plan to you.' We said: 'We want to hear from you. How can we make this plan better?' We wanted their fingerprints and their voices all over this plan. So after the focus groups, we had listening sessions, and we told everyone the plan was a living thing, and it was going to continue to grow and change based on their feedback, and on what their customers were experiencing, and on the new realities.

"To make sure the plan took root, I visited every single site every single quarter and conducted focus groups and talk-to-me sessions where we talked about the plan and the journey, so we'd get constant feedback. While this was happening, we never let up on our communications. We created something we called the *Voice of the Frontline*, an interactive, online suggestion site which helped build communities across all of our frontline teams. This wasn't just for the call centers, however. We included all the frontline teams. It was far more than a suggestion box, and we continue to use it to help us shape the future of the company.

"We also launched *Being Here Matters* to address the chronic absenteeism issue. *Being Here Matters* was about showing people how important their work was to others and how we were going to tackle the things that are keeping people from coming to work. But we needed everybody to care, so our message was 'your customers need you, your teammates on either side of you need you here, and it's important for you to be a part of this movement.' We needed to tackle absenteeism by appealing to their pride through the idea that being here matters. And so this was part of the cultural transformation. And it worked. In short order, we cut our absenteeism in half, and it's continued to get better, even years after we launched this program.

"There were plenty of other initiatives going on during this time. A big one was making sure the right people were on the bus as we plunged into the change process. I had to make lot of changes to my leadership team, but I was careful not to change the team just for the sake of changing things up. I don't believe there's such a thing as a perfect leader. I think all leaders are flawed, and all leaders have gaps in their game. But I do believe there's such a thing as a perfect team. And I think when a leader is aware of their gaps and their strengths, and is willing to make courageous decisions to bring people in to fill those gaps, then you can create a perfect team. So I went on a mission to do that.

"A critical part of the transformation process was empowering our frontline team so they could turn around and make our customers feel like the most important people in the world. And one of the most important keys to accomplishing this goal, and reinforcing it, was to create a culture of learning. So we trained our first-level leaders to become exceptional coaches. We started this process through a coaching program called LEAD, with help from a consulting company called SwitchGear. After SwitchGear completed its initial assessment, the assessors told us we had a problem: 'Your call center managers know the "hello" in the conversations the specialists are having with customers, and they know the goodbye. But they have no idea what's going on in the middle.' As a result, the managers were unable to teach the specialists how to have better, more satisfying conversations with customers. Also, our managers weren't able to find the bright spots—the specialists who have really got the journey and the conversation right—so they could model and replicate the behaviors of those specialists across the team.

"SwitchGear helped us create an operating system that enabled us to develop exceptional coaches internally, and the core of that operating system was side-by-side coaching. Team managers would sit with the call specialists every day, and listen to the calls, and coach the specialists in real time. What a difference it made! Not only did customer satisfaction soar, but the LEAD program dramatically improved the relationships between our frontline people and their managers. Coaching created the muscle we needed to begin to drive many of the cultural and procedural changes we wanted to make. It was a really powerful weapon for us across all our call centers, and helped us create a more frictionless experience between our specialists and their customers.

"But there were other issues that needed fixing as well. We noticed that our call center technology was not as up to date as we had thought, so we revamped and simplified the digital tools used to serve our customers. We encouraged our frontline teams to help shape those tools by structuring the program in a new way, and we made sure that feedback was built into the process, which was new for us. We also looked at their work environment, which was drab and uninspiring. So we brightened up the sites, upgraded the chairs, gave each specialist two monitors instead of one and put inspiring Care Nation messaging on the walls.

"These last changes may seem small, but they made a big difference to our frontline teams. Instead of words and promises, they had physical evidence of our commitment to action. They could see things changing right in front of them, and it became a big motivator. To keep the momentum going, we highlighted small wins as well as big wins. That created a constant drumbeat that things were improving. As the narrative began to evolve, others outside our group started telling the story. Joe started to tell it, and Jim started to tell it, and then, other teams in the company started saying, 'Hey, something's happening in Care Nation, and it's awesome.' And when our team started to hear other people telling the story, that gave everyone another lift and drove the flywheel even faster.

"Throughout it all, we were mindful of the stress that our frontline people might be experiencing. Change can be fearful for some, and annoying for others, and unsettling for nearly everyone, so we needed a mechanism to keep building momentum. We created something called *Frontline Certified*, which was, in effect, an approval process managed by the frontline staff themselves. No programs or initiatives could get approved unless they were certified by our frontline people, so if Care Nation didn't say it was okay, it wouldn't happen. As you can imagine, that started to spark the *Frontline Certified* story throughout the organization.

"All told, it's been an amazing journey. Our frontline people have done an incredible job of accepting and managing and driving the change. And the ongoing support we have received from our entire executive team has been invaluable. But we're not finished. Creating exceptional customer service in this industry is far from easy. But we have conviction. We believe we can become best in class. Even now, I'll hear the Care Nation team say: 'We shouldn't just benchmark ourselves against our industry. We should benchmark ourselves against the Amazons of the world, against the Ritz-Carltons of the world, against the Ubers of the world.' They would have never talked about that a couple of years ago, but they do now. Because they believe."[4]

How to Drive Successful Change

What took place at the call centers—the vision, the plan, the brand building, the empowerment of the frontlines, the feedback loop and the leaders' follow-through on their promises—is a remarkable success story. The data Rogers has collected supports the progress made. For example, the company's Likelihood to Recommend (a variation of Net Promoter Score) is up almost 70 percent since the transformation began; our First Time Resolution metrics have improved 50 percent; and our frontline team engagement is currently at 86 percent, the highest of all the divisions in the company. Eric and his team managed the change process the right way and, by doing so, created a textbook example of how to drive successful change, but this success could just as easily not have been.

Kotter's research and analysis on change led him to conclude that a successful transformation has eight phases, and "critical mistakes in any of the phases can have a devastating impact, slowing momentum and negating hard-won gains."[5] Here are the eight reasons why transformations fail, according to Kotter:

1. Lack of urgency
2. Lack of support from the top
3. Lack of vision
4. Poor communication
5. Resistance (both human and structured)
6. Lack of short-term wins
7. Celebrating too soon
8. Failure to culturally anchor the change[6]

These eight reasons explain Eric's successful transformation of Rogers's call centers. Here is how Eric succeeded.

Eric Cultivated a Sense of Urgency

The drive to transform Rogers's call centers began at the very top—with the new CEO, Joe Natale, whose number one priority was to transform the culture at Rogers by having every employee "obsess over the customer experience."[7] Joe felt that a change of this magnitude had to start at the grassroots level, so he put the call centers front and center. When Eric took the reins of the change process, he demonstrated to the frontline workers just how important their job was by visiting every call center site and reviewing the plan in detail with them, by conducting mass listening sessions to elicit feedback, and by following up with videos, town halls and leader-to-leader sessions. Further, Eric empowered frontline staff at the call centers by allowing them to help mold the plan as it was taking shape.

Eric Ensured That Top-Down Guidance and Support Were Present

The backing of the CEO and executive team gave heft and credibility to the program while helping spread Eric's story across the organization. Studies by McKinsey report that change is five times more likely to succeed if top management is actively engaged in modeling the change.[8]

At the same time, a lack of management support will almost certainly derail a change initiative, no matter how well thought out it may be.

When leaders get tentative about the change process, dysfunction can result. A case in point is Hewlett-Packard under its former CEO Carly Fiorina. As venture capitalist John Hamm noted in the *Harvard Business Review*: Fiorina "had a fixed idea that reorganizations must be managed with extreme care, and she implicitly communicated her belief by the cautious way she floated her ideas with senior managers. She worried that a reshuffling plan would open a Pandora's Box of political sensitivities, especially among middle managers." Her indecision caused a big problem:

> For two months prior to Fiorina's official announcement, work slowed or stopped as employees, not knowing precisely what to expect or fear, shifted their focus to the upcoming changes. Managers, jostling for power and position, got lost in political battles. Motivation plummeted. Contractors were put off, since no one knew who would be managing which divisions after the reorganization [...] A total of 12 weeks—a full quarter—were effectively lost.[9]

Once leadership understands that a change is needed, the commitment must be rapid and decisive. The bandage must be pulled off cleanly and quickly. As long as the company's values don't change, everything else is up for grabs, including the company's business model and culture. Satya Nadella offers us a great example. He believes that employees should have a growth mindset and be open to learning, absorbing new ideas and breaking down silos. He also believes in showing empathy to coworkers and customers, and he constantly reinforces these concepts in all his messaging and his own behavior. When he became Microsoft's CEO, he began to change the culture in subtle ways. He asked his executive team to read a small selection of books. One of them was called *Nonviolent Communication* by Marshall Rosenberg. It focused on learning to communicate with empathy and without judgment. According to Nadella, it helped transform Microsoft's culture "from cutthroat to creative."[10]

Eric Developed a Clear Path

Eric and his team created a clear, simple plan of action based on four objectives:

1. Change the culture.
2. Create a frictionless customer and frontline experience.
3. Provide better training and tools.
4. Change the way our customers see our value.

Every action was dictated by one or more of these goals. Together, they created powerful momentum and focus.

Eric Communicated Constantly and Transparently

Constant and transparent communication is critical to making change work. To develop a narrative that thousands of people could embrace, Eric had to create a believable and relevant story, one with the customer at its core. When McKinsey asked thousands of global leaders what their organizations would do differently if a transformation happened again, "nearly half of respondents (and the largest share) wish their organizations had spent more time communicating a change story."[11] Eric's constant follow-up with the call centers and the feedback loops that were initiated helped drive communication and execution to great heights.

Eric Engaged Employees through
Their Ownership in the Change Process

From the start, Eric and his team looked for ways to empower workers at the call centers. Frontline employees had to be fully engaged in the program; otherwise, it wouldn't be effective, let alone take root over the long term. When employees were asked to participate in the change process and take ownership in their work, both engagement and productivity levels—not to mention customer satisfaction—skyrocketed.

Let's be clear: emotions matter. In organizations where engagement is high and positive emotions prevail, productivity, innovation and revenue growth far outpace those in organizations in which low engagement and negative attitudes are the rule. Research by consulting firm Accenture "found that high levels of fear and frustration can reduce business outcomes by some 20%. On the other hand, high levels of passion and drive can boost them by up to 50%."[12] When teams understand the need for change and embrace the change, performance doesn't drop off during the transformation process but, in fact, increases.

Eric Celebrated Small Wins

Physical evidence that management was following through on their promises and that the change process was having an impact on customer satisfaction scores was an essential factor in keeping the momentum going. Simple but constructive steps like providing more comfortable chairs and painting the walls made it easy for employees to see tangible examples of the change process. Resistance to change is the greatest obstacle to transformational success, but resistance doesn't disappear when the momentum builds. Rather, it is "always waiting to reassert itself," said Kotter.[13] The changes made at Rogers have been deep, cathartic and extremely positive, but the process is far from finished. Small wins keep the momentum going, while big wins accelerate it.

Eric Did Not Declare Victory Too Soon

One of the most important elements of the success driven by Eric and his team was that they consistently resisted the urge to declare victory too soon. In fact, they have never declared victory at all. The message to the teams has been the opposite: "To make our call centers the best in the industry, we must continue to adapt to the changing world around us. That is what will make us better!" And Eric and his team have never stopped trying to improve.

Adapt but Never Abdicate

How leaders culturally anchor transformation can define their career and reputation because the ability to adapt is critical to personal and organizational success. Recall Collins and Porras's paradox of change (see Chapter 1), which essentially says, "Don't change your foundational values and purpose, but be open to changing everything else—your strategy, your culture and your practices." What distinguished the visionary companies from their peers, according to Collins and Porras in *Built to Last*, was that "core ideology in a visionary company works hand in hand with a relentless drive for progress that impels change and forward movement in all that is not part of your core ideology" (i.e., values and purpose).[14] I remember Jim Collins making this point crystal clear to me when I first met him. He told me that the first response to a changing world is not to ask ourselves, "How should we change?" but instead to ask, "What do we stand for and why do we exist?" These two critical questions define the core ideology of a company. With Eric's call center transformation, Rogers's values and purpose never changed. However, the world was changing, and the organizational culture and strategies in the call centers needed to follow suit.

· · · · ·

Taken together, the principles and frameworks in Kotter's *Leading Change* and Collins and Porras's *Built to Last* provide insight for leaders looking to successfully navigate the complexity of change while sustaining high performance. By the way, these powerful models and insights also apply at a personal level as well, because just as companies that thrive over time must adapt, so too must individuals.

In Chapter 8: Crisis Leadership, you will read about how a crisis tests a leader's grit, strength, determination and purpose. The theme of core values and how they contribute to resilience is amplified. Before you dive in to Chapter 8, please complete the activity and exercise for Chapter 7, which you will find in Part 3.

CHAPTER 7 TAKEAWAYS

> The world is moving too fast for leaders or organizations to think that the status quo is good enough. You either move forward and adapt or run the risk of being left behind. Virtually every leader will confront the prospect of wrenching change over their business lives, and how they manage it will largely define their careers.

> The work of John Kotter, Jim Collins and Jerry Porras offers insights and frameworks for successful change initiatives. No one is immune to change. Everyone can prepare a plan for adaptation, even transformation.

> Communication is always critical. But in times of change, it is even more critical to success. Think of increasing the pace and volume of communication by a factor of ten because this will help stabilize those impacted by the change and keep them focused on what is most important.

> Finally, people will go along with change only if they feel heard and safe. If they feel that the future will get them personally to a better place, that will also make them more likely to go along with change.

Crisis Leadership

8

Crises can go two ways: They can sow division or spur
magnanimity.
—RANDALL LANE, *FORBES*

dmiral James Stockdale was the highest-ranking U.S. military
officer incarcerated at the infamous Hanoi Hilton, a
prisoner-of-war camp during the Vietnam War, where he
was imprisoned for eight years. He was tortured, and he
had no rights, no set release date and no certainty of whether he would
ever see his family again. When Jim Collins asked the admiral how he
found the guts to survive, Stockdale simply said: "I never ever wavered
in my absolute faith that not only would I prevail—get out of this—but
I would also prevail by turning it into the defining event of my life."

Collins then asked him who hadn't escaped.

Stockdale replied, "The optimists [. . .] they died of a broken heart."

I find Stockdale's response surprising. Isn't another word for optimism *hope*? Isn't hope necessary to fight pessimism and darkness? I
asked Jim to explain this for me. He told me that Stockdale said that

the optimists were the ones who believed "we're going to be out by Christmas." Stockdale continued:

> Christmas would come, and it would go [and they were still in prison]. And there would be another Christmas. And they died of a broken heart [...] This is what I learned from those years in the prison camp [...] You must never ever ever confuse, on the one hand, the need for absolute, unwavering faith that you can prevail despite those constraints, with, on the other hand, the need for the discipline to begin by confronting the brutal facts, whatever they are. We're not getting out of here by Christmas.[1]

As leaders, we have the gift of important lessons from Admiral Stockdale. Be real and don't sugarcoat a bad situation. Face the facts. Be transparent, honest and fact based. At the same time, give people hope that together, we can get through a situation—for realistic hope in a critical moment is as essential as the oxygen we breathe. The image below shows one of the most valuable pieces of advice any leader can possess when they find themselves in the middle of a crisis, big or small.

The Stockdale Paradox		
Retain faith that you will prevail in the end, regardless of the difficulties.	AND at the same time	Confront the most brutal facts of your current reality, whatever they might be.

Source: Jim Collins, *Good to Great*, HarperCollins 2001, p. 86.

A crisis tests a leader's grit, strength, determination and purpose. It tests the leader's ability to support their team, who are often under similar duress. Coming out the other side of a crucial moment requires skillful communication and compassion in order to connect with people at a human level. Let's explore communication by way of example.

Leading When the World as We Knew It Is Gone

Joe Natale had a sixth sense that COVID-19 was going to be a threat on a global level. He sat down with me to discuss what steps we needed to take if the virus showed up in North America—something we believed was inevitable. Joe and I spoke about how the health crisis would likely become an economic crisis if it really took hold and fear set in. Sadly, we were right. On January 27, 2020, Canada had its first recorded case of COVID-19. And people began to fight for their lives.

Joe leads twenty-six thousand team members and has a genuine, heartfelt touch with people. He is a skilled communicator, and he publishes a biweekly video blog called *Joe's Take*. He has established trust with team members through monthly open mic sessions, responding directly and honestly to any question put to him. In addition, every Monday morning he emails a story to all team members outlining how we let a customer down and then emphasizes what we can learn to do better every day. This Monday morning email ritual was designed to sharpen and strengthen everyone's focus on the customer. Everyone took the lessons to heart.

When the virus hit North America, we held an open mic session with our team members to answer their questions, and Joe framed our response to the crisis by laying out two key areas of focus—and only two: 1) to keep our teams healthy and safe; and 2) to keep our customers connected to the essential wireless and internet services they needed now more than ever. Two promises to guide the company's actions during the pandemic. Within those promises were two priorities grounded in our values of people being at the heart of our success, and in our purpose of keeping Canadians connected to a world of possibilities and the memorable moments that matter most in their lives.

Throughout the crisis, Rogers held two information sessions every week with its entire workforce. First, executive leaders would share tips and tools to help employees get through the crisis, and then, ask team members to tell us how they felt and what they were experiencing. Our chief medical officer, Dr. David Satok, joined these calls to give comfort and provide evidence-based data updates about the pandemic and the impact on team members' communities. Joe also held weekly open mics, and we would often get close to ten thousand employees on our calls with Joe. As the crisis unfolded, some of the stories we heard were just heartbreaking. People were struggling mentally and worried financially. So we told our employees that no matter what happens, they would continue to receive full salary and benefits for the first few months of the crisis.

In looking back, I see how Joe set the tone for our three thousand people leaders in a remarkable way. We made a series of decisions right out of the gate that demonstrated we would stay focused on our objectives, and live our values and purpose. Here are some of the key decisions we made:

1. As soon as the crisis hit, we changed several of our customer policies. We removed all wireless roaming charges as thousands of Canadians struggled to return home from overseas.
2. We eliminated overage fees and data usage caps on all internet and wireless plans, thereby removing the biggest fear of our eleven million customers: bill shocks.
3. We provided additional TV entertainment at no charge, so families could be entertained together while the schools were closed.
4. We announced full income protection for our workforce at the height of the crisis. Joe and I discussed the fact that as a family company, we had to stand behind our people, because people who lost their jobs through no fault of their own would have nowhere to go. We knew this pandemic was nothing like the great financial crisis of 2008–9. This was different.
5. We committed to not lay anyone off permanently until we moved through the worst of the crisis. In the event of a temporary layoff, we would support the affected employee by topping up pay above

and beyond government programs, while ensuring that medical benefits continued.

6. To support our communities, we announced a donation program to Food Banks Canada. Because we saw a rise in spousal abuse, we donated to Women's Shelters Canada. Three months into the crisis, the Rogers family donated $60 million to support Canadians impacted by the pandemic. Our teams felt a deep sense of pride in how we supported the communities where our employees worked and lived.

7. Finally, we recommitted ourselves to our inclusion and diversity plans as another crisis unfolded during the pandemic. Following the tragic murder of George Floyd in Minneapolis on May 25, 2020, we acknowledged the heartbreaking loss with our teams, especially our BIPOC (Black, Indigenous, People of Color) team members. We immediately responded through our media platform of fifty radio stations along with a national TV platform to relaunch *Speaker's Corner*, which gave all Canadians a voice on how we could attack racism, social inequality and violence to make Canada stronger and our company an even better place to work. We launched "safe talk" listening sessions with our Black community, and listened, learned and gained insight into how to become a stronger company. And we launched a new five-year Inclusion and Diversity strategy to ensure that as a company, we were part of the change that our country needed.

What was the outcome of all these decisions? In June 2020, Rogers did a pulse survey, and the results showed that 93 percent of our team members said they were proud to work for Rogers. These results were a record high for the company. Externally, we saw two major data points. On the Edelman Trust Index, our customers' trust and faith in the company rose 19 percent to the highest rating in Canada among the large telecom companies. In terms of Likelihood to Recommend, a measure of customer loyalty, we saw across-the-board increases, year over year, in all our major brands and businesses.

I attribute the positive developments to bold leadership rooted in our values and purpose. We stepped up communications and spoke the truth. Consistent with the takeaways from the Stockdale Paradox, Joe and the executive team gave people hope—without diminishing the effects of a pandemic that was gripping the entire world—that we would get through this together, and we would keep our people safe and our customers connected.

CASE STUDY

How a Prime Minister Kept Her Country Calm

When New Zealand's peace was shattered by the Christchurch mosque shootings, Prime Minister Jacinda Ardern wasted no time springing into action and leading her country deftly out of crisis.

When she addressed the press, she left no doubt where she stood on racism, assuring Muslim minorities that this was an attack on all New Zealanders. She flew to Christchurch and visited with members of the Muslim community, reassuring them: "I am here today to bring with me the grief of all New Zealand [...] I am here to stand alongside you ... We feel grief, we feel injustice, and we feel anger."[2] Powerful words. The images were equally powerful because she wore a hijab as she spoke, and hugged both Muslim women and men.

Within days, she announced that the country's gun laws would change because "people will be seeking change, and I am committed to that."[3] She noted that attempts had been made to change the laws several times in the past two decades but that now was the time for real change. In the weeks that followed, Ardern was asked how she managed to deal with the crisis so calmly and decisively. She responded simply: "There is very little time to sit and think in those terms. You just do what feels right."[4]

In other words, she relied on her values and principles. "I absolutely knew what I wanted to say," she said. "That, very quickly, was clear to me, when I heard that a mosque had been targeted. I knew what I wanted to say about that straight away. But, no, I didn't think about particular words. I just thought about sentiments, and what I thought needed to be conveyed."[5]

Ardern's response to her country's COVID-19 crisis was equally effective. As an epidemic in one country swiftly mutated into a pandemic affecting hundreds of nations, she gave a remarkable speech to New Zealanders explaining exactly what action the government was taking and what sacrifices people would need to make. Most importantly, she gave meaning and context by carefully explaining the reasons:

If community transmission takes off in New Zealand the number of cases will double every five days. If that happens unchecked, our health system will be inundated, and tens of thousands of New Zealanders will die. There is no easy way to say that—but it is the reality we have seen overseas—and the possibility we must now face here. Together, we must stop that happening, and we can. Right now we have a window of opportunity to break the chain of community transmission—to contain the virus—to stop it multiplying and to protect New Zealanders from the worst. Our plan is simple. We can stop the spread by staying at home and reducing contact. Now is the time to act [...] These decisions will place the most significant restriction on New Zealanders' movements in modern history. This is not a decision taken lightly. But this is our best chance to slow the virus and to save lives. Let me set out what these changes will mean for everyone [...] We will continue to vigorously contact trace every single case. Testing will continue at pace to help us understand the current number of cases in New Zealand and where they are based. If we flush out the cases we already have and see transmission slow, we will potentially be able to move areas out of Level 4 over time. But for the next wee while, things will look worse before they look better. In the short term the number of cases will likely rise because the virus is already in our community.

But these new measures can slow the virus down and prevent our health system from being overwhelmed and ultimately save lives.[6]

Ardern didn't just relay the facts; she thoughtfully explained to New Zealanders what must happen and why, and she did it with genuine empathy. As a result, anxiety levels diminished, and people willingly followed her lead. The results of her actions speak volumes: New Zealand's coronavirus caseload is exemplary.

CASE STUDY

Principled Leadership Personified

In April 2018, Starbucks CEO Kevin Johnson faced a crisis centered on anti-Black racism. Two Black men sitting in a Philadelphia Starbucks waiting for a friend were asked to leave the store by the manager. When they refused, the police were called, and the men were arrested for "trespassing." They were taken away for no reason other than being a perceived threat because they were Black.

Kevin Johnson handled the incident by accepting full responsibility. In a video he posted to Starbucks's website and social media platforms, Johnson told the world: "I want to [issue] a personal apology to the two gentlemen who were arrested in our store [...] This is not who we are, and it's not who we are going to be [...] These two gentlemen did not deserve what happened."[7] He went on to say that he would "do everything I can to ensure it is fixed and never happens again, whether that is changes to the policy and the practice, additional store manager training, including training around unconscious bias."

Johnson announced that he would shut down Starbucks's eight thousand U.S. stores on May 29, 2018, so the company's 175,000 employees could undergo racial-bias education. Johnson and other senior management at Starbucks understood that this gesture was only the beginning. The company's chairman, Howard Schultz, noted: "We realize that four hours of training is not going to solve racial inequity [...] but we have to start the conversation."[8] The move was celebrated by some as a necessary first step and derided by others as a publicity stunt, but the real importance was that Starbucks's employees fully understood the company's stance on anti-Black racism, and discrimination and racism of any kind. Almost as importantly, Johnson's decision helped mitigate the potential shame Starbucks's employees might feel while restoring their confidence and pride as Starbucks employees.

Some critics called for Starbucks to take action against the store manager, but Johnson would have none of that. Instead, he said: "The focus of fixing this—I own it. This is a management issue, and I am accountable to ensure we address the policy and the practice and the training that led to this outcome." What happened was "reprehensible [...] We are accountable. I am accountable."[9] Johnson spent two days in Philadelphia visiting with the two men who were arrested as well as the mayor, police chief and others in the community to learn what happened and why it happened, and to make sure it would never happen again.

Johnson's unambiguous apology and his proactive handling of the Philadelphia incident are a clear illustration of +5 leadership in action. When news of the COVID-19 pandemic came out of China two years later, Johnson once again led by example. He quickly ordered Starbucks shops in China to close even though the company's revenues would be decimated. Johnson explained:

> We immediately decided there were three simple principles that would guide every decision we would have to make [...] Do what is right for our partners and for our customers; do what is right to support our government and health officials; and do what is right to show up in a positive way in our community. We have leaders in 82 markets around the world making hundreds of decisions a day in a way that's consistent with those values and principles.[10]

How leaders respond to crises goes a long way to determining their future and the culture of their organization. Although +5 leaders don't welcome crises any more than the next person does, when they do come (because crises are inevitable), these leaders respond with humility, grit, and clear purpose and action.

How do you go about handling a crisis in your own organization? As a leader, you must first take personal and immediate responsibility. When you model your response and behavior after people like Joe Natale, Jacinda Ardern and Kevin Johnson, your organization will not only survive a crisis, but it will likely emerge even stronger than before.

Do You Have a Crisis Mitigation Checklist?

No matter what the situation, a crisis is always defined by several common characteristics. First, it is unpredictable; often characterized by rapidly changing circumstances, twists and turns; and often contains mini-crises within the larger crisis. Second, because of the unpredictability, the leader often has no clear playbook to follow. Hence, defining the next decision or move can be the most important action. Third, accountability and communication are critical in any crisis. Clear communication, transparency and fact-based messaging that blends the brutal facts with hope and opportunity are essential to stabilizing and mobilizing any workforce that faces an unexpected turn of events.

Ultimately, the leader's values, communication skills and grit—plus a healthy dose of compassion and empathy—are often most critical to successfully lead a team out of a crisis. Why? In any crisis, people need hope and belief that they will get through this. To follow a leader in a crisis, people need to trust that their leaders have their best interests at heart, and that the leaders are following a path that they believe will get them and their team to a better place.

The Characteristics of a Crisis

1. A crisis occurs suddenly, and its velocity and challenges are unpredictable.
2. A leader often has no playbook for a crisis, and even if a playbook exists, it cannot anticipate a crisis's rapid twists and turns.

3. A crisis creates an extraordinary demand for information.
4. Decisions must be fact based, with all emotion removed from the equation.
5. Messaging must never be sugarcoated, but at the same time, it must be hopeful.

For leaders, crises are times when stress and uncertainty collide in ways that require exceptional clarity of values, purpose and passions. As a military pilot, I trained day after day for crises. Whether it was an aircraft emergency such as an engine failure or the need to defend your country, I was always preparing for unforeseen events. The same is true for the best leaders: they don't just think about how to lead in normal times, but they also have a game plan or checklist for the unexpected. Here is your crisis checklist.

Crisis Leadership Checklist

Establish Two or Three Major Priorities

Don't try to boil the ocean. You must pick the two or three most critical priorities for your organization or team. (These are often characterized early in a crisis and are likely to include team safety, customer issues and liquidity concerns.) If ever there was a time for establishing clarity of what is expected from everyone, a crisis is it. The more priorities you set up front, the easier it will be to get everyone on your team focused on what is essential. Finally, maintain this focus on what is important until the key indicators of your business tell you that you are through the worst and highest-risk time frame.

Act Fast

All crises are notorious for incomplete data, information overload, high anxiety and decision trade-offs. In the military, we were taught that the only bad decision in a crisis is no decision. Leaders must avoid paralysis via analysis and make a call to move forward. All decisions need to tie back to the two or three previously established priorities. Most importantly, in a crisis, speed trumps perfection in decision-making.

Own It
If a crisis is caused by an error, it is critical for the leader to take full accountability for the situation right from the beginning. Mistakes happen. Crises occur. But one of the biggest mistakes leaders make is to play victim or place blame. A crisis is a time for solutions, for moving forward, not for looking back.

Be Compassionate and Empathic
In the midst of an emergency, many people are afraid. Abraham Maslow's hierarchy of needs kicks in, and people move quickly to their personal safety and well-being. Showing up with empathy and compassion is often what is needed to meet people where they are— not where you want them to be. When people feel listened to and truly understood, it creates a dynamic for trust and psychological safety that brings people together. And standing together is needed to get to the other side.

Communicate, Communicate, Communicate
As is plain to see from the case studies, communication is always important. But it is critical during a crisis. The Stockdale Paradox lays out how leaders need to frame their communication in any crisis: confront the brutal facts that you are facing and within the facts find realistic hope. Most importantly, convey your confidence and belief that you will get through the crisis together.

· · · · ·

With this checklist in hand, let's move to the next chapter to explore the critical skill of coaching, where the leader goes behind the bench to inspire the team to exceptional levels of performance. But first, turn to Part 3 for the activity and exercise to be completed for this chapter.

CHAPTER 8 TAKEAWAYS

> When facing a crisis, in the words of Admiral Stockdale, "You must never ever ever confuse, on the one hand, the need for absolute, unwavering faith that you can prevail despite [your] constraints, with, on the other hand, the need for the discipline to begin by confronting the brutal facts, whatever they are."

> When you are experiencing a personal crisis, ask for help and support. The same goes for the workplace. Never ever feel you cannot ask for help.

> How leaders respond to crises goes a long way to determining the leaders' future and the culture of their organizations. Although +5 leaders don't welcome crises any more than the next person does, when they do come (because crises are inevitable), these leaders respond with humility, grit, and clear purpose and action.

> To follow a leader in a crisis, people need to trust that their leaders have their best interests at heart, and that the leaders are following a path that they believe will get them and their team to a better place. As the leader, you need a crisis checklist to be prepared for what can suddenly erupt in front of you.

> However, no one checklist can cover every eventuality. You will be called to be adaptable, innovative and creative. You can build this mindset through education. Building this mindset in your team is perhaps the most precious activity you can undertake.

The Leader
as Coach

> In the past, a leader was a boss. Today's leaders must be partners with their people [...] they no longer can lead solely based on positional power. —KEN BLANCHARD

It's been my experience that when an organization cares for its people, people will care about their organization. By *caring for people*, I mean having people's well-being, personal growth, career development, and rewards and recognition baked into an organization's culture. Leadership is about empowering people, not over-managing them, and while it is true that *empowerment* has become a buzzword, it perfectly encapsulates the new realities inside the modern workplace. Today's employees are expected to have entrepreneurial drive, and be self-directed and confident decision-makers. Employee empowerment is here to stay, because forward-thinking employers know it leads to a greater sense of autonomy—the employee's need to direct their own life and work. Empowerment drives engagement,[1] and engagement is the number one driver of high-performing teams. But to stay engaged, people need to find meaning in their work, and have a sense of ownership in it and pride in their team.

People not only want to grow; they need to grow. A survey by Pew Research found that over half of American workers believe it will be "essential for them to get training and develop new job skills throughout their work life in order to keep up with changes in the workplace."[2] This is not surprising. A Brookfield Institute report found that 42 percent of the tasks that Canadians are currently paid to do can be automated using existing technology,[3] while across North America, job restructuring is occurring at a breakneck pace thanks to the emergence of new technology. What other challenges are businesses facing? Cultures based on command and control no longer dominate the landscape, and hierarchical structures are becoming increasingly flatter and more democratic. The leaders advancing change do so because "people are expected to lead from where they are—not only from the C-suite or other positions of formal authority," according to an MIT Sloan report.[4] Today, everyone—not just executives—wants to be engaged in their work. But for people to become and stay engaged, they need an environment that is psychologically safe, and enables them to develop as people and professionals. That means today's leaders must be coaches, not managers.

Why Coaching?

As my HR colleagues who are reading this book will know, our days are jammed with meetings and to-do lists, yet 40 percent of our workweek is spent coaching people. I have an MBA and have completed the Advanced Management Program at Harvard, yet I took the time to become a certified coach. Why would I spend the time if I didn't see the value? Don't take my word for it. A prominent study by the Association for Talent Development found that organizations

Training differs from coaching. Training is about learning a set curriculum and testing for specific learning goals. Coaching focuses on accountability to take action, and on an individual's growth and development through their behavior, goals and needs.

with strong coaching cultures have a larger percentage of highly engaged employees (61 percent) than do their peers (53 percent) and higher revenue growth.[5] The Hay Group reported that approximately 25 to 40 percent of Fortune 500 companies use executive coaches.[6] IBM's survey of CEOs reported that people skills were ranked in the top four of "External forces impacting the enterprise."[7]

Tens of billions of dollars are spent on leadership development, but most leadership development programs fail or fall short of their objectives.[8] Why? In large part, leadership development education is designed without a sufficient understanding of the mindset shift required. "Becoming a more effective leader often requires changing behavior," noted a McKinsey report. "But although most companies recognize that this also means adjusting underlying mind-sets, too often these organizations are reluctant to address the root causes of why leaders act the way they do."[9] Coaching, however, enables mindset shifts to happen.

In the past, coaching was mainly reserved for transitioning top-tier executives or used as a last-chance intervention when a manager's behavior became unacceptable. Today, the benefits of leading by coaching and developing an organization-wide coaching culture are emerging inside many of the world's leading companies.[10] Why? In part, today's employees, especially younger ones, crave feedback and coaching. For years, Millennials have been telling us they want regular and real-time performance feedback,[11] and since they now represent the largest segment of the North American work-force,[12] leaders must incorporate continuous feedback into their leadership framework.

Leaders tend to assume that because they lead, they are de facto coaches, but I can tell you from personal experience that until you have studied and practiced a proven coaching methodology, you have to question the value of your coaching efforts. Might you actually be doing harm?

When leadership development consultancy Zenger/Folkman asked 3,761 executives to assess their own coaching skills, 24 percent of the executives who rated themselves "above average" were actually ranked in the bottom third of the group by their colleagues.[13] In other words, many executives who think they're good coaches aren't. If you want to be a great leader, one of the first things I recommend you do is get a coaching certification from a recognized institution, because that skill set is fundamental to a leader's ability to build teams, develop talent and create team loyalty.

Applying the Right Framework

Coaching requires a system and structure. The Association for Talent Development defines a coaching culture as meeting at least five of the following six criteria:

> Employees value coaching.
> Senior executives value coaching.
> The organization has a dedicated line item budget for coaching.
> Coaching is available to all employees.
> Managers, leaders, or internal coaches receive accredited coach-specific training.
> All three coaching modalities (internal coach practitioners, external coach practitioners, and managers or leaders using coaching skills) are present in the organization.[14]

The biggest mistake many leaders make, according to Dr. Ralph Shedletsky, is that they don't see the need for setting aside allocated time for coaching. "Often, I hear that the meetings between a leader and a direct report are either ad hoc or infrequent," Shedletsky said. "And the most common reason given is, 'I see this person regularly. We're working on projects together, and their office is nearby. We're constantly interacting, so I don't need to have formal meetings.' That is a mistake."[15]

Carollyne Conlinn, a founding partner of Essential Impact—one of Canada's leading executive coaching firms—notes that "coaching is a way to have people internalize their motivation." Coaching's key value, according to Carollyne, is its ability to drive and enhance long-term performance:

> High performance can certainly be generated in the short term by the more traditional management methods, which means setting a goal, following up with people and making sure that they get the job done. But coaching is a way to have team members internalize their motivation and make room for them to be more self-generating with the solutions they come up with, and whatever else is needed to get the job done. It also eliminates the need for leaders to be constantly supervising people and creating ambitious goals with arbitrary time-lines. What you really want to do is shift the accountability directly to the person doing the work.[16]

To do that effectively, a framework is required.

Selecting a coaching framework for your organization must be a rigorous process that begins with a needs analysis, assessment and research. The coaching framework we selected for Rogers, shown in Figure 9.1, was developed by Essential Impact, and it has five phases: Engage, Enlighten, Empower, Excel and Evolve. Whether our leaders are being coached one on one or we are training leaders to coach their own teams, the framework remains the same. Only the context and content change. Here is how Carollyne describes the process.

Engage
"At the beginning, it's important to establish trust between the coach and the coachee, and get clarity on direction and expected outcomes.

FIGURE 9.1: EXCELERATOR COACHING PROCESS FRAMEWORK

Philosophy of Coaching

In the Excelerator Coaching™ System, our philosophy of coaching allows
for a variety of approaches and processes that move coachees toward
their expected outcomes through dynamic engagement.

ENLIGHTEN
- Coach Inquires
- Coach Listens
- Coach Observes
- Coach Responds to Verify Understanding
- Coach Suspends Premature Advice, Judgments and Emotions
- Coach Discerns Conditions
- Both Establish Focus

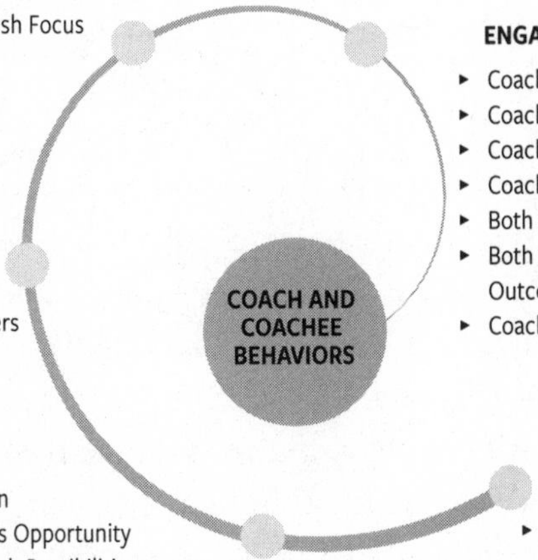

ENGAGE
- Coach Attends to Coachee
- Coach Defines Process
- Coachee Is Relaxed
- Coachee Identifies Focus
- Both State Purpose
- Both Define Measurable Outcomes
- Coachee Is Ready to Begin

EMPOWER
- Both Identify Barriers
- Both Negotiate Willingness to Move Forward
- Coach Verifies Intent and Direction
- Coachee Articulates Opportunity
- Inquires about Coach Possibilities
- Both Explore Alternate Courses of Action
- Coach Challenges Assumptions
- Coach Makes Strategic Requests

COACH AND COACHEE BEHAVIORS

EVOLVE
- Coach Supports the Coachee to Continuously Grow Into Their Best Self

EXCEL
- Coachee Takes Ownership of Opportunity
- Both Brainstorm Options
- Both Prioritize
- Both Build Action Plans
- Coachee Takes Accountability for Results
- Coach Champions Coachee
- Coachee Articulates Expected Outcomes
- Coachee Shifts to Next Level of Self-Responsibility

Source: Essential Impact Coaching Framework. Used with permission.

This is fundamental, because without some level of trust, psychological safety and engagement, coaching won't be successful. Coaching is quite different from a consulting situation where the consultant comes in after having done their due diligence to diagnose a problem and deliver a solution. We see the coaching relationship as a co-creative process that is continuously evolving. At the beginning, there's a conversation about what the coachee wants to accomplish, and depending on the situation, there might be input from others in the organization. Ideally, clear goals are set for the coachee, and they're motivated to achieve those goals. So we articulate together exactly what they want from the coaching, and how it will be measured, and how we'll know when we get to our end point."

Enlighten

"Once there's clarity about the outcome, the Enlighten phase begins. It's not linear, but rather, it's about focusing and elaborating on what the issue at hand is, along with what might be the contributing factors affecting the coachee's abilities or effectiveness at getting to the desired outcome. It's not about the coach discerning and deciding; it's about the coach supporting and then making space for the coachee to see what it is that they need to be working on. The coach's level of self-awareness is a big contributing factor, but the more self-aware the coachee is, the more powerful the coaching can be. To help in this area, we might use self-awareness or self-assessment tools and feedback from peers or the employees who report directly to the coachee. Often, an interview with the coachee about the results and questions they might have can help flesh things out. Then, we summarize the feedback so the coachee has more to work with in terms of what might need to change."

Empower

"Any objections usually show up at the Empower stage but again, not necessarily in a linear fashion. For example, the coachee might say: 'I've tried this and that already, but there's still something that isn't working that needs to change.' When a coachee appears stuck on what has not worked, the coach's role is to try to reframe the problem from 'What is not working?' to 'What could work?' in order to open the thinking to identify options which may not have been explored. Research tells us that if leaders focus their attention on what's not working, they're just going to get more of the same. So we help them focus on what is working, and leverage that to give them the confidence to tackle the things that need to be improved."

Excel and Evolve

"The Excel part of the conversation is where the commitment to change gets fully articulated into an action plan or a commitment to make a change in some way. For an executive, this whole process typically takes place over six months, so they really have the time to work on things and make changes, edit and adjust. By that time, a new behavior pattern or thinking pattern has become well ensconced. However, it's one thing to identify an issue, and make a change, and feel good about it. It's another to actually integrate this new way of thinking into other aspects of their lives. That's the Evolve part. It's people dealing with the feedback they've received at work, for example, and transferring it to other relationships in their lives. And that's really what coaching is about. It's about supporting people to make life changes that will have a long-term positive impact."[17]

· · · · ·

As you can see, coaching isn't a one-and-done process; it's ongoing. At Rogers, we came to realize that if our senior leaders were the only ones getting coached, coaching would be too big a burden. So we decided to launch our coaching skills development initiative with our director-level leaders and have them coach the employees who report directly to these leaders. Today, our coaching skills development is now offered at the VP, director and manager levels. Our leaders continuously reinforce the changes with their teams because they themselves are being coached. That's key, because if you're trying to introduce a new skill set through coaching, people are going to want to know that their bosses have experienced coaching too.

What kind of impact does coaching have on the bottom line? When the International Coaching Federation surveyed over two thousand coaching clients from sixty-four countries, 28 percent of the respondents reported an ROI of between ten and forty-nine times their investment, while 9 percent saw an ROI of at least fifty times! The median return on coaching on a company basis was 700 percent.[18] Quite remarkable.

At Rogers, the coaching we did with our frontline staff at the call centers helped us in myriad ways. Within twenty-four months from the start of the coaching program, we saw the following results:

> a significant increase in sales
> more agile response time
> improved conversion rates of calls into sales
> significantly reduced staff turnover resulting in substantial cost savings
> increased customer satisfaction scores and decreased customer escalations

Because we track the impact coaching has on our business, we know that the sites that employ coaching are outpacing their peers.

Coaching has helped us shift our culture from one of compliance orientation to one focused on talent development. Hence, people feel a sense of ownership and accountability.

Getting Clarity—Coaching's Greatest Value

There are many ways for leaders to coach, but all great leaders and coaches have the same objective: to help people become the best version of themselves. Ralph Shedletsky offered this perspective: "Coaching sessions are not about the leader jumping in and saying: 'You did this and that well, and I'm really pleased. Okay, now let's move on.' The leader's job is to ask questions, not to tell the coachee what the next steps are, so the person can fully own and fully explore what issues they might have and what's working well, and in turn, ask the leader for the input they require in order to solve their own problems. This method allows the coachee to own their own development, to understand it and to take responsibility for getting help, while allowing the leader to give input where they need to, not where they think they have to."

Shedletsky believes that coaching's greatest value lies in its enabling leaders to give their coachees clarity on three levels:

1. What are my responsibilities?
2. How do I go about doing my work well?
3. How will I learn and grow, and develop my career?

What Are My Responsibilities?

"It's important for people to know why the work they're doing is important to the organization," Shedletsky said. "They need to get clarity about how their job fits into the strategy and the specific objectives of the organization. To get that, they need to answer, through self-reflection guided by the coach's input, these important questions: 'What's the desired impact? How will I be measured?' And most important of all: 'What quality of feedback will I receive, and when?'"

How Do I Go About Doing My Work Well?

Job performance can be measured in many ways, but this question is not answered in terms of numbers of widgets produced or sales revenue achieved. According to Shedletsky, this level of coaching speaks to the leader being able to clearly identify and model the organization's values and culture.[19] Incorporated within that are such elements as integrity, accountability and collaboration—in other words, how a person behaves while they're trying to achieve their objectives. Aligning work and purpose contributes to engagement and brand loyalty.

How Will I Learn and Grow, and Develop My Career?

The engaged employee will expect more from the organization in terms of professional growth. The employee will want due recognition and the opportunity to shoulder more responsibility to prove their initiative and be set on a career path (this topic is discussed in Chapter 10). The leader-coach must have a game plan for the coachee, using questions that provide insights into the coachee's capabilities, creative thinking and relatability. Recall Carollyne Conlinn's words: "It's about supporting people to make life changes that will have a long-term positive impact."

With growth comes tangible rewards, but this doesn't necessarily mean giving the coachee a promotion. It could be as simple as sending them to a conference that aligns with their interests or offering them a lateral move to an area they feel more passionate about.

Coaching shouldn't be for just high-potential employees. As LinkedIn cofounder Reid Hoffman put it in his book *The Alliance*,

"Companies have long devoted resources to crafting personalized roles and career paths for their stars [. . .] Yet it is possible—indeed necessary—to extend this personalized approach to all employees."[20]

CASE STUDY

Coaching a World Series–Winning Team

In sports, as in business, the coach's role is to get the best out of each individual player by putting them in a position to succeed. It's about creating a psychologically safe environment where players aren't punished for making a mistake. Having a safety net builds team confidence, which enables players to collectively perform at their absolute best and win.

In the 1990s, the Toronto Blue Jays won the World Series not once but twice. Yet Cito Gaston, the manager, never got the credit he should have. In fact, he was often accused of simply riding on the coattails of a bunch of superstars. "Anyone could have managed a team with that much talent," the critics said. Nothing could be further from the truth, according to Paul Beeston, the former president and CEO of the Blue Jays, the architect of their championship run and the man responsible for hiring Gaston.

"Cito had played the game, he knew how difficult the game was, and he was a big man with a very soft voice. But more importantly than that," Beeston told me, "he commanded respect. Cito understood that players make mistakes and that they were published in the box scores for everyone to see. So he never got upset over a mistake. He made players the best they could be by playing to their strengths.

"A manager has a very difficult job because players get paid for performance, and if they're not getting into the lineup on a given day, they don't get a chance to perform. And if they don't get the chance to play, that can affect the money they get on their next contract. That's why Cito operated on a no-surprise basis. If he was going to sit someone, he would tell the player before he went home that night. If he was upset with someone's performance, he would bring them in to his office and have an honest and totally forthright discussion. Because he explained the rationale for his decisions, he had the players' backs, and they had his. And he was like that with everyone—from the role players to the stars."

Although Beeston was president of the organization, he didn't see himself as "the boss," even though he managed several hundred people. When asked how he was able to get the organization to perform at its best and win, he echoed Jim Collins's research on finding the right people: "I always considered myself the head of HR. It was my job to hire the right people and put them in a position where they could succeed. I delegated power to them, but I made myself available whenever they needed me. Most importantly, I allowed them to make mistakes—as long as they didn't make the same mistake twice [...] Different people with different styles make up a team, but if you have the right people in the right places, you can build something special. As long as they knew that I trusted them and was open and honest, and behaved with integrity and listened to them, I never had a problem. The other thing we had was the ability to laugh at ourselves. That's probably underestimated. It's important to have a sense of humor about some of your mistakes, as long as they're not too egregious, because it's too much of a grind if you don't."

Beeston credits his mentor Peter Hardy, then president of Labatt Brewing and vice-chair of the Blue Jays, with instilling these leader-coach principles in his leadership style. "Peter was tough as nails, only about five foot seven, but he had your back as long as you were honest with him. He was an exceptional leader. He was never around when the Jays were on winning streaks, but when things were bad and we were losing, you could count on seeing him. He wouldn't say much. He didn't have to, because his actions spoke volumes, and what they said was, 'I have your back, and we're all in this thing together.' I learned from Mr. Hardy that the key to a winning team is having the right culture. A company or a team has what I call a personality, and usually, it takes on the personality of the people at the top. We were an organization that had integrity, worked hard, played hard, and we had the ability to know that if we made a mistake, it would be addressed head-on and we would all move on from there. But you have to have dedication, you have to have teamwork, and you have to have people that stay together, work together and even more importantly, argue together."[21]

Beeston and the Blue Jays, just like HP or Nike, were ahead of their time when it came to the way they chose to lead. Beeston's "argue together" is exactly what I mean when I talk about "productive conflict" in Chapter 6 in the second layer of the playbook for high-performing teams (see Figure 6.3 on page 112). Paul's values—winning with integrity, honesty, candor and hard work—permeated the Blue Jays organization. He helped create a safe environment for his players as well as his staff, but he also created an atmosphere of support and learning—a place where everyone could ask questions, express their views and learn from their mistakes.

Professor Herminia Ibarra of London Business School and executive coach Anne Scoular also described this best expression of a coaching culture: "The kind that creates a true learning organization—which is ongoing and executed by those inside the organization. It's work that all managers should engage in with all their people all the time, in ways that help define the organization's culture and advance its mission."[22] Great leaders strive to build a high-performance coaching culture.

Coaching Frontline Leaders Pays Dividends

Coaching cultures are becoming increasingly common in the business world because forward-thinking leaders recognize that they attract talent and build leadership strengths. At Rogers, coaching was critical to making Eric Agius's work in changing the culture at our call centers a success. To make sure the changes stuck, we instituted a coaching culture into the front line of our organization.

"One of the first things we did," Eric said, "was to make coaching time sacred." By taking that first step, the frontline managers knew that Rogers was investing in them as people leaders.

Some team managers weren't comfortable with coaching, and Eric pointed out that initially, turnover was high. But filling the leadership ranks with people who had a passion for coaching and were going to be good at coaching was essential; again, it comes down to the right people being on the bus and in the right seats.

Listening was the primary trait Eric expected of his coaches. "They would take the time to listen to the conversations that our specialists were having with the customer and then guide the specialists toward making those conversations better. Our leaders would derive a lot of their questions from listening in. For example, they might say: 'Hey, I noticed that when the customer asked you this, you responded in this way. What if you thought about saying X instead of Y with your customer?' And the specialist might say: 'That's a fabulous idea. I'm going to try that.' And then, as part of the ongoing coaching process, the coach might say: 'Next time you try that, send me the call so I can listen to it, and I can give you feedback. And let's make sure we do that before the end of the week.'"[23]

Thanks to Eric and his team, Rogers's call centers are now an environment that thrives off a coaching-feedback cycle. The coaching culture starts at the top with leaders who understand the value of coaching and who are willing to be coached themselves. They bring in experienced coaches to train their most influential leaders, and then let those leaders filter their learnings down to their teams until coaching concepts and behaviors have become ingrained in all the teams. To make sure the changes stick, the executives make coaching a routine part of the workweek, and they hold managers accountable for coaching their teams, and building new skills by setting expectations and following through on them.

Use Coaching Techniques to Build Trust with Your Team

If you want to be a good coach, start by being a good leader. Good leaders don't believe they know more than do the employees who report directly to them. Instead, these leaders are always listening and learning. The best coaches model three important behaviors.

Listen Actively

Fundamental to becoming a great coach is building trust, and the fastest way to build trust is to become a better listener. Listening isn't the same as hearing. Hearing is passive and requires no effort. Active listening requires effort, concentration and practice. When leaders actively listen to their coachees, they pick up on many of the nuances— the hidden needs and feelings that are coloring their coachees' performance both positively and negatively. Listening builds trust because it makes people feel valued, safe and connected. A strong bond of trust between coach and coachee is critical, because a coachee is in a vulnerable position. Here is Dr. Shedletsky's strong opinion on this skill.

"Good leaders know how to listen. In fact, one of the most important arrows in the coaching quiver is active listening. By *active listening*, I mean validating what we hear from people. Conversely, one of the quickest ways to create distrust or disengagement or apathy in a person is if you in some way minimize or disregard their point of view. If I sit at a conference table and say something which I think is contributing to the conversation and I'm ignored or I'm minimized, then the next time I'm less likely to voice my opinion and offer a point of view—and in particular, a contrary point of view.

"When a person hears 'I understand what you're saying, but let me explain why I disagree,' that person understands they've been heard and their point of view is appreciated, even if it's not necessarily agreed with. And that builds a relationship and an environment where people are comfortable expressing their views."[24]

People shine when their voices are heard. When they aren't, trouble can occur. Executive coach Marshall Goldsmith, a leading figure in the coaching field and the author of the best-selling business book *What Got You Here Won't Get You There*, noted that if employees aren't listened to and fully appreciated for their enthusiasm and initiative, their performance can deteriorate. Goldsmith offered a telling example:

> Imagine an energetic, enthusiastic employee comes into your office with an idea. She excitedly shares the idea with you. You think it's a great idea. Instead of saying, "Great idea!" you say, "That's a nice idea. Why don't you add this to it?" What does this do? It deflates her enthusiasm; it dampers her commitment. While the quality of the idea may go up 5 percent, her commitment to execute it may go down 50 percent. That's because it's no longer her idea, it's now your idea.[25]

Ask, Don't Tell

The second quality of a great coach is the ability to ask the right questions. Great leaders don't tell people what they should do. They ask those people what they want to achieve and help them figure out for themselves how to get there. Asking the right questions lets the coachee own the agenda, according to Dr. Shedletsky.

"The best questions focus on how the coachee is feeling about their performance. A common issue at meetings is that the loudest voice dominates and not everyone in the room speaks up. The chairperson or leader could simply go around the room and direct the conversation so that those who haven't spoken get a chance to speak, but sometimes, you've got to go deeper than that and find out why someone isn't speaking, and what's holding them back.

"For example, at a board of directors meeting, let's say one of the board members has a marketing background, and the conversation is focused on a very legalistic or financial issue. They might feel a bit insecure asking questions out of fear that they will appear ignorant. It's up to the leader or the board chair to reassure everyone that there's no such thing as a bad question or a bad point of view. That way, each person can contribute to the discussion and help create a better solution."[26]

Change isn't easy, and changing our behavior is one of the most challenging tasks we can undertake in our lives. I know this from my own experience. In 2005 at MDS, the CEO who promoted me to CHRO was fired by the board. The new CEO arrived, and it was very clear he was on a mission to turn around performance and make his mark quickly. I remember trying to explain to him the company's history and why it was so important. After my third attempt, he stopped me in my tracks. "Jim, I don't care about the past. I only care about today and the future." It was a wake-up call for me. I had to meet him where he was—not where I wanted him to be. If we're not performing to our potential, change is not only good, but necessary. As the McKinsey studies pointed out, "identifying some of the deepest, 'below the surface' thoughts, feelings, assumptions, and beliefs is usually a precondition of behavioral change."[27] The best coaches guide this change by asking open-ended questions that spark insights in the other person, according to Ana Karakusevic. "Questions should be guided not by your own perspective on the situation, but from the subject's own perspective. It's not about you, it's always about them—and your questions must reflect this."[28]

Show Empathy

All coaches are supportive. But great coaches show empathy by putting themselves in the coachee's shoes. This helps them understand the coachee's issue on a visceral level. They actually feel the person's emotions about the issue. Studies have shown that empathy is a by-product of self-awareness.[29] Self-awareness requires a keen understanding of yourself and your strengths and weaknesses, but it also requires an awareness of the impact of our behavior on others. By asking people empathic, open-ended questions like, "What's working so far, and what isn't?" and "How can I help?" (and listening actively to the answers), we show people we care. I can tell you from years of personal experience that simple acts of appreciation like this go a long way to developing loyalty.

Satya Nadella is a great example of the empathic leader-as-coach. When he took over as Microsoft's CEO in 2014, Nadella wanted the people he worked with to develop a more collaborative mindset. "My personal philosophy and my passion," he wrote in his book, *Hit Refresh*, "is to connect new ideas with a growing sense of empathy for other people."[30] He succeeded in transforming the company's culture by relying on and modeling his own values of empathy, learning and listening. "Founder CEOs can take some things for granted because of who they are," he famously wrote, referring to Bill Gates and Steve Ballmer. "I describe myself as a 'mere-mortal CEO.' And I wanted to make much more explicit our sense of purpose and culture. Strategies and markets come and go. Those don't."[31]

Nadella had noticed employee attitudes shifting as far back as the late 1990s—a time when Microsoft grew to become the world's most valuable company. "You could see people walking around like, 'Wow, we must be God's gift to mankind,'" he said. Now that he was CEO, he felt the culture at the company needed to return to its roots. "Let's not be know-it-alls," he told employees. "Let's be 'learn-it-alls.'"[32] So the company became a "listening and learning" organization, which cared about inclusion and diversity just as much as it cared about its customers.

Nadella understood that the process of becoming "learn-it-alls" had to start with him, so he began modeling the behaviors he wanted Microsoft's managers to adopt. He solicited thoughts from everybody he talked to and listened empathically to what they had to say. He asked nondirective questions, demonstrating that his role was to support rather than judge. He encouraged people to be open about their mistakes and learn from them.

Empathy isn't something most people are born with. It's acquired through time, experience and a willingness to learn. (Nadella made that point quite dramatically in Chapter 6 when he talked about how the birth of his son, who has cerebral palsy and quadriplegia, changed him as a person.) True empathy isn't possible without humility, because we can't step into the shoes of others if we feel superior to them. Of all the traits shared by great leaders, humility may be the most essential. Humility isn't the absence of ego, however. We all have ego. Humility is admitting what you don't know. It's about asking for help and acknowledging mistakes. It's about being a "learn-it-all" instead of a know-it-all. Great leaders are in constant learning mode, and the learning never stops. Neither does the listening. That's why great leaders make great coaches. And great coaches are both humble and empathic.

In Chapter 10, we explore coaching techniques for career advancement. Please complete the activity and exercise for Chapter 9 in Part 3 before turning to the final chapter of this book.

CHAPTER 9 TAKEAWAYS

> Creating a coaching culture within an organization requires developing a culture that is psychologically safe and committed to learning. The Association for Talent Development defines a coaching culture as one that meets at least five of the following six criteria:
> > Employees value coaching.
> > Senior executives value coaching.
> > The organization has a dedicated line item budget for coaching.
> > Coaching is available to all employees.
> > Managers, leaders, or internal coaches receive accredited coach-specific training.
> > All three coaching modalities (internal coach practitioners, external coach practitioners, and managers or leaders using coaching skills) are present in the organization.[33]

> Coaching is no different from any other task or skill. It needs to be structured, systematic and built on a framework.

> Coaching is not about the answers you give but about the questions you ask. The ultimate objective is to build ownership for the outcome in the coachee.

> Creating a coaching culture that gets fully behind the development of people and teams may be the single biggest decision you can make as a leader to drive high performance. The world is changing, and the demographic changes alone will result in Millennials and Gen Z making up over 80 percent of the workforce in the next five years. They will demand leaders who are skilled as coaches.

Coaching Individual Transformation

10

> People gravitate to what gives them meaning, to what engages to the fullest their commitment, talent, energy, and skill. And that can mean changing jobs to get a better fit.
>
> —DANIEL GOLEMAN

"**T**he times, they are a-changin'," Bob Dylan famously sang. This is especially true in the job market. One-third of employees who show up for their first day at work today will move on to another company within four years,[1] and the trend is expected to accelerate. The job-hopping Millennial has become a bit of a cliché, but the characterization is based in fact.[2] According to recent research from consulting firm Deloitte, for example, close to half of Millennials are planning to leave their jobs within two years, and loyalty is even lower among Gen Z employees.[3] What's driving such disaffection for their work or company? Perhaps a Workopolis study of ten thousand young Canadians can give us some insights—the number one reason is their boss.

According to the study, employees report the following as their reasons for leaving their workplace:

> My relationship with my boss – 37%
> I was bored, unhappy with the work – 29%
> I found a better opportunity – 20%
> Poor fit with the culture/coworkers – 14%[4]

More than a third of employees quit their jobs because of their boss. Why is this happening? Are managers failing to develop, recognize and reward their people? Are they unconcerned about their people's well-being? What's really going on?

The underlying cause is not so obvious. Studies show that most managers are in fact competent and sincerely care about their employees. So there must be another reason. If you look closely at the four reasons cited, you'll notice that people are bored and unhappy. If a meaningful connection to work culture and coworkers is absent, then the employee-manager relationship is bound to suffer. The list shows that nearly two-thirds of employees who quit their jobs (63 percent) were either unhappy, wanted a better opportunity or were a poor fit—in other words, they were not fully engaged in their work. Employee engagement levels across countries and companies have remained low for decades, and the numbers haven't changed as Baby Boomers (who may be just putting in time) exit the workforce and Millennials (who you would think would be full of energy and optimism) enter it.

How do we as leaders help our people find their work more rewarding, their collaboration with coworkers richer and more productive, and their brand loyalty stronger? What has been missing from the leadership toolbox to turn engagement numbers around? The answer lies in coaching for career advancement—both your own and that of team members who need your mentorship and support.

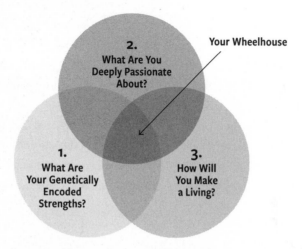

Source: Adapted from Jim Collins, *Good to Great*, HarperCollins 2001, p. 96.

A Career Path Begins with Clarity

A strong leader knows that the single biggest part of being exceptional is growing people. That also means that, unfortunately, some of your people are going to grow out of their roles and perhaps even out of your company. But this is good. They will be more satisfied in life, and in turn, they will perform at a higher level wherever they end up. Part of being a great leader means that while you are investing in people to drive the best business performance possible, you are also investing in them because it increases engagement, and will end up benefiting them and the people they touch. As corny as it sounds, that will make the world a better place.

You'll recall in Chapter 2 that I asked you to fill out your own personal hedgehog. Doing so should help you figure out your strengths and passions, and how you are going to make a living. Having this kind of clarity is extremely valuable to creating impact and building a robust path to personal success. The personal hedgehog (shown again in Figure 10.1) is the key to success for both you and your team members. By sharing with them the power of the personal hedgehog, you will empower your team members to play to their strengths and passions, focus on their impact and take stock of their careers for themselves. Almost certainly, they will gain insight and unearth something eye opening that will have far-reaching ramifications for them (and maybe even for your business).

When helping a coachee start this very personal and iterative process, encourage them to build a plan and work the plan with your support. Here are some points to keep in mind and some coaching to give as you help them on their way to building their career path—and your own.

Step 1: Know Your Wheelhouse

Career success starts and ends with being self-aware. This means having laser-like clarity on Principle 1 (Values and Purpose) and Principle 2 (Strengths and Passions). As we spoke about earlier, the ultimate test is for work to not feel like work. The people I work with often describe this feeling as being "in my sweet spot" or "in my wheelhouse." Either way, it comes from being at the intersection of the three circles defining your personal hedgehog.

The benefits to completing your personal hedgehog can be life changing, as I have witnessed in both my personal and my professional life. That said, a person does not typically find their wheelhouse overnight. It almost always takes perseverance, determination and multiple iterations over time for people to finally achieve clarity on their three circles.

What does it mean to be in your sweet spot? When I discussed this topic with organizational psychologist Dr. Tim Gilmor, he told me: "It means alignment of your internal resources, your head, your heart, your body and spirit. It's about the notion of internal synergy. It's about understanding that our purpose in life is not meant to be about us."[5]

Step 2: Early in Your Career, Pick a Company That Aligns with Your Values and Purpose

Cultural fit, as discussed earlier, is critically important for workplace engagement. When mentoring anyone (your employees or people outside your company), making sure the answer to the third circle, "How will you make a living?," points to a values-led, purpose-driven company will be a key factor to that individual's achieving career success. Having employees that are inspired by a company's mission and its contribution to society and community will make for stronger, happier workers. Ideally, a person at the beginning of their career will pick a company in a growing industry. But more important than that is finding the right fit and alignment with an individual's values and purpose.

Another key factor for engaging your employees is their desire for personal development and success. As Patrick Bliley from executive search firm Spencer Stuart put it: "The best leaders approach the early years in their career with a measure of introspection and a learning orientation. This enables them to gain a deep perspective on themselves."[6] In other words, the future leaders working for you now want opportunities to learn and grow—providing them a safe place to do that is critical in their development and your company's success.

Step 3: In Your Mid-Career, Pick the Leader

If you've done a good job by offering your future leaders exciting growth opportunities, they are going to want to accelerate their momentum. That usually involves moving to work alongside one of the most talented leaders in your organization. Pairing future leaders with respected, top talent who have an outstanding track record in driving results enriches the future leader and the current leader's team. It also helps fuel the notion of strong team building within your company.

Step 4: Ensure Your Employees Are Engaged in Their Current Role, Even When Promotion Is on the Table

You can do yourself and your employees a big favor by letting them know you can't take shortcuts when climbing the ladder. In fact, almost always, excelling in their current role is their springboard for building career success. You want top performers, and you expect consistency. A proven track record of results in their current role and the roles that came before is critical in being able to fairly evaluate an employee's success and possibilities for advancement. A team member with one foot out the door searching for the next job is not doing you, the business or themselves any favors. Too often, I see ambitious leaders who are "just okay" in their current role because they're spending too much time looking for their next assignment. Focus on showing your employees that if they beat expectations in their current role, great opportunities will present themselves. There's no need to chase these opportunities.

As Patrick Bliley noted: "When I'm doing a search for a senior executive, it's the things that are under the surface that are most important to qualify, quantify and assess for. It's about capacity and character. By capacity, I mean this: 'Do they have the intellectual horsepower to be able to be great and to step into a new context and be successful?' By character, I mean: 'Are they made of the right stuff? Do they have the right values, the integrity? When the chips are down, have they demonstrated the ability to lead in a way that's thoughtful? Are they doing the right things the right way?'"[7]

As Patrick pointed out, great leaders excel by doing the right things the right way. They are superb team players with a passion for the company and the position they hold. They don't look past the present. As Nadella, the CEO of one of the world's most valuable companies, put it: "It's easy to say, 'When am I going to be CEO?' But don't wait for your next job to do your best work. Think about every job you get as the most important job, even as possibly your last job. I thought each job was fantastic until I got the next."[8] I can't stress enough how critical it is for employees to bring all the focus and energy they can to their current role, because doing so truly does separate the winners from the also-rans. Very few people advance their career by being just average in their current job.

Step 5: For Top Leaders, It's All about the Team

As the careers of your employees advance and they begin to lead teams, it is important to note that their success, instead of being assessed on the leader's individual strengths and capabilities, will be judged by their team's strengths and capabilities. In other words, the leader's performance is now measured by the effort, skill and capabilities of the people they hire, and how well their team works together to deliver consistent, exceptional results. Bottom line: at some point, your mentorship will reach a tipping point from coaching the individual for their own success to coaching the individual for their team's success.

The best leaders know how important it is to master the fundamentals of building strong, high-performing teams. They become exceptional at selecting the right talent for their teams, and they teach and mentor the team to deliver outstanding results on a consistent basis. In my view, a leader's highest and best value lies in the ability to build high-performing teams.

This is especially true for leaders who transform from middle management to executive roles. To develop great leaders, however, you must find them first. I'm a firm believer that when selecting people for leadership, you can seldom make a silk purse out of a sow's ear. Exceptions exist, but if you're not selecting proven performers (see Step 4), the effort to build a successful team becomes harder. This takes us back to Chapter 3 and the third principle: finding and keeping the right people. How do you get the right people on the bus and into the right seats? Be rigorous without being ruthless, as Jim Collins says, and follow his three guidelines:

1. If in doubt, don't hire.
2. Put your best people on your biggest opportunities, not your biggest problems.
3. Take your time to decide about making a change on your team, but once you decide, act![9]

Choosing the right leaders for your team is not easy. When someone leaves a team, for example, a vacancy needs to be filled. Typically, the vacant job is posted internally, or a search firm is brought in to pursue and select a group of appropriate, diverse candidates. The easy part is defining the criteria for the job. The hard part is selecting the right person for the job. That's why many of the most sophisticated companies often use assessment-based hiring.

For example, let's say you have ten candidates on your long list—a mix of internal and external leaders. You might interview five and select two finalists. To decrease the risk and increase the odds of selecting the right person, best practice suggests doing an assessment with your top two candidates. To perform an assessment, a combination of methods will be used to profile a potential candidate's character qualities. After you've interviewed the individual, observed how they handle themselves, vetted their résumé, and determined whether they have the skill set and experience that increase the odds of success in their new role, you have to assess qualities that are a little more subtle and more difficult to discern. This is where professional psychologists like Dr. Gilmor enter the scene. In some ways, assessing character qualities is like looking under the hood of a car or as Dr. Gilmor put it: "It's like sending in a professional to do an inspection of a home you want to buy. They are up in the attic looking for proper insulation, and down in the basement looking for hairline fractures in the foundation and so on." Here is Dr. Gilmor's description of the assessment process.

"An assessment brings a certain objective scrutiny to the individual and what they're bringing characterologically. Our task is to be scrutineers for qualities of character. Typically, you want to establish that they do have the intelligence needed to function at the level of complexity the job's going to present. They need to have the relationship capability to enable them to work effectively with others. And they need to have the emotional maturity to make good judgments and develop credibility as someone that can be counted on as a leader. So if you think about it as a follower for a moment, would I want this person to be in command of the ship I'm putting my talent and energy into, to sail it to a particular destination? And so the assessment allows you to be a little more thorough in your evaluation of a candidate's character."

Completing an assessment of your two finalist candidates will give you powerful insight to help you make the right hiring decision. But the assessment is not the only criterion leading to selection. The candidate's experience, career trajectory and accomplishments are also important. You're looking both for fit (strengths, values and so on) and a track record of success. But the results of the assessment are critically important. For example, when Dr. Gilmor does a candidate assessment, he often leads with a single question: "What does this opportunity mean to you?"

It's a great question because how long the candidate takes to respond can indicate how serious they are about wanting to join your team. As Dr. Gilmor pointed out: "Are they trying to sell me on their answer? If they carry on too long or become oblivious to the fact that I don't need this much information, then that might be an indication of someone who is misfiring."

Other telltale signs can point to a candidate's fit (or lack thereof): the candidate's greeting, their eye contact and their awareness of their impact in a new environment in which they're going to be evaluated. How do they handle all of that? How readily can they adapt to the circumstances of the evaluation? How at ease or on edge are they? Do I see their hands shaking as they perform the more challenging tasks during the assessment? Do I hear negative self-talk?

Do I hear four-letter expletives, and are they unaware that they just swore? People who lack self-awareness tend to lose track of their impact, according to Dr. Gilmor: "It goes to the notion of being present, being fully attuned to each moment and your impact on the others in the room."[10]

To summarize Step 5, hiring right and building your team are two of the most important actions you will ever take. You simply have to learn to excel at building talent and teams if you want to fully realize your aspirations. Let's put this into context by illustrating how three individuals moved their careers, step by step, into high gear.

CASE STUDY

Early Career Success: Kevin

Let's begin with Kevin, a talented young man starting out in his career. For Kevin, building a high-performance trajectory began in high school. He pushed himself academically, and by the time he was ready to graduate, he was at the top of his class. He was also one of the starting guards on the high school basketball team and the starting quarterback on the football team. Every step of the way, he shaped the behaviors he would soon need to excel in business: grit, mission focus and a builder's mindset.

After Kevin graduated with a business degree from one of Canada's most prestigious universities, he went to work full time at one of Canada's top banks. In fact, TD Bank liked him so much they hired him in his third year, well before he graduated at the end of the four-year program. He stood out at the bank as one of their up-and-coming leaders, but over time, he realized that something was missing. He simply wasn't passionate about the work, so he joined Oliver Wyman, a management consulting firm with more than sixty offices and clients spanning five continents.

Kevin had a unique combination of strong analytical skills and excellent people skills. His move to Oliver Wyman was a great test of his consulting and analytical abilities. But after almost two years, the constant travel and work away from home led him to interview with Fengate, a multibillion-dollar infrastructure company based in Toronto. He met Lou Serafini Jr., who is a dynamic leader and the second-generation founder of the company. Lou took him under his wing and put a lot of faith in him. Kevin delivered, and soon, Lou created a new role that was a perfect fit. Within two years of joining, Kevin had vaulted into a senior executive role, and at the tender age of thirty-one, he was leading the firm's international fundraising while working with the company's executive team. Today, Kevin is an executive vice-president and on a vertical learning curve. He is challenged and excited, and is pinching himself about how he is working his plan and how his first three career moves accelerated his trajectory so beautifully. His parents must be so proud of him. Actually, Pattie and I are, as he is our younger son!

CASE STUDY

Mid-Career Success: Tracy

Second, let's look at Tracy Moore, a young woman who did what lots of people said couldn't be done. She built a trajectory that led her to host a national TV show, and she designs her own fashion line, Tracy Moore by Freda's. Tracy told me that her career might have stalled if she hadn't picked the right leaders to work with—many of whom went on to become her mentors and champions. Of course, it helped that she was driven to succeed from an early age. Thanks to some wise counsel from her high school teachers, she began to understand the importance of the three circles. "I've always loved to present," she said, "and I had teachers who really encouraged me. They would bring other classes in to listen to my independent study units. I had a teacher tell me I was a very strong writer, and I asked her: 'What do I do with that? Does this mean I become a novelist?' She said, 'No, you can be a politician, you can be a lawyer or you can be a journalist.' It was the first time I had ever thought that way."

Tracy ended up volunteering at the campus radio station, and that was her first taste of broadcast journalism. "I liked it. I liked to talk, and I liked to write and I had strong opinions. I didn't really know what all that meant, but I think that if you're in a situation where you've got those strengths, you have to lean into them.

"I definitely agree that the intersection of strengths and passions and a thriving industry, the three circles, is a really good equation for finding career success. Having said that, I came into a shrinking industry—broadcast television—so I knew it was likely to be the weakest link in those three circles. That meant I was going to have to work twice as hard as anyone around me. It also meant I was going to have to be strategic about meeting people who could help me in the industry. And that's what I did. But hard work, being honest with people, and being collaborative and empathic—these are my values.

"I think values are crucial for feeling fulfillment in the line of work that you take. Yet I also think that showing up fully, as who you really are, in the workplace might be a process. We all have to make sure that those values are front and center. And showing up completely in the workplace is a lesson that you learn over time. I think for a lot of people, including me, it's a process."[11]

CASE STUDY

Full Career Success: Pattie

Finally, the person who has most inspired me in my life is my wife, Pattie. In fact, not only does she inspire me, but her career has inspired and helped millions of other Canadians. Here is her story.

We are all shaped by our experiences, and Pattie's life changed at the age of nine when her father died of a heart attack at age thirty-six. It was a devastating blow for her and her family. This event would go on to influence her throughout her life.

Several years after her dad died, her mom remarried a wonderful man who also brought two children into the marriage. When the decision came to decide who should attend college or university after high school, two children went and two did not. With tears in her eyes, Pattie told me that at the time, she believed she was not smart enough to be sent to university, so she left home and got a job as a bank teller with one of Canada's leading banks. When I first met her, she was separated and had taken on a management job in training frontline bank employees. One of our first conversations was about her dad dying and how she had struggled to get her career fired up. I remember sending her a famous quotation by Walt Disney: "If you dream it, you can do it!"

The rest, as they say, is history. In the next eighteen months, Pattie was promoted to bank manager, then assistant VP and finally VP, and ran one of the bank's largest call centers. Three years later, she was promoted to SVP. During that time, her passion for helping women become equal financial partners in a marriage led her to write the first of several books on personal finance. She tapped into the memories of her mom's struggles following the death of her husband, and from here, Pattie's trajectory and impact went vertical:

> She wrote seven books on personal finance, many targeted at women.
> She hosted one hundred episodes of a personal finance show that aired weekly on one of Canada's major TV networks.
> She was honored as one of Canada's most powerful women.
> She took early retirement from the bank and kept chasing her dream, which was to be on national television as the chief financial commentator for CTV News. She succeeded in fulfilling this goal.

> Along the way, she has been the love of my life and a fabulous mother to our four amazing children.

When I think of Pattie's career, I just smile with incredible pride. It's a textbook example of how to get on and stay on a high-performance trajectory in life. Best of all, the trajectory she built has resulted in helping hundreds of thousands of Canadians take charge of their personal finances, which made a meaningful difference in their lives.

Avoid Costly Career Mistakes

I often get calls to coach executives who need to fine-tune their development plans to maintain their career momentum, and I also get calls to step in to help executives who are driving an out-of-control train, just one or two turns away from a total derailment that may lead to termination. In working with leaders who are struggling, I almost always find they are aware of how tenuous their situation is. They are overwhelmed, quickly losing confidence and unable to make even the smallest of decisions.

Sometimes, I see executives who are angry. Many are frustrated with their boss for not being clear on what is expected of them. Others are angry with their teams or peers, who they feel are not being supportive. Ultimately, I always coach executives to let go of any kind of victim mentality and conduct a deep assessment of what they are facing, how they got there and what they need to do to recover.

Let's go to the balcony for a moment and have a look at the major causes of career derailment for leaders. According to the Center for Creative Leadership, one of the most prestigious authorities and think tanks on effective leadership, the five major causes of career derailment have not materially changed over the last few decades: an inability to adapt to change, difficulty building and leading a team, failure to deliver business results, absence of strategic direction and poor interpersonal relationships.[12]

In addition to these five reasons, I would add a sixth: failure to get along with your boss, an issue discussed earlier in the chapter. When executives or leaders come to me for help with their boss, my counsel is always the same: If you're having a problem in your relationship with your boss, this is your problem, not your boss's. You simply have to resolve this and quickly. One of my favorite pieces of advice on this topic was published in the *Harvard Business Review* many years ago. The counsel of John Kotter and John Gabarro is as valid today as it was when it was written:

> The fact is that bosses need cooperation, reliability, and honesty from their direct reports. Managers, for their part, rely on bosses for making connections with the rest of the company, for setting priorities, and for obtaining critical resources. If the relationship between you and your boss is rocky, then it is you who must begin to manage it. When you take the time to cultivate a productive working relationship by understanding your boss's strengths and weaknesses, priorities and work style—everyone wins.[13]

You have to manage your boss and build a trusted relationship with them that works in the good times and the challenging times. But make no mistake: you have to own this relationship. If you don't, the results can be fatal to your career. In my experience as a coach, the most serious derailers, the ones that often lead to termination, are

> failure to deliver results
> not getting along with your boss
> not getting along with your peers

Interestingly, often the presence of hard skills gets you hired and the absence of soft skills gets you fired. The lesson for all leaders is important. Get serious about building your soft skills, including communication, teamwork, relatability, and understanding how to build teams with strong trust and psychological safety. Learn to become skilled at working cross-functionally because teams are increasingly being built this way. Don't just brush up on these skills—make it a goal to build and refine them throughout your career because if you're weak in the soft skills, becoming a great leader will be a huge challenge.

An essential step in strengthening your soft skills is building and honing your level of self-awareness. As I've said before, self-awareness, as I define it, is a combination of two things: knowing your strengths and understanding your impact on others. Leaders have a huge impact on others, either positive or negative—what Patrick Bliley calls a "multiplier" effect. Great leaders understand this: "Great leaders really manage their own energy and tone and posture in their individual interactions as they go about their day-to-day work in their organizations. There are multipliers of stress, and there are smoothers of stress, and it's critical to be aware of your own energy level and be aware of the wider consequences of the small decisions you make about how you communicate. This level of self-awareness is absolutely critical to being a great leader."[14]

Find a Champion to Be in Your Corner

Before wrapping up this chapter, I think it's worth mentioning one other factor that can help you take advantage of opportunities. When I think of my own career and the opportunities that have come my way, I've managed to land the bigger roles thanks to champions who spoke up for me at key moments. As you become more senior, the competition for landing any job becomes more intense. There are always multiple candidates, each of whom is highly qualified to do the job. For me, what often made the difference was having a champion who stepped up to support me. Frequently, it was someone who knew the hiring manager and was prepared to make a call of support at a critical moment to tip the decision my way.

If you ask the best executives about their career success, you'll seldom hear them say they did it on their own without the support of people around them who championed their candidacy or mentored and supported them along the way. Champions are people who know your work well, either through having been your boss or worked with you in some capacity. Keep in mind, however, that champions will go out on a limb for you only if they know you can deliver the goods—which is why you must always be focused on, and excel in, your current job.

Mentors are equally important, and not just in the early stages of your career. Approximately 80 percent of CEOs have had a mentor at some point.[15] Even the most high-profile leaders have mentors. When I interviewed Paul Beeston, he told me that Peter Hardy, who was vice-chairman of the Toronto Blue Jays at the time, was instrumental to Beeston's success as a CEO.

"Mr. Hardy taught me that you need to treat everybody equally, but you can't do it in the same manner all the time. If you listen to your people and trust them to do their jobs, then they will trust you. And don't be afraid to say you don't know when you don't know about something. Always be honest and open with people.

"He taught me a lot about managing people. When the Blue Jays started winning in 1984 and 1985, on the clubhouse wall there was a motto that said, 'What we can achieve is unlimited, and we don't care who gets the credit.' Well, that was all bull because everybody was trying to take credit for us winning. So Mr. Hardy brought us all down to earth in a hurry by reminding us that we couldn't have won anything if we hadn't done it together. He believed in the ability of the team, and the team included all the people we didn't see, such as the scouts on the road and the development people who worked the dustiest ballparks in North America. I learned so much from him."[16]

CEOs like Paul Beeston made it to the top by listening, learning and focusing on being the best they could be at their current job (Beeston started out as the Blue Jays' accountant), not the one they aspired to. That's key to building a successful career.

One final point. While I don't have any data to support this, it's been my experience that, all things being equal (and assuming your strengths and passions line up with the role), the person who gets the job generally makes three winning moves during their interviews with the hiring manager. First, they explicitly say they want the job. You'd be shocked how many candidates "do the dance" but never declare themselves. You have to say you want the job! Second, they link their strengths and passions to the role in such a way that the hiring manager clearly sees the connection between what the candidate brings and what the role demands. Third, they don't try to negotiate or put barriers in front of a job offer until they're offered the role. When I'm coaching leaders in a competitive job search, my advice is always the same: earn the right to say no! Think about it for a moment. Until you're offered the role—which is the only concrete signal that the employer prefers you to all the other candidates—you simply have no leverage.

· · · · ·

The key takeaway in this chapter is that for you or those that you coach, a plan like the five steps outlined in this chapter is the best way for you and the key talent you lead to realize career goals and aspirations. Understand that following a plan doesn't guarantee you won't have setbacks. Everyone has them. But if you have a clear plan, your career and the careers of those you coach—and the impact of those careers—will almost certainly be extraordinary. Please give a lot of thought to the activity and exercise for this chapter because developing your people is a leader's highest calling.

CHAPTER 10 TAKEAWAYS

> More than a third of employees quit their job because of their boss. Why? How do we as leaders help our people find their work more rewarding, their collaboration with coworkers richer and more

productive, and their brand loyalty stronger? What has been missing from the leadership toolbox to turn engagement numbers around? The answer lies in coaching for career advancement—both your own and that of the team members who need your mentorship and support.

> I cannot stress enough how important charting a clear path is to career success. It builds momentum, and enables people to be in the right place with the right approach and the right mindset for personal success. When it comes to coaching individuals about their career, there is almost always a sequence to building a rewarding career path that enables them to fully achieve their long-term goals.

> Encourage people to get on an innovative team with a values-led company in a growing industry. Focus on the right company, and their career will get off to a great start.

> Within your organization, pair future leaders with a leader with a reputation for outstanding delivery because they're incredibly skilled at hiring the right people and building strong teams.

> Focus on employees who beat expectations in their current role.

> The best leaders know how important it is to master the fundamentals of building strong, high-performing teams. They become exceptional at selecting the right talent for their teams, and they develop a deep and teachable point of view on how to build a culture within the team that delivers outstanding results on a consistent basis.

> To accelerate your career, engage a mentor and a sponsor. You need to build sponsorship early and often in your career to make sure you have the support ready when a new role that is aligned with your career plan becomes open.

LEADERSHIP COACHING TECHNIQUES

Part 3 is your workbook. I encourage you to take the time necessary to work thoughtfully through these activities and exercises. They are designed to help you grow as a leader, build a high-performance team and have a positive, enduring influence on your organization's culture.

1: Self-Insight Drives Purpose

Just as core values and purpose are foundational for the built-to-last companies, the same is true for individuals. The most talented leaders lead by design based on a rock-solid foundation of clear, basic human values and a well-defined purpose that lays out a path to achieve their goals. As you know, leaders are tested all the time. Resilience is needed to prevail. But it relies upon the foundation the leader has built.

When I coach executives, I ask questions about the strength and clarity of their personal values and purpose. This bedrock of values and purpose is timeless and does not change materially. If anything, life's experiences often deepen the clarity and intensity of beliefs and purpose. The leaders' clarity and deep sense of what they believe and what they stand for only help them make better decisions about business, people and life.

So let's go to the balcony together, and test the clarity of your personal values and purpose, the essential foundation of the +5 leader. In the next chapter, we will move from values and purpose to the second principle of +5 leaders, which is playing to your strengths and passions.

While you are on the balcony, take a few moments to reflect on your past behavior in as nonjudgmental a way as possible. To do this, we're going to focus on your positive experiences, not your negative ones. Always focus on strengths, not weaknesses. As Peter Drucker liked to argue: if you focus on your strengths, you make your weaknesses irrelevant. But remember to take your time as you go through the exercises because this is a life-changing process. The questions I ask you to consider aren't easy to answer, but after you've tackled them, you'll have a sense of clarity that few others have. And you'll have taken the first step to becoming a +5 leader.

Activity 1.1: Journal Exercise

Reflect on the following statement, and write down your thoughts. Do you agree, somewhat agree or disagree with the statement? Why?

> In their best seller *Built to Last*, coauthors Jim Collins and Jerry Porras view values and purpose as the core ideology of companies that are "built to last": "A set of basic precepts that plant a fixed stake in the ground: This is who we are; this is what we stand for; this is what we're all about."[1] Both values and purpose are foundational for organizational success.

Activity 1.2: Journal Exercise

Reflect on the following statement, and write down your thoughts. Do you agree, somewhat agree or disagree with the statement? Why?

> When you're thinking about change, the first thing you should consider is what not to change. During their long years of research for their book, *Built to Last*, coauthors Jim Collins, Jerry Porras and their team discovered that the built-to-last companies embraced something called *the paradox of change*: On one hand, you don't ever want to change your core—your foundational values and purpose. On the other hand, you need to be willing to change everything else—your strategy, your culture, your practices.

Exercise 1.1: Clarify Your Values

1. Clarify your values by identifying the three to five events in your life that you might describe as crucial moments, or in other words, events that influenced your values, ethics and character. For example, think of the impact your parents and family environment

have had on you, and reflect on those emotional roller-coaster rides in your life that tested and challenged you in deep ways, and how you responded.

2. Think back to the experiences you've had in your life where your deep beliefs were tested or challenged by situations or people as you were pushed to take actions contrary to your values and ethics. How did you respond?

3. Make a list of three to five core values or beliefs that guide your behavior and provide you with a framework for making the big decisions in your life. Include two kinds of values in your list. First, include basic human values such as integrity, respect, caring for others, giving back and mutual trust. Then, include what I call *performance values*, such as teamwork, innovation and commitment to deliver. Performance values drive your behavior when you are at your best at work.

4. Share these values with the handful of people you trust most. Validate the values, and lock them down.

Exercise 1.2: Clarify Your Purpose

1. Clarify your purpose by fast-forwarding to your sixty-five-year-old self. Assume you are healthy and engaged in life, put yourself on the balcony and reflect on your life by asking yourself these questions:
   > What kind of difference have I made in the lives of those who are most important to me?
   > What do members of the teams I have led remember most about our work together?
   > How well or badly have I treated people and made them feel?
   > Have I helped make the world a better place, even in a small way?
   > What are my next steps to continue to grow as a leader of my community?
   > If I am taking on a new business venture, how will I lead in ways that are different?

2. Write down what you want your legacy to be. Ask yourself what you need to pursue in order to have no regrets in life.

3. Go back to the present and identify two or three elements that distill the journey you're on and the difference you want to make. This is your purpose in life.

4. Share your purpose with three or four people you trust. Validate it, and lock it down.

Exercise 1.3: Link Values to Purpose

The third step is to link the values you have articulated and assess those values in the context of your legacy. Do you live those values 24/7? Is your purpose defined, clear and constant? Where is more work required to make your legacy an assured acknowledgment of who you are? Write down in a list the places you are confident you are excelling (and why), and in a separate list, write down what you need to work on to define your legacy.

2: Play to Your Strengths—Live with Passion

It is time to go back to the balcony and engage in self-reflection about the path you are on. Fill out the three circles framework (personal hedgehog) for yourself, and validate it on two levels: with your spouse, partner or best friend, and then, with key colleagues. After you have completed and shared your three circles, the test of whether your hedgehog accurately reflects you is whether you can say this: "Yes, this is me. This is definitely me. When I'm at my best, I'm playing to these strengths and following these passions. For me to be the best I can be, to spread my wings and feel great about my contribution, this is the lane I need to be in. This is my wheelhouse. It not only feels right for me—this *is* me."

If you find the process frustrating, if you are struggling to determine your strengths and passions, go back to the balcony, and reflect on what is working and what is not in your life and career (see page 20 for a discussion of The Balcony and the Dance Floor metaphor). When you've gotten added perspective and have a description of your strengths and passions, follow the process described in Exercise 2.1, including validating them with people you know and trust. You can even go a step further and validate your strengths and passions through an assessment with an organizational psychologist (like I did). You can also go through a formal 360-degree feedback process to gain insights on how others see your strengths. Whichever way you choose, don't do it on your own. Refine, validate and adjust for clarity.

Activity 2.1: Journal Exercise

Reflect on the following statement and write down your thoughts. Do you agree, somewhat agree or disagree with the statement? Why?

> Jim Collins said: "If you make a lot of money doing things at which you could never be the best, you'll only build a successful company, not a great one. If you become the best at something, you'll never remain on top if you don't have intrinsic passion for what you are doing. Finally, you can be passionate all you want, but if you can't be the best at it or it doesn't drive economic success, then you might have a lot of fun, but you won't produce great results."[2]

Exercise 2.1: Complete the Three Circles Framework

To make sure you're crystal clear about your strengths and passions, go back to the balcony and gain perspective on your life. If you want to drive impact and build high-performing teams that consistently exceed expectations, you have to be absolutely clear about your own drive and focus.

Step 1: Clarify your strengths and passions by completing the three circles framework to shape your personal hedgehog (see Figure 2.2: Create Your Personal Hedgehog on page 27).

1. Look back on your life and think of your greatest success—a time when you were at your very best.
2. In relation to that success, write down the strengths you leveraged to deliver the outcome you're most proud of accomplishing.
   > Use simple, clear language that anyone can understand and relate to.
   > Be sure to include a performance strength as well (e.g., one that delivers strong results).
3. In terms of your passions, think of your life (personal and work), and write down a list of things that you love to spend time on and are very good at.
4. Prioritize this list in terms of impact in your life, from highest to lowest (family, sports, team building, problem solving, etc.).
5. Finally, to assess circle three, "make a living," list all the industries you've worked in and categorize them each as a growing or shrinking industry. The key point is to assess whether the jobs and industries you've worked in have enabled you to grow personally—and economically.

Step 2: Validate your strengths and passions.
1. Take your completed three circles framework and review it with your spouse, partner or best friend. You are looking for feedback on how you describe your deep strengths and passions from someone you trust and who has your back. Once again, be sure to relate your biggest successes and accomplishments to your strengths and passions.
   > Refine as necessary based on feedback.
2. Further validate your strengths and passions with your colleagues to see if what you believe captures the essence of you also resonates with how others see you.
   > Refine as necessary.

Step 3: Reflect on your new self-awareness, and test your findings against your career aspirations. Take thirty days, and reflect on your personal hedgehog.

1. Think about your current role and how you can excel. Excelling in your current role is the springboard for your next opportunity.
2. Test your strengths, passions and personal focus against your career aspirations.

3: Finding the Right People and Building a Strong Team

As I wrote at the beginning of Chapter 3, the most important decisions we make in life, whether personally or professionally, relate to people. The choices we make about the person who will journey through life with us, those whom we will be able to count on as friends and those who will make our time at work that much more pleasant—these choices are at least important and potentially life altering.

To make the right choices, we need to understand who we are. This is also true of organizations. Purpose directs our actions, and those actions are an expression of what we are meant to do. Our collective actions are an expression of the organization's purpose. We work hard to ensure that the organization succeeds and thrives, and benefits accrue to the community.

Getting clarity on these foundational principles is the first step on your journey to becoming a +5 leader. The next step is to translate this foundation into tangible results. In other words, the question now becomes: "How does the work get done, and who's going to do it?"

Now, we turn to activities and an exercise for you to complete based on the topics covered in Chapter 3.

Activity 3.1: Journal Exercise

Reflect on the following statement, and write down your thoughts. Do you agree, somewhat agree or disagree with the statement? Why?

> Leaders help shape and build the culture within their teams, and culture is changed one leader at a time, one team at a time. You behave your way to restoring a culture to its center or starting a new culture.

Activity 3.2: Assess Your People Quotient

Reflect on the following questions. Write down your thoughts, but do not think of them as fixed. Your "right people" practices in work and life should change as your organization's priorities and goals change, as do your own and those of the people around you:

> *Examine your foundation*: Review your values, purpose, strengths and passions (see Chapters 1 and 2). Do you have clarity on these foundational principles?

> *Right people*: Do you have the right people in your work life and your personal life?

> *Your personal life*: Are you surrounded by close friends and family who share your values, celebrate your successes and care about you? If not, what can you do to change that?

> *Your organization*: Are you reporting to people who have clarity of purpose and values, and who support you and share your values? If not, what can you do to change that?

> *Your team*: Are you part of a group that shares a common purpose, moves in the same direction and has your back? If not, what can you do to change that?

> *People decisions*: Do you have enough rigor and discipline to make the right people decisions? Are they one of your signature qualities as a leader?

Exercise 3.1: Hire for the Right Fit, Always

Jim Collins provides three rules to help leaders make the right people decisions:

1. If in doubt, don't hire.
2. Put your best people on your biggest opportunities.
3. When you know you need to make a change, take your time deciding on the change, but once you decide, act![3]

For each principle, we will break them down as follows to help you create a checklist for reference. In building your own leadership playbook, make notes about the points below, including from your own experience as a leader:

1. Finding the right people is all about fit and finding people who
   > share the organization's values and purpose
   > have the right strengths
   > have the right character, including a willingness to adapt and learn
   > are team players who celebrate others' success

2. The biggest people-related mistakes are
   > not putting enough rigor into the selection process
   > making quick hiring decisions instead of the right hiring decisions
   > trying to change the behaviors of the wrong people instead of letting them go

3. The right people are those who
   > immediately live the values of the organization
   > are inspired by purpose
   > are passionate about their work
   > don't have to be managed

When you hire the right people, work doesn't feel like work.

4: Getting to Full Engagement

In your role as a leader, you are far from alone in wondering why—with all the time, effort and money being spent driving employee engagement—so many employees, including your own team members, fail to be inspired to do their best work. As the author of this book, I am accountable for helping you answer that question. Let's turn to activities and an exercise that may lead to productive reflection.

Activity 4.1: Journal Exercise

Reflect on the following statement, and write down your thoughts. Do you agree, somewhat agree or disagree with the statement? Why?

> Achieving a personal state of ideal performance requires making choices that will advance and not derail your progress in each of the four levels of the High-Performance Pyramid (see Figure 4.1 on page 57). Your progress as a leader will have beneficial effects on the physical, mental, emotional and spiritual/purposeful energy of your colleagues generally and your team directly.

Activity 4.2: Compare the Paradigms

TABLE 4.1: THE POWER OF FULL ENGAGEMENT

Old Paradigm	New Paradigm
Manage time	Manage energy
Avoid stress	Seek stress
Life is a marathon	Life is a series of sprints
Downtime is wasted time	Downtime is productive time
Rewards fuel performance	Purpose fuels performance
Self-discipline rules	Rituals rule
The power of positive thinking	The power of full engagement

Source: Jim Loehr and Tony Schwartz, *The Power of Full Engagement*, Free Press 2003, p. 6.

Table 4.1 shows the seven dimensions for each of the old and new paradigms used by leaders to increase self-engagement and productivity, and team engagement and productivity. Create three columns:

> Old Paradigms
> New Paradigms
> My Comparison of the Old and the New

When you have completed the activity, ask what strategies emerge that you can use to elevate your engagement and that of your team.

Exercise 4.1: Increase Your Engagement Capability

Engagement is at the core of life. Personal engagement enables individuals to consistently perform at their best when needed most by managing their energy to reach their Ideal Performance State on demand. Organizational engagement enables companies to harness the collective energy of tens of thousands of people in a focused way.

Part 1: Increase Your Personal Engagement Capability

Step 1: Using the checklist below, assess your capacities according to the four building blocks of energy needed to drive high levels of personal engagement.

	Personal Checklist		
1.	Physical Capacity (fitness, sleep, nutrition)	O Yes O No	If no, actions . .
2.	Emotional Capacity (stress, friends, relationships)	O Yes O No	If no, actions . .

	Personal Checklist		
3.	Mental Capacity (focus, priorities, results)	O Yes O No	If no, actions . . .
4.	Purposeful Capacity (clarity of purpose and values)	O Yes O No	If no, actions . . .

Source: Created by Jim Reid.

Step 2: Assess your levels of stress and recovery, and their related dimensions, in your work life and personal life. Remember: life is a series of sprints followed by recovery. Without recovery, we are unable to achieve high levels of performance. Comment on your levels of each of the following, being sure to list both stressors and recovery methods for each:

1. stress
2. concentration/focus
3. problem solving
4. relatability
5. energy

Step 3: Write down the rituals you use (or plan to use) to strike the balance between stress and recovery:

1. Ritual #1:
2. Ritual #2:
3. Ritual #3:

Step 4: Assess your personal level of engagement as measured against the four dimensions:

1. *Pride*: I am proud to say I work for my company.
2. *Advocacy*: I would recommend my company as a great place to work.

3. *Loyalty*: If I were offered a comparable job with similar pay and benefits at another company, I would stay at my company.
4. *Satisfaction*: Overall, I am satisfied with my company as a place to work.

Part 2: Increase Your Team Engagement Capability

Step 1: Answer these questions:
1. Do you have the right people on the bus?
2. Have you moved or will you move the wrong people off the bus?
3. Are the people on the bus in the right seats?

Step 2: Do you have a process in place to measure, communicate and improve engagement for your team? Describe the process, using short, clear sentences:
1.
2.
3.
4.
5.

Step 3: Do you know the top three drivers of engagement for your team? Describe them:
1.
2.
3.

5: Inner Discipline

The framework for the activity and exercises in this chapter is based on Jim Collins's argument that a "culture of discipline" separates the great companies from their lesser-performing peers. Recall that he defined the culture of a great company as one composed of disciplined people, engaged in disciplined thought, taking disciplined action (see page 42). The kind of discipline he was referring to created freedom for people to act in the right way. It was far from a strait-jacket but was rather a launching pad for greatness, because discipline provides people with the confidence to confront the brutal facts and adjust course when necessary. Discipline rooted in purpose enables people to rely on their purpose to guide the toughest of decisions.

Now, we turn to the activity and exercises for you to complete based on the topics covered in Chapter 5.

Activity 5.1: Journal Exercise
Reflect on the following statement, and write down your thoughts. Do you agree, somewhat agree or disagree with the statement? Why?
> People receive encouragement and support in a culture of psychological safety, where trust in one another is paramount. When leaders say, "We're all in this together" and "Let's move in the same direction," they demonstrate a team-first attitude. If they consistently act that way, their culture grows stronger because culture is behavior driven.

Exercise 5.1: Assess Your Leadership Behaviors
What are your hallmark behaviors as a leader? If you want to build and grow a high-performing and resilient culture, be truthful about how you lead. Answer each of the five sections in the image to follow on a scale from 1 (needs a lot of work) to 5 (I always lead this way). Be honest in your answers, and know that very few leaders scale all the way to 5. When you complete the assessment, ask what behaviors require work. For each behavior that needs improvement, write three action items you will take. For example, to grow your humility, an action item could be to read about emotional intelligence or take a webinar from an accredited source.

1. Humility—I put the team and company first, always

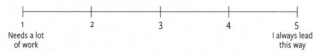

1	2	3	4	5
Needs a lot of work				I always lead this way

2. Builder—I am committed to building my people, team and culture

1	2	3	4	5
Needs a lot of work				I always lead this way

3. Mission—I am a mission-focused leader

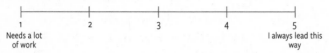

1	2	3	4	5
Needs a lot of work				I always lead this way

4. Grit—I never give up

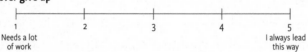

1	2	3	4	5
Needs a lot of work				I always lead this way

5. Storytelling—I communicate in an impactful way so my team is committed to the change journey

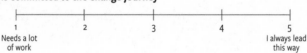

1	2	3	4	5
Needs a lot of work				I always lead this way

Source: Created by Jim Reid.

Exercise 5.2: Assess Your Understanding of Culture

How deeply do you understand the role of culture in driving performance? Get clarity by answering the following questions:

1. In sixty seconds or less, can you describe what culture is and why it is important?
2. Is building the team's culture one of your most critical roles? If not, why not?
3. How much time do you spend building culture?
4. What are the worst behaviors you as a leader are willing to tolerate? Write them down using this checklist:

> blaming others
> having a victim mentality
> bullying others
> intimidating others
> engaging in other inappropriate behaviors

6: Building a Winning Team

One of the hard truths I have observed as a coach is that the best leaders understand the two fundamental drivers of success: 1) getting the right people into the right seats; and 2) building and coaching the team to achieve high levels of trust, collaboration and innovation that produce excellent results. Teams are the critical performance unit of any organization. They are the building block of a high-performance culture, and the most effective way to change culture is to change it one leader and one team at a time.

Let's step into the activity and exercises to assess how well you are doing in building your team and strengthening your culture.

Activity 6.1: Journal Exercise

Reflect on the following statement, and write down your thoughts. Do you agree, somewhat agree or disagree with the statement? Why?

> People perform at their highest level when they possess a clear sense of purpose and are led by an engaged, trustworthy and inspiring leader. The leader must unequivocally provide the team with the environment to share their thoughts, constructive ideas and opinions without fear of recrimination or ridicule. Team members need to feel psychologically safe. This is more than just feeling safe from harassment or ridicule. They need to feel that their ideas and concerns merit the attention of the leader and fellow team members. They need to believe that they can open up, share their emotions and occasionally make mistakes without being penalized or losing their job.

Exercise 6.1: Assess Your Progress in Building a Winning Team

For this exercise, ask yourself the following question: "In my role as a leader, am I taking necessary and sufficient action to create the right environment for the team to flourish and produce outstanding results?" Rate each of the following five sections on a scale from 1 (needs a lot of work) to 5 (I always lead this way). Be honest in your answers, and know that very few leaders scale all the way to 5. When you complete the assessment, write three action items you will take to improve a weaker aspect.

1. I understand the importance of psychological safety, and have researched its application and benefits. I focus on building trust and psychological safety every day.
2. I understand the principle of productive conflict and encourage healthy debate in my team.
3. I am fully committed to achieving our goals, and I provide the resources and tools necessary to the team to ensure full commitment to and alignment with the work we need to do.
4. I hold myself and my team members accountable.
5. I lead for results but know this is a team effort, and that acknowledgment and reward are given when we are successful.

Exercise 6.2: The Seven Steps for Renewing Organizational Culture

For this exercise, you are required to assess the current state of your organization's culture and cast your mind into the culture's future state. The learning outcomes are to strengthen best practices and illustrate gaps that require leadership to close them. Successful culture change requires systematic planning and rigorous discipline.

Step 1: First, determine what should not change. What is foundational? What has made the organization sustainable and needs to be present in twenty years? This step requires reflecting on the organization's core values and purpose, and looking for misalignment that negatively impacts the work of leaders.

Step 2: Do you have the right people on the bus? Have you gotten the wrong people off the bus? A disciplined approach to team building is critical to driving successful culture change. Recall the three keys to team building:

1. If in doubt, don't hire.
2. Put your best people on your biggest opportunities.
3. When you know you need to make a change, act!

Having the right people is all about fit. You need to have people on your team who:

1. share and espouse the organization's values and purpose
2. possess the right strengths
3. possess the right character—a willingness to adapt and learn
4. are team players who celebrate others' success

Step 3: In your view, is the organization aligned to a clear, compelling vision of where you are going, and does the organization make it safe for people to sign up for the journey?

Step 4: Gather insights and data by asking all members of your team what is working and what is not. If engagement across the team is not uniform, what steps do you need to take to fix the situation?

Step 5: Are you providing sufficient support to team leads on how to create customer value? Are you holding them accountable to build their people and their teams?

Step 6: Are you aligning your processes and compensation to the behaviors you need to engage in to win? Are you practicing zero tolerance for unhealthy behaviors and doing so consistently?

Step 7: Do you constantly communicate, celebrate wins and reinforce Steps 1 to 6?

7: Driving Successful Change

The research done by John Kotter on change suggests that most large-scale change efforts fall well short of success—in fact, most fail. But it does not have to be that way.

The best leaders step into change. They understand that the anchor point for successful change is being clear about not changing what is core (values and purpose) and being open to changing everything else (strategy, practices, process, culture). But the best leaders also understand the need for a clear, simple framework for driving successful change, and they follow it in a disciplined way.

Complete the following activity and exercise to assess how you think about and approach change to drive better results for your business.

Activity 7.1: Journal Exercise

Reflect on the following statement, and write down your thoughts. Do you agree, somewhat agree or disagree with the statement? Why?

> The hard work of making change happen over the long term—permanently shifting the way we interact with our colleagues and customers—requires the skill and commitment of a truly people-oriented leader. Most of all, people need to feel safe to move forward.

Exercise 7.1: Six Steps to Manage Change

Here are six action steps for your leadership playbook that provide a framework to lead and manage change. At the end of each step, I ask questions that are intended to give you pause and cause you to reflect. A framework is static, but it can be dynamic when used to its fullest capability.

Step 1: Be Clear on What Not to Change

When you as a leader are faced with significant change, the first question to ask yourself is, "What should I not change?" Being clear on this provides an anchor point for people to rally around when everything around them is changing. This anchor point is almost always tied to the organization's or team's fundamental values and purpose—which are timeless and endure over time.

1. Are you clear on your organization's fundamental values, purpose, ethics and principles, which will sustain and anchor the organization through change and adaptation?
2. Are your personal values, purpose, ethics and principles aligned with those of the organization? If not (and there may be valid reasons for the discrepancy), why not? Is a discussion with your manager in order? Are you on the right bus?
3. How often do you and your team discuss values, purpose, ethics and principles? Are the discussions merely nice to have, or do you insist on meaningful discussion and debate?

Step 2: Select a Framework for Change

Select a framework that provides a clear roadmap for you and your team. I recommend Kotter's eight-point framework (see page 140) because it is simple, comprehensive and relatable. But other models exist. What's important is that you follow and apply a consistent set of steps, so you can make change happen in a systematic and disciplined way.

1. Do you have a change model to provide a roadmap for you and your team? If not, or if the one you have is not satisfactory, what will you do to address this situation?
2. Have you listened to ideas from your team about how to implement change? Do you listen well to your team, or could you improve?

Step 3: Inform Your Change with Data

One of the most critical determinants of successful change is learning what is working and what is not. Use reliable data from multiple sources to inform and validate next steps.

1. Do you have valid and sufficient data to help you make decisions? If not, what resources are at your disposal to obtain the necessary data to establish a baseline for change?
2. If your culture is a strong learning culture, you have an advantage over many other leaders. If your organization has a weak learning culture, what steps can you take to influence growing a learning culture?

Step 4: Don't Try to Boil the Ocean

In the first wave of change, select the three to five things that must change to drive improved results, and tie those priorities back to your values and purpose. Once you have accomplished the first phase of transformation, select the next set of priorities while again connecting those priorities with your values and purpose. Successful change is often characterized by wave after wave of consistent, focused changes that build upon each other, often over several years.

1. Do you have a roadmap that includes at least the first two waves of what needs to change?
2. Have you prepared your team for change? Do you have a list of action items that are critical to success?

3. Do your action items take into account Kotter's reasons why transformation sometimes fails? What strategies do you have to mitigate the challenges?

Step 5: Put Your Best People on the Change Team

One of the most powerful principles of driving change requires leaders to select the best people to drive the change. Your best leaders are respected and have credibility, and their personal support in backing the changes can bring swifter and more widespread acceptance of the change process.

1. Have you evaluated the skills of the team members who are tasked with implementing change? Are they your best people?
2. Have you assessed the team members' skill sets against the overall strategy? What will you do to address any gaps?

Step 6: Don't Underestimate the Need for Increased Communication

It is often said that communication in times of change needs to increase tenfold over that in more stable times. The bigger the changes you want to drive, the more critical communication becomes. Creating a narrative where people feel safe to journey with you is almost always one of the crucial determinants of successful transformation.

1. How do you rate yourself as a storyteller? How do you rate other colleagues as storytellers? Have you crafted a simple change narrative that your teams can get behind?
2. Do you believe that stories can empower others?
3. To whom can you look for advice on becoming an effective storyteller?

8: Crisis Leadership

A crisis is unexpected and unpredictable. Navigating through a crisis can test a leader's grit, perseverance and determination. That is why the most effective leaders make a concerted effort to understand how a crisis will affect team performance, and they always have a plan to prepare for and respond when a crisis hits.

So let's go back to the balcony and reflect on how prepared you are as a leader to handle the next crisis that may be around the corner.

Activity 8.1: Journal Exercise

Reflect on the following actions taken by Starbucks CEO Kevin Johnson. What do they mean to you? Why?

> After the anti-Black racism incident in Philadelphia, some people called for Starbucks to take action against the store manager, but CEO Kevin Johnson would have none of that. Instead, he said: "The focus of fixing this—I own it. This is a management issue, and I am accountable to ensure we address the policy and the practice and the training that led to this outcome." What happened was "reprehensible [...] We are accountable. I am accountable."[4] Johnson spent two days in Philadelphia visiting with the two men who were arrested as well as the mayor, police chief and others in the community to learn what happened and why it happened, and to make sure it would never happen again.

Exercise 8.1: Prepare for a Crisis

This exercise is designed to help you refine a crisis playbook if you have one or begin to build a framework for one. For this exercise, I want you to apply the five steps we discussed in this chapter (see Crisis Leadership Checklist on page 158) to help you mitigate or solve a crisis that is in front of you. Alternatively, use an example of a crisis that is occurring in your industry and that may be affecting your business.

Based on the information you have, complete the following steps:

1. List two or three priorities that will guide your actions and decisions. What is the rationale for choosing these priorities? How do the outcomes for these priorities outweigh those of other priorities you might have identified?
2. Supporting your team requires that you be confident and demonstrate that accountability for outcomes rests with you. Speed is required, and a lack of confidence will inhibit decision-making. Are you confident? Will the team members' confidence in themselves bend if they make mistakes? Write down your reflections.
3. Are you leading your team to the best of your ability? Are you listening to your team? Do you need to bolster their resilience? Should you be doing more coaching with your team? Make a list of coaching initiatives you need to take and how you are going to implement them. For example, you see a need to improve team collaboration. What exercises can you use to make collaboration more efficient?
4. Are you getting feedback from your team on how you are communicating? Is your messaging clear, authentic and consistent? Are team efforts aligned with priorities? Is any team energy being wasted? Keep a journal of communication action steps and results, because wasted effort might be a result of not understanding what you are asking of your team.

9: The Leader as Coach

The world is changing, and a key element of this change is being driven by demographics. The emergence of a younger workforce of Millennial and Gen Z team members is requiring leaders to show up differently. Younger workers are asking for more feedback, opportunity to grow and coaching from their managers.

The best leaders today are deepening their coaching skills, so they can truly empower their teams and create ownership for results at the individual level. Let's work through the following activity and exercise to assess your effectiveness as a coach, and to build a plan for you to be seen as the best coach for your team.

Activity 9.1: Journal Exercise

Reflect on the following description of coaching by Carollyne Conlinn and write down your thoughts. Do you agree, somewhat agree or disagree with the statement? Why?

> "High performance can certainly be generated in the short term by the more traditional management methods, which means setting a goal, following up with people and making sure that they get the job done. But coaching is a way to have team members internalize their motivation and make room for them to be more self-generating with the solutions they come up with, and whatever else is needed to be successful. It also eliminates the need for leaders to be constantly supervising people and creating ambitious goals with arbitrary timelines. What you really want to do is shift the accountability directly to the person doing the work."[5]

Exercise 9.1: Assess Your Coaching Capability

This exercise is intended to have you take stock of how you need to prepare to begin the process of learning about coaching or to grow your coaching skill set and methodology.

On a scale of 1 (very low proficiency) to 5 (very high proficiency), self-assess the following skills and how you will take steps to improve your weaker skills:

1. I listen actively and carefully consider my colleagues' ideas and points of view.

2. I ask questions to increase my understanding of the big picture from different perspectives.
3. I understand that communicating with colleagues requires empathy and positivity.
4. I encourage accountability by guiding coachees to make their own decisions and come up with creative solutions.
5. I create room for all ideas and healthy debate by practicing psychological safety.
6. My coaching is guided by absolute respect for confidentiality and privacy.

10: Coaching Individual Transformation

The vast majority of people want to grow and make a difference during their life. Hence, leaders who excel at developing people and helping team members reach their goals are in high demand.

Over the years, much of the research on driving engagement has been rooted in getting behind your team's personal and career development. Not only do the strongest leaders navigate their own career extremely well, but they also demonstrate this same commitment for the people they lead.

Let's go to the balcony one last time to think about how effective you are at driving the development and careers of each member of your team.

Activity 10.1: Journal Exercise

Reflect on the following statement, and write down your thoughts. Do you agree, somewhat agree or disagree with the statement? Why?

> Early in your career, your success is often driven by you and you alone. But as your career advances and you begin to lead a team, your success is measured and defined quite differently. Instead of being assessed on your individual strengths and capabilities, you

as a top leader are judged by your team's strengths and capabilities. In other words, your performance is now measured by the effort, skill and capabilities of the people you hire, and how well your team works together to deliver consistent, exceptional results. Bottom line: at some point in your career, the levers of success will shift from you to your team. So developing your team members becomes a critical success factor for you as a leader.

Exercise 10.1: Describe the Five-Step Career Development Plan for You and Your Team Members

For each of the five steps, note your responses:

1. Do you know your wheelhouse, your sweet spot? Do you help each of your team members get clarity on their own wheelhouse for themselves?
    > What feelings do you have or what signals have you been given by others or circumstances that may suggest your team members do not have a firm handle on their sweet spot? One example is projects that are not being completed on time or to the standards you have set for the team. Another signal might be finding that you are intervening to manage team conflict or make decisions when the team is quite capable of making their own decisions.
    > What steps are you taking to further assess if you and each team member are in the right wheelhouse and making progress? For example, have you completed the personal hedgehog exercise for your team members?
2. Are you with a company that is in a growing industry and can offer you professional development and career advancement? How does your team think about this?
    > Growth creates opportunity. Pushing a career forward is much easier if you're able to ride a wave. Is the company you are

with values-led and purpose driven? You and your team want to feel inspired by the company's mission, and its contribution to society and community.

> What steps are you taking to ensure that your organization can meet team members' career ambitions? How do you see this for your own ambitions?

3. Is the leader you report to of a high caliber? Is the leader a model for you? Are you being mentored? Are you operating this way with your team?

> People want to work with one of the most talented leaders in the organization. Help your team members look for someone with a reputation for outstanding delivery because they're incredibly skilled at hiring the right people and building strong teams. Great leaders will challenge aspiring leaders more and develop them faster.

> What action steps will you take to connect your team with a leader who will mentor them and hold them accountable for growing their leadership skills?

4. Are you laser focused on your current role? Is your team operating this way?

> The next opportunity for you and your team will almost always arrive because you excel in your current job. When the best leaders are building out their teams, they're looking for people with a proven track record of success. And they're not just looking for high performance; they're looking for consistency.

> What steps will you take to ensure that you and your team are working at an optimum level? Are you displaying capacity, character, values and integrity? Are your team members leading in this way?

5. Are you identifying potential in your team and developing leadership capability through stretch assignments, coaching and professional development?

> Within a high-performing team are individuals who are ready to begin the process of moving from middle management roles to executive roles. What steps have you taken or will you take to identify team members who have the potential to take on more responsibility? What coaching framework do you have in your toolkit to help these potential leaders grow? What hiring process do you have, knowing that you will see team members leave in due course for more senior roles?

Well done on completing the Leadership Coaching Techniques workbook. Please keep it handy as a reference to guide decisions, provide feedback, intervene when you need to and build a high-performance team that is excited to outperform every day.

Epilogue

> Most people overestimate what they can do in one year and underestimate what they can do in ten years.
>
> —BILL GATES

For most of my life, I have observed the differences in mindset, behaviors and actions between the best leaders, and those who are highly competent but fall short of making an indelible impact on their organization. Why are some leaders highly successful and others less so? How do the most successful leaders motivate their teams and come up with innovative solutions to challenges that evade other leaders and teams? Do the best leaders also experience remarkable success in their broader life as a friend, partner or parent?

My observation of studying leadership in the military, in work and in life—and especially my work with Jim Collins—has taught me this: I believe there is a set of five principles in life that, if learned fully and applied consistently, will get you to a better place. I guarantee it. I see it happen every day. These five principles of personal growth and organizational success are

> having a clear purpose and set of values,
> understanding your strengths and passions,
> having the right people in the right seats,
> getting to full engagement, and
> being guided by inner discipline to outperform.

These five principles work in the real world for three reasons:

> They are simple.
> They are actionable.
> They are timeless.

The formative years I spent as an officer and military pilot made me a better person. I learned about putting country before self, I learned to serve others, and I learned that the choice to become a better leader, friend, partner and parent was mine to make. My journey in life has taught me that achieving higher levels of performance in all aspects of work and life is a choice. Those who are most committed and work hardest to realize that choice will be the most successful. So I have chosen a path to build and make things better, and to live my personal hedgehog every day.

Personal growth comes through listening and learning. Every great leader I know, and know of, is a lifelong learner, including such notables as Colin Powell, Satya Nadella, Jamie Dimon, Marc Benioff and Jacinda Ardern. So too are Joe Natale, Eric Agius, Nancy Nazer and other leaders whose stories are inspiring and insightful. They are all intensely curious, humble, tenacious leaders, and they understand that success is seldom the result of a leap of faith or insight but rather a series of small, often laborious steps over time. But as the saying goes, small steps make a big difference. As Collins discovered in his exhaustive research of business leaders, "Good to Great transition comes about by a cumulative process—step by step, action by action, decision by decision, turn by turn of the flywheel—that adds up to sustained and spectacular results."[1]

I believe a similar compounding effect happens when leaders learn and apply the five principles. We all know about the power of compound interest, but a blog post by a venture capitalist named Tomasz Tunguz really helped reinforce the power of compounding for me. He asked: "What if you could improve how you do something by 1% each day for a year? What would happen? You'd be 37× better."[2]

Remarkable. By committing to a 1 percent improvement every day, by the end of a year we would be thirty-seven times better! Here's the equation that proves his point:

$$1.01^{365} = 37.8$$

Imagine the compounding effect of this over a lifetime!

I believe that both personal and professional success come about by consistently committing to small steps that compound over time—but those steps must be taken in the right direction. The direction of your personal roadmap makes all the difference. That's what the five principles are all about. They put us on the right path, and they keep us on that path, guiding us throughout our lives, much like a compass will always set us on the true path.

· · · · ·

Without a higher purpose, we risk becoming rudderless, noted the estimable Clayton Christensen, author of *The Innovator's Dilemma*. "Having a clear purpose in my life has been essential," he wrote. "But it was something I had to think long and hard about before I understood it [...] I was conflicted about whether I could really afford to take that time away from my studies, but I stuck with it—and ultimately figured out the purpose of my life. Doing deals doesn't yield the deep rewards that come from building up people."[3]

Christensen went on to note that many of his brilliant classmates at Harvard Business School lost their way because they lacked purpose:

> Over the years I've watched the fates of my HBS classmates from 1979 unfold. I've seen more and more of them come to reunions unhappy, divorced and alienated from their children. I can guarantee you that not a single one of them graduated with the deliberate strategy of getting divorced and raising children who would become estranged from them. And yet a shocking number of them implemented that strategy. The reason? They didn't keep the purpose of their lives front and center as they decided how to spend their time, talents and energy. It's quite startling that a significant fraction of the 900 students that HBS draws each year from the world's best have given little thought to the purpose of their lives.[4]

Some people just can't seem to find their purpose. For fifteen years, Apple's CEO Tim Cook was one of those people: "I went through a period of time that I was rudderless," he shared. "I thought I should be looking for my purpose [...] I looked under every sheet, behind every door, and everywhere, and I couldn't find it. I thought, 'Oh my God, there's something wrong with me.'"[5] Cook found it years later, after he met Steve Jobs and joined Apple in 1998, thereby finding a company that believed in something big. Cook learned from Jobs that Apple's job was "to serve humanity," said Cook. "It was just that simple. Serve humanity. And it was in that moment, after fifteen years of searching, something clicked. I finally felt aligned."[6]

Cook expanded on the notion of finding purpose:

> Whatever you do with your life, be a builder. You don't have to start from scratch to build something monumental. And, conversely, the

best founders—the ones whose creations last and whose reputations grow rather than shrink with passing time—they spend most of their time building, piece by piece. Builders are comfortable in the belief that their life's work will one day be bigger than them—bigger than any one person. They're mindful that its effects will span generations. That's not an accident. In a way, it's the whole point.[7]

Jim Collins emphasized that great leaders are able to dissolve their ego into the company and always put the company's interests first. This requires the leader's highest character trait—humility. Humility is often perceived as a weakness by those who do not know its power. On the contrary, humble leaders feel secure about themselves and the team they have around them. Phil Knight might be the perfect example: "There was none of that smartest-guy-in-the-room foolishness," he said.[8]

I believe these principles also apply to your personal growth. As Christensen has noted, building a successful life is even more important than building a winning team or a successful company. His thinking aligns closely with my own. "Don't worry about the level of individual prominence you have achieved," he wrote. "Worry about the individuals you have helped become better people."[9] Ultimately, these principles are about making a difference in our lives. If this book has helped just a single reader become a better person, I will be a fortunate man.

Acknowledgments

Over two decades ago, I first met Jim Collins. Many years later, after having had multiple conversations with him about his research, he challenged me to write a book on leadership. So my first thank-you is to Jim Collins for the inspiration he gave me to shape a simple, actionable framework to help aspiring leaders be the best they can be in their work and life.

Many other people have helped me on my journey to completing this work.

In addition to Jim Collins, over my career I have benefited greatly by learning from some of the best management thinkers working in the business world, like Jeffrey Pfeffer, Dave Ulrich, Jim Loehr, John Kotter and Laura Delizonna, to name just a few.

I have learned tremendously from the seven CEOs I have worked with: John Rogers, Stephen DeFalco, John Galt, Nadir Mohamed, Guy Laurence and Lou Serafini Jr. A special shout-out to Joe Natale, with whom I have worked with over the last five years. Joe, in particular, has been a phenomenal leader who invited me into his world as CEO—and trusted me every step of the way.

During my career, I have also worked alongside and had the privilege of coaching some extraordinary executives, such as Dean Prevost, Sevaun Palvetzian, Lisa Durocher, Eric Agius, Lisa Damiani, Jordan Banks, Jorge Fernandes, Graeme McPhail, Dirk Woessner, Gerardo Chiaia, George Halatsis, Deepak Khandelwal, Pranav Pandya, Terrie Tweddle, Linda Jojo and Janet Ko.

A special thank-you to the executive team that welcomed me to Rogers when I joined in 2011. Led by Nadir Mohamed—who was such a talented CEO—and the core team of Rob Bruce, Bill Linton, Keith Pelley, Bob Berner, Tony Staffieri and David Miller.

My HR leadership team at Rogers is without a doubt one of the very best people and culture teams in North America. Tony Cimino, Sandra Pasquini, Moheni Singh, Camille Gendreau, John Mallovy, Dr. David Satok, Glenda Oldenburg, Vatche Rubenyan, Stacie Bumbacco and Allison Fitton are some of the most talented HR and communications executives anywhere. I am honored to work with such a gifted team. In addition, several HR leaders that I have worked very closely with have gone on to lead HR functions of their own. These include executives such as Mary Federau, Nancy Nazer, Anne Berend, Anna Filipopoulos, Lara Root, Jennifer Honey Brannon and Peter Neufeld.

Given that this is my first book, I am grateful for the support from Jonathan Verney and Don Loney. This book would not have happened without the incredible support of my assistant, Roisin Spinello. She has worked with me every day for over a decade and has been spectacular.

I will always be grateful to the critical readers who gave me rich and valuable feedback on the manuscript as it became a book. They are my lifelong friend Klaus Ehrenfellner, with whom I served as a pilot in the military, and Debi King, Mike Weddel, Allison Fitton, Stacie Bumbacco, Ashlea Kay, Jocelyn Yacoub and Dr. Tim Gilmor.

Finally, I cannot thank my family enough for their encouragement, support and inspiration to write this book. Thank to my four children—Carolyn, Dave, Kevin and Jane. Thank you especially to my incredible wife, Pattie, who has been with me every step of the way. More than anyone, Pattie has been the inspiration for me in writing this book.

And for all the leaders I have worked with, encouraged and coached over the years, this book reflects your incredible spirit and determination to build strong teams, and an amazing culture for those you lead.

Notes

PART 1: The +5 Leadership Development Model

1: SELF-INSIGHT DRIVES PURPOSE

1   Jim Collins and Jerry I. Porras, *Built to Last: Successful Habits of Visionary Companies*, rev. ed. (New York: HarperCollins, 2001), 85.

2   Collins and Porras, *Built to Last*, 74.

3   Kathy Caprino, "The Changing Face of Leadership: 10 New Research Findings All Leaders Need to Understand," *Forbes*, February 28, 2018, forbes.com/sites/ kathycaprino/2018/02/28/the-changing-face-of-leadership-10-new-research -findings-all-leaders-need-to-understand/#773605a66197.

4   Jeffrey Pfeffer, *Leadership BS: Fixing Workplaces and Careers One Truth at a Time* (New York: HarperBusiness, 2015), 53. See also an interview with Amir Dan Rubin: "A 'Lean' Vision Drives Stanford Hospital & Clinics Performance: Q&A with CEO Amir Dan Rubin," *Becker's Hospital Review*, April 2, 2012, beckershospitalreview.com/ hospital-management-administration/a-qleanq-vision-drives-stanford-hospital -a-clinics-performance-qaa-with-ceo-amir-dan-rubin.html.

5   J.Y. Smith and Noel Epstein, "Katharine Graham Dies at 84," *Washington Post*, July 18, 2001, washingtonpost.com/archive/politics/2001/07/18/katharine-graham-dies -at-84/6182825e-caa2-4a1e-b582-f94ac9764bfc/.

6   "Katherine Graham Offers Advice on Leadership," *Harvard Business School*, June 1, 1998, alumni.hbs.edu/stories/Pages/story-bulletin.aspx?num=5522.

7   Smith and Epstein, "Katharine Graham Dies."

8   Smith and Epstein, "Katharine Graham Dies."

9   Kenly Craighill, "The Jack Welch Legacy: Rank It or Yank It?," *Woodenworks*, March 19, 2020, wodenworks.medium.com/the-jack-welch-legacy-rank-it-or-yank-it-869e0fb9ff63.

10   Lisa Vollmer, "Reward Candor, Top Performers in the Workplace, Welch Says," *Stanford News*, May 25, 2005, news.stanford.edu/news/2005/may25/welch-052505.html.

11   Tim Gilmor, in discussion with the author, June 2020.

12   Shayne Tilley, "Are You on the Balcony or the Dance Floor?," *Shayne Tilley*, November 8, 2012, shaynetilley.com/are-you-on-the-balcony-or-the-dance-floor/.

2: PLAY TO YOUR STRENGTHS — LIVE WITH PASSION

1   Jim Collins, *Good to Great: Why Some Companies Make the Leap . . . and Others Don't* (New York: HarperCollins, 2001), 90.

2   Collins, *Good to Great*, 92.

3   Based on Collins, *Good to Great*, 95–97.

4   Sharon Briggs, "Genetics Has Proven That You're Unique—Just Like Everyone Else," *Quartz*, March 21, 2017, qz.com/936525/personal-dna-testing-and-genetic-scientists-are-proving-that-youre-unique-just-like-everyone-else/.

5   Jane Yarnall, "The Genetics of Leadership," *HR*, September 11, 2015, hrmagazine.co.uk/article-details/the-genetics-of-leadership.

3: FINDING THE RIGHT PEOPLE AND BUILDING A STRONG TEAM

1   "Enduring Ideas: The 7-S Framework," *McKinsey Quarterly*, March 1, 2008, mckinsey.com/business-functions/strategy-and-corporate-finance/our-insights/enduring-ideas-the-7-s-framework#.

2   David Packard, *The HP Way: How Bill Hewlett and I Built Our Company*, illustrated ed. (New York: HarperCollins, 2006).

3   Jim Collins and Jerry I. Porras, *Built to Last: Successful Habits of Visionary Companies*, rev. ed. (New York: HarperCollins, 2001), 4–6.

4   Jim Collins, *Good to Great: Why Some Companies Make the Leap . . . and Others Don't* (New York: HarperCollins, 2001), 52.

5   This section is based on Collins, *Good to Great*, 54–59.

6   Patty McCord, "How Netflix Reinvented HR," *Harvard Business Review*, January–February 2014, hbr.org/2014/01/how-netflix-reinvented-hr.

7   Collins, *Good to Great*, 58.

8   Diane Coutu, "Leadership Lessons from Abraham Lincoln," *Harvard Business Review*, April 2009, hbr.org/2009/04/leadership-lessons-from-abraham-lincoln.

9   Coutu, "Leadership Lessons."

10   Phil Knight, *Shoe Dog: A Memoir by the Creator of Nike* (New York: Scribner, 2016), 302.

11   Knight, *Shoe Dog*, 302.

4: GETTING TO FULL ENGAGEMENT

1   Jim Loehr and Tony Schwartz, *The Power of Full Engagement: Managing Energy, Not Time, Is the Key to High Performance and Personal Renewal* (New York: Free Press, 2003), 9, read.amazon.ca/?asin=B000FCOSWS&language=en-CA.

2 Loehr and Schwartz, *Power of Full Engagement*, 33–34.

3 Loehr and Schwartz, *Power of Full Engagement*, 29.

4 Loehr and Schwartz, *Power of Full Engagement*, 12.

5 Loehr and Schwartz, *Power of Full Engagement*, 32.

6 Jim Loehr and Tony Schwartz, "The Making of a Corporate Athlete," *Harvard Business Review*, January 2001, hbr.org/2001/01/the-making-of-a-corporate-athlete.

7 Loehr and Schwartz, *Power of Full Engagement*, 11.

8 "Study Finds Significant 'Engagement Gap' among Global Workforce," *Chief Learning Officer*, November 5, 2007, multiclo.chieflearningofficer.com/2007/11/05/study-finds-significant-engagement-gap-among-global-workforce/.

9 James Harter, "If Your Managers Aren't Engaged, Your Employees Won't Be Either," *Harvard Business Review*, June 6, 2019, hbr.org/2019/06/if-your-managers-arent-engaged-your-employees-wont-be-either.

10 Patrick Bliley, in discussion with the author, August 2020.

11 Based on Kristin Stoller, "2021 Canada's Best Employers," *Forbes*, January 26, 2021, forbes.com/canada-best-employers/#304b38fa241f.

12 "Becoming Irresistible: A New Model for Employee Engagement," *Deloitte Review*, issue 16, January 27, 2015, deloitte.com/us/en/insights/deloitte-review/issue-16/employee-engagement-strategies.html.

13 Austin Smith, "An Interview with Costco CEO Craig Jelinek," *The Motley Fool*, August 1, 2013, fool.com/investing/general/2013/08/01/an-interview-with-costco-ceo-craig-jelinek.aspx.

14 Smith, "Costco CEO Craig Jelinek."

15 David Gelles, "Marc Benioff of Salesforce: 'Are We Not All Connected?,'" *New York Times*, June 15, 2018, nytimes.com/2018/06/15/business/marc-benioff-salesforce-corner-office.html.

16 Dana Brownlee, "How the 'Best Companies to Work For' Engage Employees and Retain Top Talent," *Forbes*, September 4, 2019, forbes.com/sites/danabrownlee/2019/09/04/how-the-best-companies-to-work-for-engage-employees-and-retain-top-talent/#704552011eca.

17 These six factors are based on research by Gallup, The Engagement Institute and my own research. To see Gallup's complete list of twelve engagement drivers, visit their website: Jennifer Robison, "Leading Engagement from the Top," *Gallup*, November 2, 2010, news.gallup.com/businessjournal/144140/leading-engagement-top.aspx.

18 Alex Camp, Hortense de la Boutetière and Gila Vadnai-Tolub, "Linking Employee Engagement to Customer Satisfaction at Starwood," *McKinsey*, April 15, 2019, mckinsey.com/business-functions/organization/our-insights/the-organization-blog/linking-employee-engagement-to-customer-satisfaction-at-starwood?cid=other-soc-twi-mip-mck-oth-1905--&sid=2355349662&linkId=68111511.

19 Natalia Peart, "Making Work Less Stressful and More Engaging for Your Employees," *Harvard Business Review*, November 5, 2019, hbr.org/2019/11/making-work-less-stressful-and-more-engaging-for-your-employees. See also Jim Harter and Amy Atkins, "Engaged Employees Less Likely to Have Health Problems,"

Gallup, December 18, 2015, news.gallup.com/poll/187865/engaged-employees
-less-likely-health-problems.aspx.

20 Loehr and Schwartz, *Power of Full Engagement*, 29.

5: INNER DISCIPLINE

1   John P. Kotter, "Does Corporate Culture Drive Financial Performance?," *Forbes*,
    February 10, 2011, forbes.com/sites/johnkotter/2011/02/10/does-corporate-culture
    -drive-financial-performance/#14dce2277e9e.

2   Kotter, "Does Corporate Culture Drive."

3   Kotter, "Does Corporate Culture Drive."

4   Jim Collins, *Good to Great: Why Some Companies Make the Leap ... and Others Don't*
    (New York: HarperCollins, 2001).

5   Jim Collins, "A Culture of Discipline," *Jim Collins*, no date, jimcollins.com/
    concepts/a-culture-of-discipline.html.

6   Collins, *Good to Great*, 27.

7   Amy Ou, David Waldman and Suzanne Peterson, "Do Humble CEOs Matter?
    An Examination of CEO Humility and Firm Outcomes," *Journal of Management*,
    September 21, 2015, createvalue.org/wp-content/uploads/Do-Humble-CEOs
    -Matter.pdf, 21.

8   Ou, Waldman and Peterson, "Do Humble CEOs Matter?," 7.

9   Collins, *Good to Great*, 35.

10 Jim Collins and Jerry I. Porras, *Built to Last: Successful Habits of Visionary Companies*,
    rev. ed. (New York: HarperCollins, 2001), 23.

11 Charles Benvegar (Carmelo Benvenga), "The Wreckers" from *Songs of the Free State
    Bards*, ed. Vincent Godfrey Burns (Washington: New World Books, 1967), 7.

12 Thomas W. Malnight, Ivy Buche and Charles Dhanaraj, "Put Purpose at the Core of
    Your Strategy," *Harvard Business Review*, September–October 2019, hbr.org/2019/
    09/put-purpose-at-the-core-of-your-strategy.

13 Kurt Eichenwald, "Microsoft's Lost Decade," *Vanity Fair*, August 2012, vanityfair.
    com/news/business/2012/08/microsoft-lost-mojo-steve-ballmer.

14 Carmine Gallo, "Microsoft CEO Satya Nadella's Clear and Consistent Vision Rallies
    Employees around a Common Purpose," *Forbes*, March 31, 2018, forbes.com/sites/
    carminegallo/2018/03/31/microsoft-ceo-satya-nadellas-clear-and-consistent
    -vision-rallies-employees-around-a-common-purpose/#699ab8a924b7.

15 "Microsoft's Next Act," *McKinsey Quarterly*, April 3, 2018, mckinsey.com/industries/
    technology-media-and-telecommunications/our-insights/microsofts-next-act.

16 "Satya Nadella: When Empathy Is Good for Business," *Morning Future*, June 18,
    2018, morningfuture.com/en/article/2018/06/18/microsoft-satya-nadella-empathy
    -business-management/337.

17 Larry W. Sharp, "Critical Clarity: Customers and Culture," *IBEC Ventures*, August 31,
    2015, ibecventures.com/blog/critical-clarity-customers-and-culture.

18 Simon Sinek, *Start with Why: How Great Leaders Inspire Everyone to Take Action* (New
    York: Portfolio, 2009), 65–66.

19 Dean Madhav Rajan, "Top Three Attributes Microsoft CEO Satya Nadella Looks for in a Leader," *Chicago Booth*, October 31, 2018, news.chicagobooth.edu/newsroom/top-three-attributes-microsoft-ceo-satya-nadella-looks-leader/.

20 Leah Fessler, "'You're No Genius': Her Father's Shutdowns Made Angela Duckworth a World Expert on Grit," *Quartz*, March 26, 2018, qz.com/work/1233940/angela-duckworth-explains-grit-is-the-key-to-success-and-self-confidence/.

21 Jamie Dimon, "Chairman & CEO Letter to Shareholders," *JPMorgan Chase*, no date, reports.jpmorganchase.com/investor-relations/2019/ar-ceo-letters.htm?mod=article_inline.

22 Jim Loehr, *The Power of Story: Change Your Story, Change Your Destiny in Business and in Life* (New York: Free Press, 2007), 137.

23 Polly Mosendz, "Microsoft's CEO Sent a 3,187-Word Memo and We Read It So You Don't Have To," *The Atlantic*, July 10, 2014, theatlantic.com/technology/archive/2014/07/microsofts-ceo-sent-a-3187-word-memo-and-we-read-it-so-you-dont-have-to/374230/.

24 "The Best-Performing CEOs in the World, 2019," *Harvard Business Review*, November–December 2019, hbr.org/2019/11/the-ceo-100-2019-edition#the-ceo-life-cycle.

25 "Our Company," *Stryker*, no date, stryker.com/us/en/about.html.

26 Dan Bigman, "Inside the Growth Engine: Stryker CEO Kevin Lobo on Building an M&A Machine," *Chief Executive*, April 21, 2020, chiefexecutive.net/inside-kevin-lobos-growth-engine/.

27 Rebecca Cheung, "A Medical Technology CEO on Why Every Workday Should Feel Like a 'Home Game,'" *Rotman School of Management*, September 27, 2017, rotman.utoronto.ca/Degrees/LifeAtRotman/StudentStories/Alum-Lobo.

28 Ursula Zerilli, "Stryker CEO Kevin Lobo Reflects on Leadership, Early Successes after Nearly a Year on the Job," *mLIVE*, January 20, 2019, mlive.com/business/west-michigan/2013/08/stryker_ceo_kevin_postpones_mo.html.

29 Cheung, "Medical Technology CEO."

30 Rob Bernshteyn, *Value as a Service: Embracing the Coming Disruption* (Austin: Greenleaf Book Group Press, 2016).

31 Rob Bernshteyn, "Why Spend Management Requires an Open Approach," *Coupa*, September 5, 2017, coupa.com/blog/why-spend-management-requires-an-open-approach.

32 Damanick Dantes, "Values Are the Binding Principles of Our Organization, Says This Software CEO," *Fortune*, September 11, 2019, fortune.com/2019/09/11/coupa-ceo-rob-bernshteyn-ceo-initiative-2019/.

33 Chad Storlie, "Military Veteran Alex Gorsky, CEO of Johnson & Johnson, on the Value of Military Service to Business Success," LinkedIn, February 29, 2016, linkedin.com/pulse/military-veteran-alex-gorsky-ceo-johnson-value-service-chad-storlie.

34 Valerie Young, "Rising through the Ranks: Interview with Johnson & Johnson CEO Alex Gorsky," *The Street*, March 28, 2016, thestreet.com/investing/rising-through-the-ranks-interview-with-johnson-amp-johnson-ceo-alex-gorsky-13509225.

35   Ideagen, "3 Key Lessons That Have the Potential to Change the World—An Interview with J&J's Alex Gorsky with Ideagen's George Sifakis," *Medium*, September 30, 2019, medium.com/@ideagen/3-key-lessons-that-have-the -potential-to-change-the-world-an-interview-with-j-js-alex-gorsky-ccc4e91c43be.

36   "Our Credo," *Johnson & Johnson*, no date, jnj.com/credo/.

37   Michael Useem and Adam Grant, "Leadership Challenges at Johnson & Johnson," *Knowledge@Wharton*, January 9, 2014, knowledge.wharton.upenn.edu/article/ alex-gorsky-leadership-moments-jj/.

38   J&J, "Alex Gorsky Shares His Advice on Career Development," YouTube, December 17, 2013, youtube.com/watch?v=4mIZs5VlkB8.

39   Colin Powell and Joseph E. Persico, *My American Journey* (New York: Random House, 1995), 3ad.com/history/cold.war/feature.pages/powell.html.

40   "Colin Powell Biography," *Biography.com*, April 23, 2021, biography.com/political -figure/colin-powell#awesm=~0FANWDG9jnFwbm.

41   Colin Powell, "Commencement Address at Howard University," May 14, 1994. Available at *American RadioWorks*, americanradioworks.publicradio.org/features/ blackspeech/cpowell.html.

42   Abdallah Alaili, "There Are No Secrets to Success: It Is the Result of Preparation, Hard Work and Learning from Failure—Colin Powell," *Entrepreneur Post*, November 18, 2020, entrepreneurpost.com/2020/11/18/there-are-no-secrets-to-success-it-is-the -result-of-preparation-hard-work-and-learning-from-failure-colin-powell/.

43   Powell and Persico, *My American Journey*, 3ad.com/history/cold.war/feature.pages/ powell.htm.

44   Cloudingo, "The Importance of Women in Technology According to YouTube CEO Susan Wojcicki," *Medium*, September 24, 2015, medium.com/@cloudingo/the -importance-of-women-in-technology-according-to-youtube-ceo-susan-wojcicki -f4f856d31f09.

45   Masters of Scale and Susan Wojcicki, "How to Find—and Keep—True North," *Masters of Scale*, no date, mastersofscale.com/susan-wojcicki/.

46   Masters of Scale and Wojcicki, "True North."

47   Dylan Byers and Susan Wojcicki, "Transcript: YouTube's Susan Wojcicki," *NBC News*, April 8, 2020, nbcnews.com/podcast/byers-market/youtube-s-susan-wojcicki-n1179316.

48   Byers and Wojcicki, "YouTube's Susan Wojcicki."

49   Byers and Wojcicki, "YouTube's Susan Wojcicki."

50   "YouTube to Task 10,000 Workers with 'Curbing' Problematic Videos," *BNN Bloomberg*, December 5, 2017, bnnbloomberg.ca/youtube-to-task-10-000-workers -with-curbing-problematic-videos-1.935125.

51   Byers and Wojcicki, "YouTube's Susan Wojcicki."

52   Susan Wojcicki, "Letter from Susan: Our 2021 Priorities," *YouTube Official Blog*, January 26, 2021, blog.youtube/inside-youtube/letter-from-susan-our-2021 -priorities/.

PART 2: The +5 Team Coaching Model

6: BUILDING A WINNING TEAM

1   Phil Knight, *Shoe Dog: A Memoir by the Creator of Nike* (New York: Scribner, 2016), 302.

2   Knight, *Shoe Dog*, 299.

3   Based on Laura Delizonna, "Building High Performance Teams through Psychological Safety" (presentation, Rogers Management Conference, Toronto, ON, November 4, 2019).

4   Julia Rozovsky, "The Five Keys to a Successful Google Team," *re:Work*, November 17, 2015, rework.withgoogle.com/blog/five-keys-to-a-successful-google-team/; emphasis in original. Five factors drive effective teams, according to Google's research: "1. Psychological safety: Can we take risks on this team without feeling insecure or embarrassed? 2. Dependability: Can we count on each other to do high quality work on time? 3. Structure & clarity: Are goals, roles, and execution plans on our team clear? 4. Meaning of work: Are we working on something that is personally important for each of us? 5. Impact of work: Do we fundamentally believe that the work we're doing matters?"

5   Rozovsky, "Five Keys."

6   Patrick Lencioni, *The 5 Dysfunctions of a Team: A Leadership Fable* (San Francisco: Jossey-Bass, 2002), 92.

7   Lencioni, *5 Dysfunctions*, 195.

8   Lencioni, *5 Dysfunctions*, 188.

9   Lencioni, *5 Dysfunctions*, 208.

10 Muhammad Shloul, "Patrick Lencioni: Inattention to Results," YouTube, April 7, 2015, youtube.com/watch?v=Gjr3IZ1mFf8.

11 Nancy Nazer, in discussion with the author, August 2020.

12 Kyle Novak, in discussion with the author, August 2020.

13 Geoff Ho, in discussion with the author, August 2020.

14 Delizonna, "Building High Performance Teams."

15 Sachin Waikar, "Microsoft CEO Satya Nadella: Be Bold and Be Right," *Stanford Business*, November 26, 2019, gsb.stanford.edu/insights/microsoft-ceo-satya-nadella-be-bold-be-right.

16 Jeanne Sahadi, "This CEO's Tip for Success: Always Go Home for Dinner," CNN *Business*, February 4, 2020, cnn.com/2020/02/03/success/okta-ceo-todd-mckinnon/index.html.

17 Excerpt(s) from Simon Sinek, *Leaders Eat Last: Why Some Teams Pull Together and Others Don't*, copyright © 2014 by Sinek Partners LLC. Used by permission of Portfolio, an imprint of Penguin Publishing Group, a division of Penguin Random House LLC. All rights reserved.

7: DRIVING SUCCESSFUL CHANGE

1   Eric Agius, in discussion with the author, July 2020.
2   John P. Kotter, "Leading Change: Why Transformation Efforts Fail," *Harvard Business Review*, May–June 1995, hbr.org/1995/05/leading-change-why-transformation -efforts-fail-2.
3   Kotter, "Leading Change."
4   Agius, in discussion with the author.
5   Kotter, "Leading Change."
6   Kotter, "Leading Change."
7   Jennifer Wells, "Rogers CEO's New Obsession with Customer Service Just Makes Good Business Sense: Wells," *Toronto Star*, April 21, 2017, thestar.com/business/ 2017/04/21/rogers-ceos-new-obsession-with-customer-service-just-makes-good -business-sense-wells.html.
8   "How to Beat the Transformation Odds," *McKinsey*, April 1, 2015, mckinsey.com/ business-functions/organization/our-insights/how-to-beat-the-transformation -odds#.
9   John Hamm, "The Five Messages Leaders Must Manage," *Harvard Business Review*, May 2006, hbr.org/2006/05/the-five-messages-leaders-must-manage.
10 Jessica Stillman, "The 1 Book That Transformed Microsoft's Culture from Cutthroat to Creative," *Inc.*, October 8, 2018, inc.com/jessica-stillman/this-1-book-that -transformed-microsofts-culture-from-cutthroat-to-creative.html.
11 "Beat the Transformation Odds."
12 Warren Parry, "6 Myths about Change in Business," *Fast Company*, no date, fastcompany.com/3054866/6-myths-about-change-in-business.
13 Kotter, "Leading Change."
14 Jim Collins and Jerry I. Porras, *Built to Last: Successful Habits of Visionary Companies*, rev. ed. (New York: HarperCollins, 2001), 82.

8: CRISIS LEADERSHIP

1   Jim Collins, "The Stockdale Paradox," *Jim Collins*, 2017, jimcollins.com/media_topics/ TheStockdaleParadox.html.
2   Toby Manhire, "Jacinda Ardern: 'Very Little of What I Have Done Has Been Deliberate. It's Intuitive,'" *The Guardian*, April 6, 2019, theguardian.com/world/2019/apr/06/ jacinda-ardern-intuitive-courage-new-zealand.
3   "Gun Law in New Zealand," *Wikipedia*, June 28, 2021, wikipedia.org/wiki/Gun_law _in_New_Zealand#cite_note-NYTGuns-46.
4   Manhire, "Jacinda Ardern."
5   Manhire, "Jacinda Ardern."
6   "Prime Minister: COVID-19 Alert Level Increased," *Beehive.govt.nz*, March 23, 2020, beehive.govt.nz/speech/prime-minister-covid-19-alert-level-increased.
7   "A Follow-Up Message from Starbucks CEO in Philadelphia," *Starbucks*, April 15, 2018, stories.starbucks.com/stories/2018/a-follow-up-message-from-starbucks-ceo -in-philadelphia/.

8   Shep Hyken, "Starbucks Closes 8,000 Stores for Racial Bias Training—Is It Enough?," *Forbes*, June 1, 2018, forbes.com/sites/shephyken/2018/06/01/starbucks-closes-8000 -stores-for-racial-bias-training-is-it-enough/?sh=16c10d1e2831.
9   "Follow-Up Message from Starbucks."
10 Matt Jaffe, "Starbucks CEO Kevin Johnson Discusses Crisis Response and Recovery," *Salesforce*, May 15, 2020, salesforce.com/blog/2020/05/starbucks-ceo -crisis-response.html.

9: THE LEADER AS COACH

1   Scott Seibert, Gang Wang and Stephen H. Courtright, "Antecedents and Conse-quences of Psychological and Team Empowerment in Organizations: A Meta-Analytic Review," *Journal of Applied Psychology*, vol. 96, issue 5, March 2011, researchgate.net/publication/50890449.
2   "The State of American Jobs," Pew Research Center, October 6, 2016, pewsocialtrends .org/2016/10/06/the-state-of-american-jobs/.
3   Creig Lamb, "The Talented Mr. Robot: The Impact of Automation on Canada's Workforce," Brookfield Institute, June 15, 2016, brookfieldinstitute.ca/ the-talented-mr-robot/.
4   Kristin Viera Zecca, "Coaching Leaders to Solve Complex Problems, Build Relationships, and Spark Creativity," MIT Sloan, April 24, 2019, exec.mit.edu/s/ blog-post/coaching-leaders-to-solve-complex-problems-build-relationships -and-spark-creativ-MCIVCGFIWXFVEKHDENWZ336OTZKE.
5   Shauna Robinson, "The Case for a Coaching Culture," *TD Magazine*, January 2, 2018, td.org/magazines/td-magazine/the-case-for-a-coaching-culture.
6   "The Business Case for Executive Coaching—the ICF Coaching ROI Global Study," *WMP*, February 25, 2021, wmpmagazine.com/the-business-case-for-executive -coaching-the-icf-coaching-roi-global-study/.
7   IBM, *The Value of Training*, 2014, ibm.com/training/pdfs/IBMTraining -TheValueofTraining.pdf.
8   Pierre Gurdjian, Thomas Halbeisen and Kevin Lane, "Why Leadership-Development Programs Fail," *McKinsey Quarterly*, January 1, 2014, mckinsey.com/ featured-insights/leadership/why-leadership-development-programs-fail#.
9   Gurdjian, Halbeisen and Lane, "Leadership-Development Programs Fail."
10 The *Globe and Mail* defines a coaching culture in organizations as a culture characterized by constructive feedback and frequent developmental discus-sions between managers and their direct reports. Leann Schneider and Tim Jackson, "How to Create a Coaching Culture in Your Company," *Globe and Mail*, February 2, 2016, theglobeandmail.com/report-on-business/ careers/leadership-lab/creating-a-coaching-culture-in-organizations/ article28477122/.
11 Jean M. Twenge and Stacy M. Campbell, "Generational Differences in Psychologi-cal Traits and Their Impact on the Workplace," *Journal of Managerial Psychology*, vol. 23, issue 8, 2008, pp. 862–77, doi.org/10.1108/02683940810904367.

12 Richard Fry, "Millennials Are the Largest Generation in the U.S. Labor Force," Pew Research Center, April 11, 2018, pewresearch.org/fact-tank/2018/04/11/millennials-largest-generation-us-labor-force/.

13 Jack Zenger and Joseph Folkman, "People Who Think They're Great Coaches Often Aren't," *Harvard Business Review*, June 23, 2016, hbr.org/2016/06/people-who-think-theyre-great-coaches-often-arent.

14 Robinson, "Case for a Coaching Culture."

15 Ralph Shedletsky, in discussion with the author, August 2020.

16 Carollyne Conlinn, in discussion with the author, August 2020.

17 Conlinn, in discussion with the author.

18 "The Business Case for Executive Coaching."

19 Shedletsky, in discussion with the author.

20 Reid Hoffman, Ben Casnocha and Chris Yeh, *The Alliance: Managing Talent in the Networked Age* (Boston: Harvard Business Review Press, 2014), 42.

21 Paul Beeston, in discussion with the author, September 2020.

22 Herminia Ibarra and Anne Scoular, "The Leader as Coach: How to Unleash Innovation, Energy, and Commitment," *Harvard Business Review*, November–December 2019, hbr.org/2019/11/the-leader-as-coach.

23 Eric Agius, in discussion with the author, July 2020.

24 Shedletsky, in discussion with the author.

25 Marshall Goldsmith, "Marshall Goldsmith: Don't One-Up Your Employees' Ideas. Here's Why," *Inc.*, June 4, 2014, inc.com/marshall-goldsmith/mistake-of-one-upping-your-employees-ideas.html.

26 Shedletsky, in discussion with the author.

27 Gurdjian, Halbeisen and Lane, "Leadership-Development Programs Fail."

28 Ana Karakusevic, "The Five Key Skills of an Effective Executive Coach," *HR Magazine*, October 17, 2016, hrmagazine.co.uk/content/features/the-five-key-skills-of-an-effective-executive-coach.

29 Kira M. Newman, "Can Self-Awareness Help You Be More Empathic?," *Greater Good Magazine*, April 11, 2018, greatergood.berkeley.edu/article/item/can_self_awareness_help_you_be_more_empathic.

30 Susanna Ray, "Empathy and Innovation: How Microsoft's Cultural Shift Is Leading to New Product Development," Microsoft, February 13, 2019, news.microsoft.com/innovation-stories/empathy-innovation-accessibility/.

31 Sachin Waikar, "Microsoft CEO Satya Nadella: Be Bold and Be Right," *Stanford Business*, November 26, 2019, gsb.stanford.edu/insights/microsoft-ceo-satya-nadella-be-bold-be-right.

32 Waikar, "Microsoft CEO Satya Nadella."

33 Robinson, "Case for a Coaching Culture."

10: COACHING INDIVIDUAL TRANSFORMATION

1 "Job Hopping Is the New Normal," Workopolis, April 17, 2014, careers.workopolis.com/advice/job-hopping-is-the-new-normal/.

2   Amy Adkins, "Millennials: The Job-Hopping Generation," Gallup, no date, gallup
    .com/workplace/231587/millennials-job-hopping-generation.aspx.

3   "Deloitte Finds Millennials' Confidence in Business Takes a Sharp Turn; They Feel
    Unprepared for Industry 4.0," Deloitte, May 15, 2018, deloitte.com/global/en/
    pages/about-deloitte/press-releases/deloitte-finds-millennials-confidence
    -business-takes-sharp-turn.html.

4   "Job Hopping."

5   Tim Gilmor, in discussion with the author, June 2020.

6   Patrick Bliley, in discussion with the author, August 2020.

7   Bliley, in discussion with the author.

8   Sachin Waikar, "Microsoft CEO Satya Nadella: Be Bold and Be Right," *Stanford
    Business*, November 26, 2019, gsb.stanford.edu/insights/microsoft-ceo-satya
    -nadella-be-bold-be-right.

9   Jim Collins, *Good to Great: Why Some Companies Make the Leap ... and Others Don't*
    (New York: HarperCollins, 2001), 41–64. These three points are a distillation of
    Chapter 3: First Who ... Then What.

10 Gilmor, in discussion with the author.

11 Tracy Moore, in discussion with the author, September 2020.

12 "Keep a Promising Career on Track & Prevent Derailment," Center for Creative
    Leadership, February 16, 2020, ccl.org/articles/leading-effectively-articles/
    5-ways-avoid-derailing-career/.

13 Reprinted by permission of *Harvard Business Review*. From "Managing Your Boss"
    by John J. Gabarro and John P. Kotter, *Harvard Business Review*, January 2005,
    by Harvard Business Publishing, hbr.org/2005/01/managing-your-boss; all
    rights reserved.

14 Bliley, in discussion with the author.

15 Sheila Eugenio, "7 Reasons You Need a Mentor for Entrepreneurial Success,"
    Entrepreneur, August 17, 2016, entrepreneur.com/article/280134.

16 Paul Beeston, in discussion with the author, September 2020.

PART 3: Leadership Coaching Techniques

1   Jim Collins, *Built to Last: Successful Habits of Visionary Companies*, rev. ed. (New
    York: HarperCollins, 2001), 85.

2   Jim Collins, *Good to Great: Why Some Companies Make the Leap ... and Others Don't*
    (New York: HarperCollins, 2001), 97.

3   Collins, *Good to Great*, 41–64. These three points are a distillation of Chapter 3:
    First Who ... Then What.

4   "A Follow-Up Message from Starbucks CEO in Philadelphia," *Starbucks*, April 15,
    2018, stories.starbucks.com/stories/2018/a-follow-up-message-from-starbucks
    -ceo-in-philadelphia/.

5   Carollyne Conlinn, in discussion with the author, August 2020.

EPILOGUE

1   Jim Collins, *Good to Great: Why Some Companies Make the Leap ... and Others Don't* (New York: HarperCollins, 2001), 165.

2   Tomasz Tunguz, "1.01^365 = 37.7," *Tomasz Tunguz*, February 7, 2019, tomtunguz.com/1-01365-37-7/.

3   Clayton M. Christensen, "How Will You Measure Your Life?," *Harvard Business Review*, July–August 2010, hbr.org/2010/07/how-will-you-measure-your-life.

4   Christensen, "Measure Your Life."

5   Tom Huddleston Jr., "This Is the Advice Apple CEO Tim Cook Would Give His Younger Self—and It Came from Steve Jobs," *CNBC*, April 6, 2018, cnbc.com/2018/04/06/the-lesson-steve-jobs-taught-apple-ceo-tim-cook.html.

6   Massachusetts Institute of Technology, "Tim Cook's MIT Commencement Address 2017," YouTube, June 9, 2017, youtube.com/watch?v=2C2VJWGBRRw.youtube.com/watch?v=ckjkz8zuMMs.

7   Stanford, "2019 Stanford Commencement Address by Tim Cook," YouTube, June 17, 2019, youtube.com/watch?v=2C2VJWGBRRw.youtube.com/watch?v=ckjkz8zuMMs.

8   Phil Knight, *Shoe Dog: A Memoir by the Creator of Nike* (New York: Scribner, 2016), 298–99.

9   Christensen, "Measure Your Life."

Credits and Permissions

Index

Note: Page numbers in italics indicate
figures and tables.

+5 leaders, defined, 7
+5 Leadership Development Model:
    approach to, 3, 4–5; overview of, 2, 7–8,
    9, 235–39; sources for, 2. *See also*
    discipline; engagement; passions;
    purpose; right people; strengths; values
+5 Team Coaching Model: approach to, 3,
    4–5; overview of, 101–2, *103*; sources
    for, 2. *See also* coaching; coaching
    individual transformation; crisis
    leadership; Customer Care (Rogers),
    transformation of; team building
7-S Framework, 40
100 Best Companies to Work For, 65, 90

absenteeism, 131, 137
Accenture, 144
accountability: avoidance of, *110*, 111;
    coaching and, 163, 166, 171, 172, 229;

for communicating employee survey
    results, 70; in crisis leadership, 154,
    155, 157, 159, 227; culture and, 78, 115,
    118; humble leaders take, 80; in
    playbook for high-performing teams,
    112, 113; at Rogers, 122; workbook
    exercises on, 221, 222, 230; at
    YouTube, 96–98
active listening, 177–78
activities. *See* workbook activities and
    exercises
adaptability, *103*. *See also* change
Advanced Management Program
    (Harvard), 4, 132, 162
advocacy, 69, 216
Agius, Eric. *See* Customer Care (Rogers),
    transformation of
Agius, Marcia, 130
Alliance, The (Hoffman), 172–73
anger management, 58–59, 196
anti-Black racism, 151, 154–55, 227
Apple, 238

Archilochus (Greek poet), 23
Ardern, Jacinda, 152–54, 157
Arthur, Heather, 136
asking *vs.* telling, 178–80
assessment-based hiring, 190–92
Association for Talent Development, 162, 164, 165
athletes, 53–58, 59
attrition, 131, 132
awards, 47, 94

Baby Boomers, 184
Baker, Josephine, 60
balance. *See* energy management
Balcony and the Dance Floor, The (case study), 20–21. *See also* self-awareness
Ballmer, Steve, 84, 180
baseball, 92, 173–75, 199
Bates, Edward, 49
Beeston, Paul, 173–75, 199
behaviors, five hallmark: builder's mindset, 81–82, 92, 219, 238–39; workbook exercise on, 218–19. *See also* clarity of mission; grit; humility; storytelling
Being Here Matters (program at Rogers), 137
beliefs. *See* values
belonging, 124
benefits and rewards, employee, 65–66, 172, 188–89
Benioff, Marc, 65
Benvegar, Charles, 82
Berlin, Isaiah, 23
Bernshteyn, Rob, 91–92
Bersin, Josh, 64
biases, 42, 154–55
Black community, 151, 154–55, 227
Blanchard, Ken, 161
Bliley, Patrick, 63, 187, 188, 198
boss-direct report relationships, 183–84, 197
bottom-up culture change, 120
branding, 135–36

Briggs, Sharon, 31
Brin, Sergey, 95–96
Brookfield Institute, 162
Buche, Ivy, 83
builder's mindset, 81–82, 92, 219, 238–39
Built to Last (Collins and Porras), 13, 76, 81, 145, 206
Burroughs, 76–77
Bush, George W., 17
Businessweek, 114
bus metaphor, 40. *See also* right people

call centers. *See* Customer Care (Rogers), transformation of
Camp Pono (virtual wellness site), 66
Canada, 32, 86, 162, 183–84
capacity, 188. *See also* High-Performance Pyramid
career development. *See* growth and development
career mistakes, 196–98
careers: early, 187, 192–93; full, 194–96; mid-career, 187, 193–94
Care Nation. *See* Customer Care (Rogers), transformation of
caring for people, 161, 184
case studies: The Balcony and the Dance Floor, 20–21; Costco, 64–65; crisis leadership at Rogers, 149–52; culture change at Rogers, 114–24; Customer Care Transformation at Rogers, 131–40; High-Performance Pyramid in Action, 60–61; Jacinda Ardern, 152–54; Kevin Johnson, 154–55; Kevin Reid, 192–93; Microsoft, 84–85; Pattie Lovett-Reid, 194–96; Salesforce, 65–66; Steve, 33–35; The Three Disciplines and Team Building, 46–47; Toronto Blue Jays, 173–75; Tracy Moore, 193–94
Cava, Jeff, 68–69
Center for Creative Leadership, 196

champions (sponsors), 198–99
change: acceleration of, 48; career
    derailment and, 196; coaching and,
    164, 179; daily *vs.* lasting, 20; failures
    in change initiatives, 132, 133, 140–41,
    223–26; paradox of, 13–14, 145, 206;
    psychological impacts of, 133, 134, 139;
    in Rogers's culture, 114–24, *116*, 171;
    top takeaways about, 146; workbook
    activity and exercise on, 223–26. *See*
    also crisis leadership; Customer Care
    (Rogers), transformation of
character, 14–18, 29, 188, 190–91
charity, 151
Chase, Salmon P., 49
Chiaia, Gerardo, 73–75
China, 155
Christchurch mosque shootings, 152–53
Christensen, Clayton, 237–38, 239
Chrysler, 76–77
Churchill, Winston, 60
Citigroup, 87
clarity: coaching provides, 171–73; of
    Customer Care transformation plan,
    143; in Google's five dynamics of a
    team, *109*; of Nadella's mission
    statement, 89; needed for finding the
    right people, 39–40; of strengths and
    passions, 28, 29, 32, 35, 36–37, 158, 185,
    186, 209; of values and purpose, 12,
    17, 20–21, 73, 74, 156, 158, 186, 205–8
clarity of mission, 90–98; at Coupa, 91–92;
    at Johnson & Johnson, 92–94; overview
    of, 83–85, 91, *103*, 107; Powell's, 94–95;
    storytelling and, 88, 89; at Stryker,
    90–91; at YouTube, 95–98
Clock Builders, 81–82
coaching, 161–82; benefits of, 162, 164; of
    Care Nation, 138–39, 170, 176; case
    study on, 173–75; clarity provided by,
    171–73; of D. Reid, 60, 61; Excelerator
    Coaching Process Framework for,

166–69, *167*; of Jim Reid, 4; need for
    framework in, 164–65, 166; at Rogers,
    176–77; of Steve, 34; top takeaways
    about, 182; trust and, 166, 168, 177–81,
    199; *vs.* training, 163; workbook
    activity and exercise on, 228–30. *See*
    also +5 Team Coaching Model
coaching culture, 164, 165, 172, 175, 176.
    See also organizational culture
coaching individual transformation,
    183–201; avoiding career mistakes,
    196–98; case studies on, 192–96;
    finding a champion, 198–99;
    framework for, 185–92, 200, 231–33;
    job hopping and, 183–84; top
    takeaways about, 200–1; workbook
    activity and exercise on, 230–33
cognitive performance therapy, 59
Collins, Jim: on Graham, 16; interview
    with Stockdale, 147–48; as source of
    leadership and coaching concepts, 2, 4,
    235; Stanford Executive Program run
    by, 82; on success as cumulative, 1, 237;
    on values and purpose as foundational,
    12. See also *Built to Last* (Collins and
    Porras); *Good to Great* (Collins)
commitment: in coaching, 169; culture
    change and, 119; lack of, *110*, 111;
    listening and, 178; in playbook for
    high-performing teams, *112*, 113; of
    team members to one another, 106;
    workbook exercise on, 221
communication: during a crisis, 148–55,
    157–58, 159; of employee survey results,
    70; high-empathy, 125; nonviolent,
    142–43; at Okta, 126; at Rogers, 116,
    137, 143; workbook exercise on, 228.
    See also feedback; storytelling
communities: Black, 151, 154–55, 227;
    Muslim, 152–53; pandemic support
    for, 151
compassion, 148, 157, 159

compensation, 132
competitive advantage, 106
compounding effect, 1, 5, 237
CompuGroup Medical, 74
confidence, 35, 49, 111, 228
conflict: fear of, *110*, 111; productive, *112*,
   122, 175, 221
Conlinn, Carollyne, 166, 168–69, 172, 229
Cook, Tim, 238–39
Corporate Culture and Performance (Kotter
   and Heskett), 75
Costco, 64–65, 66
costs of Customer Care, 133, 135
Coupa Software, 91–92
COVID-19 pandemic, 149–52, 153–54, 155
crises, 87, 157–58
crisis leadership, 147–60; Ardern's,
   152–54, 157; checklist for, 158–59,
   227–28; culture and, 156; K. Johnson's,
   154–55, 157, 227; at Rogers, 149–52,
   157; Stockdale Paradox and, *148*, 152,
   157–58, 159; top takeaways about,
   160; workbook activity and exercise
   on, 227–28
cross-training, 64
CTV News, 195
Cullman, Joe, 44
culture. *See* coaching culture;
   organizational culture
Customer Care (Rogers), transformation
   of, 129–45; hope for Customer Care,
   133, 134; initiation of, 129–30;
   initiatives undertaken in, 135–40; as
   ongoing, 140, 144–45; plan for, 135,
   137, 141, 143; problems with Customer
   Care, 131, 132, 133; reasons for success
   of, 141–45; rebranding as Care Nation,
   136; success of, 139, 140, 170, 176
customer experience: at Coupa, 92;
   employee engagement and, *68*, 69;
   leaders' role in enhancing, 114–15; at
   Rogers, *116*, 122, 151 (*See also*

Customer Care (Rogers),
   transformation of); at Stryker, 90

data and surveys: at Rogers, 118, 120–22,
   123–24, 130, 133, 140, 151; and top
   quartile engagement, 70; use in change
   initiatives, 225. *See also* feedback
DDI (consulting firm), 12–13
decentralization, 90
deliver, ability to. *See* high performance
Delizonna, Laura, 108, 124
Deloitte, 183
Dennis (S. Wojcicki's husband), 96
dependability, *109*
development. *See* growth and development
Dhanaraj, Charles, 83
Dimon, Jamie, 87, 105
discipline, 73–99; builder's mindset,
   81–82, 92, 219, 238–39; Chiaia's and
   Woessner's, 74, 75; interplay between
   culture and performance, 75–77, *76*, 98;
   overview of, 9; as secret sauce of high
   performance, 77–79; top takeaways
   about, 99; workbook activity and
   exercises on, 217–20. *See also* clarity
   of mission; grit; humility; storytelling
Disney, 12
Disney, Walt, 195
diversity, 90–91, 151
DNA, 31
donations, charitable, 151
Drucker, Peter, 4, 32, 75, 205
Duckworth, Angela, 87
Dylan, Bob, 183
dynamics of a team, *109*, 110, 121
dysfunctions of a team, *110*, 111

early career, 187, 192–93
Edelman Trust Index, 151
education. *See* learning; training
EduTubers, 97
Eichenwald, Kurt, 84

emotional capacity, *57, 58*–59, 61, *214, 215*

empathy: in crisis leadership, 154, 157, 159; humility and, 80, 181; S. Nadella and, 84–85, 124–25, 142–43, 180–81; workbook exercise on, 230

employee engagement. *See* engagement

employees. *See also* coaching individual transformation; Customer Care (Rogers), transformation of; right people

Empower (step in coaching framework), *167*, 169

empowerment: coaching enables, 166, 171, 178, 186, 229; culture and, 115; humble leaders provide, 80; importance in today's workforce, 161–62; at Rogers, 138, 141, 143

energy, 59

energy management: overview of, *9, 53*–56, *55, 214*; in physical capacity, 57–58; self-awareness about, 63, 198

Engage (step in coaching framework), 166–68, *167*

engagement, 53–72; case studies on employee, 64–66; case study on student, 60–61; Chiaia and Woessner create environment of, 74; coaching and, 164, 168, 172, 185, 187, 188–89, 199; discipline's importance to, 77; Employee Engagement Playbook, *66*, 67–69; empowerment drives employee, 161–62; job hopping and, 184; as organic, 67; overview of, *9*; rituals' importance to, 61–62; at Rogers, 46, 122, *123*, 135, 140, 143; storytelling and, 88, 89; summary of Loehr and Schwartz's paradigm for, *55, 214, 215*; taking stock to improve employee, 62–64; top quartile employee, 69–71; top takeaways about, 71–72; workbook activities and exercises on, 214–17, 232. *See also* High-Performance Pyramid

England, 86

Enlighten (step in coaching framework), *167*, 168

Enron, 50

environment: physical, 132, 139, 144; right, 107–10, 119, 220–23 (*See also* organizational culture; team building)

equation for compounding, 237

Essential Impact (coaching firm), 166

Evolve (step in coaching framework), *167*, 169

Excel (step in coaching framework), *167*, 169

Excelerator Coaching Process Framework, 166–69, *167*

exercises. *See* workbook activities and exercises

expenditure, energy, 54, 56, *57*–58

expenses of Customer Care, 133, 135

experience, hiring decisions and, 42, 43

Farnam Street, 16

Fast Company, 114

feedback: from Customer Care at Rogers, 131, 134, 137, 139, 141, 143; as part of employee engagement, *66. See also* coaching; communication; data and surveys; storytelling

Fengate, 193

finger-pointing, 118

Fiorina, Carly, 142

firing decisions and layoffs, 44–45, 46, 150–51, 197

First Time Resolution (data metric), 133, 140

fit, hiring for. *See* hiring decisions

five dynamics of a team, *109*, 110, 121

five dysfunctions of a team, *110*, 111

Five Dysfunctions of a Team, The (Lencioni), 110

five hallmark behaviors. *See* behaviors, five hallmark

five situations, 102
Floyd, George, 151
focus groups. *See* feedback
Food Banks Canada, 151
Forbes, 114, 147
Fortune, 65, 90
Fortune 500, 91, 164
foxes *vs.* hedgehogs, 23–24
Franklin, Benjamin, 53
Frontline Certified (program at Rogers), 139
frontline teams. *See* Customer Care (Rogers), transformation of
full career, 194–96

Gabarro, John, 197
Gallup, 32, 62, 68
Gaston, Cito, 173–74
Gates, Bill, 84, 180, 235
General Electric, 17–18, 84
genetic encoding, 31
genome, 31
Gen Z, 183–84, 228
German military, 83
Gilmor, Tim, 18, 186, 190–92
goals: building soft skills, 198; in coaching, 163, 166, 168, 229; hiring and, 29, 43; individual *vs.* collective, 111, 120; in Jim Reid's personal hedgehog, 30; passions, strengths and, 35; of Project Aristotle, 121; purpose and, 205; at Rogers, 116, 135, 138, 143. *See also* clarity of mission
Goldsmith, Marshall, 178
Goleman, Daniel, 183
golf, 54–55, 58, 59
Good to Great (Collins): on culture of discipline, 76, 217–18; on finding the right people, 40, 41–45, 107, 174, 189–90, 213; on hedgehog concept, 23–24, 28, 209; on humble leaders, 80, 239
Goodwin, Doris Kearns, 49

Google, 95–96, 97, 108, *109*, 120–21
Gorsky, Alex, 92–94
Graham, Katharine, 15–17, 23
Grant, Adam, 93
grit, 89–98; Bernshteyn's, 91–92; in crisis leadership, 148, 156, 157; Gorsky's, 92–94; Lobo's, 90–91; overview of, 85–87; Powell's, 94–95; S. Wojcicki's, 95–98; workbook exercise on, 219
Grit (Duckworth), 87
growing industries, 35–36, 187, 231
growth and development: caring for people's, 161; coaching and, 163, 171, 172–73; in hedgehog concept, 36; importance to Rogers's employees, 123–24; need for, 162. *See also* coaching individual transformation
gun laws, 152

Hamm, John, 142
Hanoi Hilton, 147–48
hard skills, 197
Hardy, Peter, 174–75, 199
Harter, James, 62
Harvard Business Review, 49, 89, 132, 142, 197
Harvard Business School, 16, 238
Harvard University, 4, 132, 162
Hay Group, 164
health, 71
"Hedgehog and the Fox, The" (Berlin), 23
hedgehog concept, 23–24, 25, 28. *See also* personal hedgehog
Heskett, James, 75
Hewlett, Bill, 41
Hewlett-Packard (HP), 40–41, 142, 175
hierarchy of needs, Maslow's, 159
high performance: coaching's influence on, 166, 185, 229; discipline's importance to, 77–79; drivers of employee engagement leading to, 68; Jim Reid's personal hedgehog and, 30–31; Loehr

and Schwartz on, 53–54; organizational culture and, 71, 75–77, 76, 98. *See also* results, business and financial

High-Performance Pyramid, 54–62, 57; case study on, 60–61; emotional capacity, 57, 58–59, 61, 214, 215; mental capacity, 57, 59, 61, 214, 216; physical capacity, 56–58, 57, 214, 215; spiritual capacity, 57, 59–60, 214, 216; workbook activity and exercise on, 214, 215–16

high-performance teams. *See* right people; team building

High Trust Teams (program at Rogers), 121

hiring decisions: assessment-based, 190–92; champions' role in, 198; choosing the right people, 42–44; at Costco, 64–65; hard skills' influence on, 197; questions for candidates, 28, 29, 86, 191; at Rogers, 46; at Stryker, 91; winning moves by candidates, 200; workbook exercises on, 213, 233

Hit Refresh (S. Nadella), 180

Ho, Geoff, 117, 120–24

Hoffman, Reed, 96, 172–73

Holtz, Lou, 82

hope: during a crisis, 147–48, 152, 157, 159; for Customer Care, 133, 134

House, The (program at Rogers), 118–19

Howard University, 94

HP (Hewlett-Packard), 40–41, 142, 175

HP Way, The (Packard), 40–41

HR, 46, 116, 162, 174

humility, 89–98; Bernshteyn's, 91–92; in crisis leadership, 156; Dimon on, 105; empathy and, 80, 181; Gorsky's, 92–94; of Knight's team, 107; Lobo's, 90–91; overview of, 79–81; Powell's, 94–95; security and, 239; S. Wojcicki's, 95–98; workbook exercise on, 219

humor, sense of, 174

Husky Injection Molding, 74

Iacocca, Lee, 76–77

Ibarra, Herminia, 175

IBM, 164

Ideal Performance State, 55–56, 58, 62, 214

impact, *109*, 110

Inclusion and Diversity strategy (Rogers Communications), 151

income, 132

income protection, 150–51

Innovator's Dilemma, The (Christensen), 237

International Coaching Federation, 170

Iran, 86

Islamophobia, 152–53

Jack Welch School of Management, 17

Jelinek, Craig, 64–65

job hopping, 183–84

Jobs, Steve, 39, 238

Joe's Take (video blog), 149

Johnson, Jeff, 50

Johnson, Kevin, 154–55, 157, 227

Johnson, Robert, Jr., 93

Johnson & Johnson (J&J), 92–94

journalism, 193–94

Journal of Management, 80

JPMorgan Chase, 87

Karakusevic, Ana, 179–80

Karen (actress), 26

Kenexa, 69

Knight, Phil, 49–50, 106–7, 239

Kotter, John: on accelerating rate of change, 129; on culture and performance, 75; on failure of change initiatives, 132, 133, 140–41, 223, 226; framework for change, 140, 145, 224; on relationships with bosses, 197; on resistance to change, 144; as source of leadership and coaching concepts, 2

Labatt Brewing, 174
Lane, Randall, 147
layoffs and firing decisions, 44–45, 46,
    150–51, 197
LEAD (coaching program), 138
Leaders Eat Last (Sinek), 126–27
leadership. *See* +5 Leadership
    Development Model
Leadership BS (Pfeffer), 14
leadership coaching techniques. *See*
    workbook activities and exercises
leadership programs: failure of, 164; at
    Rogers, 118–19
leadership theories, current, 1
"Leading Change" (article by Kotter), 132,
    133
Leading Change (book by Kotter), 132, 145
learning: in coaching, 175, 199; culture of,
    138, 142, 180–81, 225; great leaders
    seek lifelong, 236; overview of, 101.
    See also training
legacy, 208
Lencioni, Patrick, 110–11, 113, 119–20, 121–22
Likelihood to Recommend (data metric),
    140, 151
Lincoln, Abraham, 49, 60
LinkedIn, 172
listening: in coaching, 176, 177–78, 199; at
    Microsoft, 180–81; at Rogers, 151, 176;
    at Stryker, 90; workbook exercise on,
    229
listening sessions. *See* feedback
Lobo, Kevin, 90–91
Loehr, Jim: *The Power of Full Engagement*,
    53, 54–60, 73, 214–15; as source of
    leadership and coaching concepts, 2;
    on storytelling, 88; tips for anger
    management, 58
Logoplaste, 74
London Bridge terror attack, 97
Lovett-Reid, Pattie, 26, 47–48, 193, 194–96
loyalty, 69, 183, 217

MacDonald, Ray, 76–77
Major League Baseball, 92, 173–75, 199
making a living: alignment with values
    and purpose, 187; C. Reid's personal
    hedgehog and, 26–27; elements of,
    35–36; in hedgehog concept, 27, *78*,
    185; hiring decisions and, 29; Jim
    Reid's personal hedgehog and, *30*;
    Moore's personal hedgehog and, 194;
    workbook activity and exercise on,
    209, 210. *See also* results, business and
    financial
Malnight, Thomas W., 83
Mandela, Nelson, 60, 73
Maslow's hierarchy of needs, 159
Masters Tournament, 58
McCord, Patty, 43–44
McKinnon, Todd, 126
McKinsey: 7-S Framework of, 40; Cava's
    interview with, 69; on change, 141,
    143, 164, 179
MDS Inc., 4, 14, 179
meaning, *109*, 110
measurements: of employee engagement,
    69, 70, 122, *123*, 140; of reasons for job
    hopping, 184; of team performance,
    121; in workbook exercises, 218–19,
    221, 229–30; of workers using their
    strengths, *32*. *See also* results, business
    and financial
media, 151
meetings, 179
mental capacity, *57*, 59, 61, 214, 216
mentoring. *See* coaching
Microsoft. *See* Nadella, Satya
mid-career, 187, 193–94
military: crisis leadership in, 158; great *vs.*
    poor leadership in, 3; mission in, 83,
    93, 126; passion in, 18–19, 36; Powell's
    experience in, 94–95; as source of
    leadership and coaching concepts,
    235–36

Millennials, 91, 164, 183–84, 228
mindset, builder's, 81–82, 92, 219, 238–39
mission, 15, 123, 126, 219. *See also* clarity of
    mission
MIT Sloan, 162
Moore, Tracy, 193–94
Morneau Sobeco, 4
Most Admired Corporate Cultures
    award, 47
Muslim community, 152–53

Nadella, Satya: empathy and, 84–85, 124–25,
    142–43, 180–81; on engagement, 188;
    storytelling by, 88–89
Nadella, Zain, 125
Natale, Joe: crisis leadership of, 149–52,
    157; on culture, 117; on putting the
    customer first, 122; on Rogers's
    purpose, 116; support for Customer
    Care transformation, 134, 135, 136,
    139, 141
NATO, 83
Nazer, Nancy, 20, 86–87, 116–19
Netflix, 43–44
Net Promoter Scores, 130, 140, 151
New York Times, 16, 65
New Zealand, 152–54
Nick (Jane Reid's partner), 47–48
Nicklaus, Jack, 54–55
Nike, 49–50, 106–7, 136, 175
Nixon, Richard, 16
Nonviolent Communication (Rosenberg),
    142–43
Novak, Kyle, 117, 119–20, 121
nucleotides, 31

objectivity, 20
Okta, 126
Oliver Wyman (management consulting
    firm), 192–93
One Medical, 15
openness, 92, 105

opportunities, right people and, 44, 46
organizational culture: caring for people
    as part of, 161; changes in Rogers's,
    114–24, *116*, 135–36, 137, 138, 141, 145,
    171; changing nature of today's, 162;
    Collins on discipline's role in, 76,
    217–18; crisis leadership and, 156;
    diversity's importance to, 90;
    engagement and, 68, 184, 187; as
    execution engine, 125–26; high
    performance and, 71, 75–77, *76*, 98;
    hiring decisions and, 42; at Microsoft,
    142–43, 180–81; overview of, 9; right
    people and fixing, 50–51; at
    Salesforce, 65–66; as top down,
    78–79, 116–24, 141–42, 176; workbook
    activities and exercises on, 212,
    219–20, 225. *See also* coaching culture
organizational design frameworks, 40.
    See also right people
organizational support, 122. *See also*
    Natale, Joe: support for Customer
    Care transformation
Ou, Amy, 80

Packard, David, 40–41
Page, Larry, 95–96
pandemic, COVID-19, 149–52, 153–54, 155
paradox of change, 13–14, 145, 206
Parrish, Shane, 16
passions, 23–38; Chiaia's and Woessner's,
    74; coaching and, 185, 186; C. Reid's,
    26, 27; crisis leadership and, 158;
    defining, 32–35; discipline's importance
    to, 77; Gorsky's, 94; in hedgehog
    concept, 23–24, *25*, 27, *78*, *185*; and
    hiring decisions, 28, 29, 200;
    importance in personal lives, 47;
    iterative relationship with strengths,
    35; Jim Reid's, *30*, 36; in the military,
    18–19, 36; Moore's, 193–94; Nazer's, 87;
    overview of, 9; results influenced by,

144; right people and, 39–40, 50; top takeaways about, 38; workbook activity and exercise on, 208–9, 210, 211

pay, 132

Pentagon Papers, 17

people decisions. *See* right people

People Plan (Rogers Communications), 116, *117*

performance. *See* high performance; High-Performance Pyramid; results, business and financial

performance values, 207

personal finance, 195, 196

personal growth. *See* growth and development

personal hedgehog, 25–30, *27*, *78*, *185*; coaching and, 186; creating a, 37–38; Jim Reid's, 29, *30*; Moore's, *193*, *194*; workbook activities and exercises on, 208, 209–11. *See also* making a living; passions; strengths

personal lives: change models for, 145–46; coaching carries over into, 169; leadership framework applies to, 5, 239; purpose's influence on, 238; right people decisions in, 39, 47–48

perspective, objective, 20

Peterson, Suzanne, 80

Pew Research, 162

Pfeffer, Jeffrey, 2, 14–15

Philadelphia, 154–55, 227

Philip Morris, 44

physical capacity, 56–58, *57*, 214, 215

physical environment, 132, 139, 144

pilots, 3, 18–19, 158, 236

poems, 82, 126–27

Porras, Jerry, 12, 82. See also *Built to Last* (Collins and Porras)

Powell, Colin, 94–95

Power of Full Engagement, The (Loehr and Schwartz), 53, 54–60, 73, 214–15

Power of Story, The (Loehr), 88

pride, 69, 216

priorities: during a crisis, 158–59, 228; Lobo's, 90–91; in the military, 83; overview of, *103*; at Rogers, 117, 141, 149. *See also* clarity of mission

productive conflict, *112*, 122, 175, 221

profit. *See* results, business and financial

Project Aristotle, 108–9, 120–21

promotions, 188–89

psychological impacts of change, 133, 134, 139

psychological safety: in coaching, 168, 173, 175; creating, 124; during a crisis, 150, 159; culture of, 78; employee engagement and, *66*; in Google's five dynamics of a team, *109*, 121; overview of, *103*, 107–8; in playbook for high-performing teams, 111, *112*; at Rogers, 122; workbook activity and exercise on, 220, 221, 230; at YouTube, 97

purpose, 11–22; The Balcony and the Dance Floor case study, 20–21; character and, 14–18; Chiaia's and Woessner's, *73*, *74*; Christensen and Cook on, 237–39; and clarity of mission, 83–85, 91; coaching and, 172, 186–87; crisis leadership and, 148, 149, 150, 152, 156, 158; discipline and, 76, 77; employee engagement and, 66–67; grit and, 85–87; and hiring decisions, 28, 29, 42; importance in personal lives, 47, 238; at Microsoft, 180; overview of, *9*; and the paradox of change, 13–14; right people and, 39–40, 50, 107; at Rogers, 116, 132, 145, 149, 150, 152; as starting point for great leadership, 73; in storytelling, 88–89; S. Wojcicki's, 96; synchronicity with values, 11–12; top takeaways about, 21–22; as the *why*, 12; workbook activities and exercises on, 205, 206, 207–8

purposeful/spiritual capacity, 57, 59–60, 214, 216
Putting Purpose to Work (PWC), 11
PWC, 11

racism, 151, 152–53, 154–55, 227
ranking system, 84
recovery: in mental capacity, 59; overview of, 54–56, *55, 214*; in physical capacity, 57, 58; rituals' importance to, 61; workbook exercise on, 216
Reid, Carolyn, 25–27, 28
Reid, David, 60–61
Reid, Jane, 47–48
Reid, Kevin, 192–93
remuneration, 132
renewal. *See* recovery
resilience, 77, 205
resistance to change, 134, 144
responsibilities, 120, 171–72. *See also* accountability
results, business and financial: career derailment and, 196, 197; coaching's influence on, 164, 170; at Costco, 64–65; and crisis leadership at Rogers, 151; culture and, *75, 76, 116*; emotions' influence on, 144; employee engagement and, 63, *68*, 188; in hedgehog concept, 24, *25*; Hewlett-Packard's, 41; inattention to, *110*, 111; Lovett-Reid's accomplishments, 195–96; overview of, *103*; in playbook for high-performing teams, *112*, 113–14; purpose's importance to, 83–85; workbook exercise on, 221. *See also* high performance; making a living; measurements
return on investment, 170
rewards and benefits, employee, 65–66, 172, 188–89
re:Work (blog), 108–9

right environment, 107–10, 119, 220–23. *See also* organizational culture; team building
right people, 39–52; Beeston on, 174–75; case study on, 46–47; Chiaia's and Woessner's ability to find, 74; clarity needed for finding, 39–40; coaching and, 189–92; culture and, 50–51, 125; in Customer Care transformation, 137–38, 176; discipline's importance to having, 77; hiring decisions about, 42–44; the HP Way, 40–41; moving or firing people, 44–45, 46, 197; opportunities given to, 44, 46; overview of, *9, 103*; in personal lives, 39, 47–48; shared values, unique strengths and, 48–50; team building and, 107; top takeaways about, 52; workbook activities and exercise on, 211–13. *See also* team building; teams
Right People Playbook, 48
Right Stuff, The (book), 19
rituals: in emotional capacity, 58–59; importance of, 61–62; in mental capacity, 59; overview of, *55, 56, 214*; in physical capacity, 57, 58; workbook exercise on, 216
Rogers, John, 4, 14
Rogers, Ted, 46, 47
Rogers Communications: The Balcony and the Dance Floor and, 20; coaching at, 166, 170–71; crisis leadership at, 149–52, 157; Nazer's interview with, 86; right people approach applied to, 46–47; Woessner's work at, 74. *See also* Customer Care (Rogers), transformation of; organizational culture: changes in Rogers's
ROI, 170
Rosenberg, Marshall, 142–43

Rotman School of Management, 90
routines. *See* rituals
Rozovsky, Julia, 108-9
Rubin, Amir Dan, 14-15, 17

safety. *See* psychological safety
sales channels, 130
Salesforce, 65-66
satisfaction, 69, 217
Satok, David, 150
Schultz, Howard, 155
Schwartz, Tony, 53, 54-60, 73, 214-15
Scoular, Anne, 175
self-acceptance, 32
self-awareness: breeds clarity, 32; career
    success and, 186; and choosing the
    right people, 49; coaching and, 165,
    168, 171-72; empathy as by-product
    of, 180; in engagement, 63; hiring
    decisions and, 29, 192; of purpose
    and values, 20-21; as soft skill, 198;
    in team building, 105. *See also*
    workbook activities and exercises
self-confidence, 49
self-sacrifice, 126-27
Serafini, Lou, Jr., 193
service, 65, 150
Seward, William H., 49
Shedletsky, Ralph, 165-66, 171-72, 177-79
Shoe Dog (Knight), 50, 106-7, 239
side-by-side coaching, 138-39
Sinegal, Jim, 64
Sinek, Simon, 85, 126-27
social inequality, 151
soft skills, 148, 157, 159, 197-98. *See also*
    empathy
software industry, 11-12, 65-66, 91-92. *See
    also* Google; Nadella, Satya
Soviet Union, 92
Speaker's Corner (TV show), 151
Spencer Stuart (executive search firm),
    63, 187

spiritual/purposeful capacity, 57, 59-60,
    214, 216
sponsors, 198-99
sports: baseball, 92, 173-75, 199; golf, 54-55,
    58, 59; Loehr's work with stars of, 53-55,
    57-58; scientific research in, 56-57
Stanford Executive Program, 82
Stanford Hospital and Clinics, 14-15
Starbucks, 154-55, 227
Start with Why (Sinek), 85
Starwood Hotels and Resorts Worldwide,
    68-69
Steve (coachee), 33-35
Stockdale, James, 147-48
Stockdale Paradox, *148*, 152, 157-58, 159
storytelling: overview of, 88-89; at
    Rogers, 136-37, 139, 143; workbook
    exercises on, 219, 226; at YouTube,
    95-98. *See also* communication
Strasser, Rob, 50
strategy, 40-41, 75, 90, 91, 151
strengths, 23-38; Chiaia's and Woessner's,
    74; coaching and, 185, 186; C. Reid's,
    25-26, 27; daily use of, 32; discipline's
    importance to, 77; as genetically
    encoded, 31; in hedgehog concept,
    23-24, *25*, 27, *78*, *185*; and hiring
    decisions, 28, 29, 43, 200; importance
    in personal lives, 47; iterative
    relationship with passions, 35; Jim
    Reid's, *30*; Moore's, 194; overview of, *9*;
    right people and, 39-40, 48-50;
    self-awareness and, 198; Steve's, 33-35;
    top takeaways about, 38; workbook
    activity and exercise on, 208-9, 210, 211
Strengths-Based Leadership (Gallup), 32
stress, *55*, 57, 198, *214*, 216
structure, *109*
Stryker Corporation, 90-91
success: as cumulative, 1, 5, 236-37;
    leaders judged by teams', 189, 230-31;
    Powell on, 94. *See also* Customer Care

(Rogers), transformation of; results, business and financial

support, organizational, 122. *See also* Natale, Joe: support for Customer Care transformation

surveys. *See* data and surveys

SwitchGear, 138

talents. *See* strengths

TD, 27, 192

team building, 105–28; career derailment and, 196; case studies on, 114–24; coaching and, 187; creating the perfect team, 138; empathy and, 124–25; engagement's role in, 69–71; five dynamics of a team, *109*, 110, 121; five dysfunctions of a team, *110*, 111; importance of, 106; playbook for high-performing teams, 111–14, *112*, 122, 175; principle of leaders eat last, 126–27; right environment's importance for, 107–10; right people's importance for, 107; self-awareness about, 105; top takeaways about, 127–28; workbook activity and exercises on, 220–23. *See also* right people

team coaching. *See* +5 Team Coaching Model

Team One *vs.* Team Two, 114, 119–20

teams: culture lives at level of, 98; drivers of engagement for, 70; humble leaders' treatment of, 80–81; leaders judged by capabilities of their, 189, 230–31; as performance units of organization, 106; shared passions important for strong, 35; team-first *vs.* me-first attitude, 78–79. *See also* right people

technology and tools, 132, 135, 139, 162

television industry, 26, 193, 194, 195

telling *vs.* asking, 178–80

terrorism, 97, 152–53

Texas Instruments, 41

theater, 25–26

three circles framework. *See* personal hedgehog

three disciplines, 42–47

Three Disciplines and Team Building, The (case study), 46–47

Tilley, Shayne, 20

Time Tellers, 81

tools and technology, 132, 135, 139, 162

top-down approaches, 78–79, 116–24, 141–42, 176

top quartile engagement, 69–71

Toronto Blue Jays, 173–75, 199

Toronto-Dominion Bank, 27, 192

Torrie, Alan, 4

toughness. *See* grit

Tracy Moore by Freda's, 193

training: cross-training, 64; employee engagement and, 66; as essential for today's workforce, 162; on racial bias, 154–55; at Rogers, 132, 135, 138; *vs.* coaching, 163. *See also* learning

transfers, decisions about, 44–45

trust: absence of, *110*, 111; Bernshteyn's desire to build, 92; coaching and, 166, 168, 177–81, 199; during a crisis, 157, 159; culture of, 78; Dimon on, 105; employee engagement and, 66; importance in team building, 108; of Knight in his team, 106; overview of, *103*; in playbook for high-performing teams, 111, *112*; at Rogers, 122

truth in storytelling, 88–89

Tunguz, Tomasz, 237

turnover, 65, 131, 170, 176

Ulrich, Dave, 2, 114, 116

United States, 32, 49, 83, 93, 162

urgency, 141

Useem, Michael, 93

Value as a Service (Bernshteyn), 91

value chain, *68*

values, 11–22; The Balcony and the Dance Floor case study, 20–21; character and, 14–18; Chiaia's and Woessner's, 73, 74; coaching and, 172, 186, 187; at Coupa, 91–92; creating, 12; crisis leadership and, 149, 150, 152, 153, 157, 158; culture and, 125; discipline's importance to, 77; and hiring decisions, 28, 29, 42; importance in personal lives, 47–48; at Johnson & Johnson, 93–94; Moore's, 194; overview of, *9*; and the paradox of change, 13–14; right people and, 39–40, 48–50, 107; at Rogers, 145, 149, 150, 152; spiritual energy derived from, 59; at Starbucks, 155; as starting point for great leadership, 73; synchronicity with purpose, 11–12; top takeaways about, 21–22; of Toronto Blue Jays, 175; as the *what*, 12; workbook activities and exercises on, 205, 206–7, 208

Vanity Fair, 84

Vietnam War, 147–48

violence, 151, 152–53

vision, 15, 50, 123

visualization, 59

Voice of the Frontline (online suggestion site), 137

volunteering, 65

vulnerability, 124

Waldman, David, 80

Walmart, 12

Walton, Sam, 12

Washington Post, 15–17

Weill, Sandy, 87

Weir, Mike, 58

Weissman, George, 44

Welch, Jack, 17–18, 84

Wellness Reimbursement Program, 65–66

What Got You Here Won't Get You There (Goldsmith), 178

wheelhouse, *185*, 186, 208, 231

Window and the Mirror, The (analogy), 80

Winning (Welch), 17

wins, small, 139, 144

Woessner, Dirk, 73, 74–75, 129–30

Wojcicki, Esther, 95–96

Wojcicki, Susan, 95–98

Women's Shelters Canada, 151

Woodell, Bob, 50

Woods, Earl, 59

Woods, Tiger, 59

workbook activities and exercises, 203–33; approach to, 3, 203; change, 223–26; coaching, 228–30; coaching individual transformation, 230–33; crisis leadership, 227–28; discipline, 217–20; engagement, 214–17; passions and strengths, 208–9, 210, 211; purpose and values, 205, 206–7, 208; right people, 211–13; team building, 220–23

Workopolis, 183–84

World Series, 173

wreckers *vs.* builders, 82

Yeager, Chuck, 19

YouTube, 95–98

Zenger/Folkman (consultants), 165

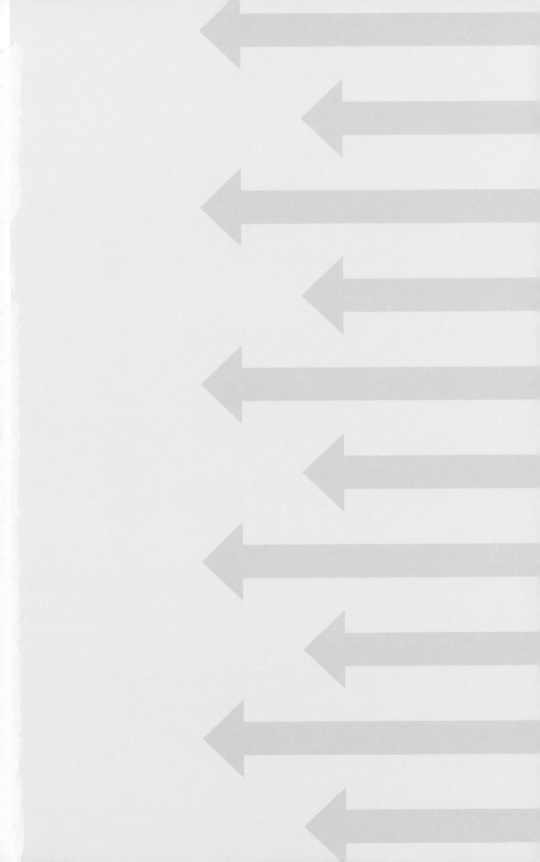